Learning Microsoft Power BI

Transforming Data into Insights

Jeremey Arnold

Beijing · Boston · Farnham · Sebastopol · Tokyo

Learning Microsoft Power BI

by Jeremey Arnold

Copyright © 2022 Onebridge. All rights reserved.

Published by O'Reilly Media, Inc., 1005 Gravenstein Highway North, Sebastopol, CA 95472.

O'Reilly books may be purchased for educational, business, or sales promotional use. Online editions are also available for most titles (*http://oreilly.com*). For more information, contact our corporate/institutional sales department: 800-998-9938 or *corporate@oreilly.com*.

Acquisitions Editor: Michelle Smith	**Indexer:** Ellen Troutman-Zaig
Development Editor: Jeff Bleiel	**Interior Designer:** David Futato
Production Editor: Christopher Faucher	**Cover Designer:** Karen Montgomery
Copyeditor: nSight, Inc.	**Illustrator:** Kate Dullea
Proofreader: Sharon Wilkey	

September 2022:   First Edition

Revision History for the First Edition
2022-09-19:   First Release

See *http://oreilly.com/catalog/errata.csp?isbn=9781098112844* for release details.

978-1-098-11284-4

[LSI]

I dedicate this book to my wife, Katherine, and my children, Elainamia and Makayla.
They are my constant source of encouragement and joy.

Table of Contents

Preface

I was a senior at Ball State University when one of my professors, Dr. James McClure, and I were discussing classic challenges to the perfectly competitive market model. We were having a back-and-forth, and throughout our entire discussion, I kept bringing all the critiques back to a single problem: asymmetric information. *Asymmetric information* is the condition in which one party knows more about the topic at hand than the other party, to the point where they can use that for some sort of advantage.

We live in a world in which Google, Facebook, Amazon, Netflix, and others know so much about you that they can try to figure out what you want before you know you even want it. However, you have access to that same information. In the information age, we don't have an asymmetric information problem as much as we have an asymmetric *comprehension* problem. What we historically haven't had is the ability to process data in the same way. Or at least, we didn't until recently.

Tools that would allow you to aggregate information at scale were historically tools of organizations that could afford complicated investments into data platforms that the ordinary person could neither comprehend nor afford. However, today there exists a piece of software that puts one of, if not *the* most powerful analytics engines ever made into your hands with an initial investment cost of zero dollars and zero cents. We have never been more awash in data, and that data is more available to people like you and me than it ever has been in human history.

Microsoft's Power BI platform gives users a tool to aggregate incredibly large amounts of data to discover insights that can give you just as much, if not more, information than those around you. Whether you are using it for personal reasons or as an organization looking to get a competitive edge in the marketplace by making data more meaningful within your company, there has never been a lower-cost entry to data processing with the ease of use of Power BI Desktop.

Microsoft has spent years working with companies all over the world on a technology for complicated data analytics. Power BI is built on that technology, and Microsoft is literally putting all that know-how into your hands. Data is the great equalizer. It's not just about having more or less of it. It's about using the data you do have effectively.

Organizations all over the world collect more data than you and I could ever comprehend in a lifetime, and yet they do nothing with it because they have no idea how to use it, and they find themselves losing market share to smaller competitors who are using the data they have effectively. Nonprofits are using Power BI to do data analysis that makes the world a better place to live, on issues from conservation to climate change to healthcare access. Citizen data analysts are using publicly available datasets to uncover financial misbehavior and to double-check results from data provided by organizations and governments around the world. If the ability to process and make data meaningful is truly the great equalizer of the information age, then Power BI is a tool that gives you the ability to sit at a table and look giants in the eye.

You might be an accountant looking to automate complicated data cleaning processes for regulatory purposes and want a tool to quickly visualize profit and loss statements. You might be a citizen data analyst looking for a tool to help crunch millions of records of data for a personal project. You could be a data scientist looking for a tool to accelerate adoption of your work by end users. If you are a person who works with data in any capacity and want to get more out of that data than you ever have, then Power BI is an ecosystem that you should have exposure to.

I wrote this book because, first, I'm super passionate about data being used effectively and I truly believe that everyone in the 21st century can interact with data in some way to improve, either professionally or personally. Second, Power BI has been a vehicle for me to better understand all sorts of important data concepts, and I think those ideas are important to accomplishing that first goal. How do we put data from different sources together? How do we deal with tables that are too large for Microsoft Excel? How do we target specific groups or slices of a group for analysis effectively? How do we visualize those results to make them comprehensible to our audience? My early career was spent deep in the bowels of corporate finance, and if I had Power BI then, I would have saved so much time and heartache in manually manipulating data and doing simple groupings and pivot tables.

Our 21st-century data requires a 21st-century tool to unlock it. I believe Power BI is the best tool to do that. It can store the data. It can analyze the data. It has the reach to be available to anyone who uses Windows. No other data visualization or exploration tool can make that claim, and that's why I'm excited you're picking up this book. And I hope you find your data journey as fulfilling as mine has been and continues to be.

Navigating This Book

This book is organized roughly as follows:

- Chapter 1, "Intro to Power BI", provides a brief history of Microsoft's previous business intelligence efforts and how those products have evolved into the Power BI we know today. Alongside that, it goes into detail about how Power BI works under the hood, in terms of how it stores and queries that data.

- Chapter 2, "The Report and Data Views", and Chapter 3, "Importing and Modeling Our Data", introduce portions of the Power BI user interface, including how to navigate the various ribbons and how to bring your data into Power BI for analysis.

- Chapter 4, "Let's Make Some Pictures (Visualizing Data 101)", and Chapter 5, "Aggregations, Measures, and DAX", go into basic principles of visualization and utilizing data aggregations.

- Chapter 6, "Putting the Puzzle Pieces Together: From Raw Data to Report", is a walk-through using the work of the previous chapters to go from nothing in Power BI to a fully functional report page.

- Chapter 7, "Advanced Reporting Topics in Power BI", discusses some advanced analytics topics in Power BI, including AI visuals and what-if analysis.

- Chapter 8, "Introduction to the Power BI Service", and Chapter 9, "Licensing and Deployment Tips", introduce the Power BI service, the cloud-based platform for sharing reports and insights.

- Chapter 10, "Third-Party Tools", introduces useful third-party tools to accelerate or ease future development.

- Appendix A, "Commonly Used DAX Expressions", and Appendix B, "Some Favorite Custom Visuals", provide examples of DAX functions for you to take and modify for your own future data, and a valuable list of some of my favorite custom visuals and their various functionalities, respectively.

Conventions Used in This Book

The following typographical conventions are used in this book:

Italic
> Indicates new terms, URLs, email addresses, filenames, and file extensions.

`Constant width`
> Used for program listings, as well as within paragraphs to refer to program elements such as variable or function names, databases, data types, environment variables, statements, and keywords.

Using Code Examples

Supplemental material (code examples, exercises, etc.) is available for download at *https://oreil.ly/MS-power-BI-files*.

If you have a technical question or a problem using the code examples, please send email to *bookquestions@oreilly.com*.

This book is here to help you get your job done. In general, if example code is offered with this book, you may use it in your programs and documentation. You do not need to contact us for permission unless you're reproducing a significant portion of the code. For example, writing a program that uses several chunks of code from this book does not require permission. Selling or distributing examples from O'Reilly books does require permission. Answering a question by citing this book and quoting example code does not require permission. Incorporating a significant amount of example code from this book into your product's documentation does require permission.

We appreciate, but generally do not require, attribution. An attribution usually includes the title, author, publisher, and ISBN. For example: "*Learning Microsoft Power BI* by Jeremey Arnold (O'Reilly). Copyright 2022 Onebridge, 978-1-098-11284-4."

If you feel your use of code examples falls outside fair use or the permission given above, feel free to contact us at *permissions@oreilly.com*.

O'Reilly Online Learning

O'REILLY® For more than 40 years, *O'Reilly Media* has provided technology and business training, knowledge, and insight to help companies succeed.

Our unique network of experts and innovators share their knowledge and expertise through books, articles, and our online learning platform. O'Reilly's online learning platform gives you on-demand access to live training courses, in-depth learning paths, interactive coding environments, and a vast collection of text and video from O'Reilly and 200+ other publishers. For more information, visit *https://oreilly.com*.

How to Contact Us

Please address comments and questions concerning this book to the publisher:

O'Reilly Media, Inc.
1005 Gravenstein Highway North
Sebastopol, CA 95472
800-998-9938 (in the United States or Canada)
707-829-0515 (international or local)
707-829-0104 (fax)

We have a web page for this book, where we list errata, examples, and any additional information. You can access this page at *https://oreil.ly/microsoft-power-BI*.

Email *bookquestions@oreilly.com* to comment or ask technical questions about this book.

For news and information about our books and courses, visit *https://oreilly.com*.

Find us on LinkedIn: *https://linkedin.com/company/oreilly-media*.

Follow us on Twitter: *https://twitter.com/oreillymedia*.

Watch us on YouTube: *https://youtube.com/oreillymedia*.

Acknowledgments

I want to thank everyone at Onebridge who believed in me and gave me the space to write this text. I want to give a special thanks to Sheryl Ricci for helping me with internal editing. Thanks to the book's technical reviewers—Bradley Nielsen, Belinda Allen, and Bill McLellan. I want to thank the team at O'Reilly who gave me this opportunity, especially Michelle Smith, Jeff Bleiel, and Chris Faucher. Finally, I want to thank you, the reader, for taking the time to pick up this text and give it a chance.

CHAPTER 1

Intro to Power BI

You're a data person. You understand your data. You know how spreadsheets work. But there's so much data to process, and your spreadsheets aren't cutting it.

You need a way to visualize the data and share it with business users so that they can see the analytics, understand the data as you do, and even manipulate the visualizations with little to no training.

If that's why you're looking at this book, you made the right move. Microsoft Power BI is exactly what you need. This book will show you how to get up to speed quickly—so quickly that you'll be building and publishing reports that will wow your colleagues and make your mom proud.

Microsoft Power BI is a data analytics and visualization tool powerful enough for the most demanding data scientists but accessible enough for everyday use by anyone needing to get more from their data.

In the beginning, back when life was simpler (in 2011), Power BI was just a simple piece of desktop software. But it isn't anymore. It's an entire business intelligence ecosystem that can fit into multiple diverse technology stacks.

This chapter introduces Microsoft Power BI, discusses the entire Power BI family of products, provides an overview of how Power BI works, and looks at what distinguishes it from other similar tools. By the end of this chapter, you'll:

- Know what components fit in the Power BI ecosystem and why they're important.
- Learn the history of Microsoft's business intelligence work to learn how that got us to Power BI.
- Discover what makes Power BI different from its competitors.

What Is Power BI?

Power BI is both a piece of software and a larger ecosystem of products. Usually when people throw out the term "Power BI," it's in reference to the desktop authorship software. However, when discussing how most people will (visually) share the fruits of their work with others, it's done in the context of the Power BI service, a software-as-a-service (SaaS) solution that hosts Power BI datasets and reports that can be used by others who have access.

Even beyond these two features, a wide variety of products in the family allow you to embed reports into websites and other applications, view reports on your mobile device, and even have your own version of the SaaS solution on premises.

This book focuses on Power BI Desktop and the Power BI service since they are your most basic and valuable building blocks.

Power BI Desktop is a tool for data investigation and visualization. Analysts can take data and create interactive reports that enable end users to garner insights that were previously buried. In finance, you might use Power BI to automate the generation of profit and loss (P&L) statements or analyze costs over time. In construction, you could use Power BI to identify variances in times to complete projects based on team composition or geographical factors. In retail, you might identify which of your products are the most successful, while pinpointing which ones might be on the cusp of taking off if given a bit more of a push via a what-if analysis.

According to Microsoft at the 2021 Business Applications Summit, 97% of the Fortune 500 uses Power BI in some capacity. That means it's a technology you can trust putting your time and effort into, especially if you're looking for the kind of insight that transforms your enterprise. Or in my case, it's the excuse to build a Pokédex for my daughter. Sometimes you just really want to be the best, like no one ever was.

Power BI Components

Power BI today consists of a wide variety of products that allow users to create and consume reports from your data. According to Microsoft (at the time of publishing), here are all the components that make up the Power BI family of products:

- Power BI Desktop
- Power BI service
- Power BI Mobile

- Power BI Report Builder
- Power BI Report Server on premises
- Power BI Embedded

There is much to unpack in these products, but the main focus of this book is on the first two components. We'll spend most of our time learning Power BI Desktop because that's the foundation you need; it's what the whole ecosystem is built around. Then we'll discuss the Power BI service in more detail toward the end because you're going to need that knowledge to publish (and then share) your amazing work that'll make you the envy of your department.

With that in mind, a quick overview of these components will be useful in the future, so here they are:

Power BI Desktop
> A free application you install on a local computer that you can use to connect to, transform, and visualize data. This is the building block for all the other portions of the Power BI ecosystem.

Power BI service
> An online SaaS solution that lets end users share reports created in Power BI Desktop or Power BI Report Builder with users across an organization. (In case you're wondering, the "s" in "service" is lowercase on purpose; that's just how Microsoft named it.)

Power BI Mobile
> A set of applications for Windows, iOS, and Android that allows end users to view reports in the Power BI service from their mobile devices without having to use a web browser.

Power BI Report Builder
> A free application you install on a local computer that you use to generate pixel-perfect paginated reports in the same form as SQL Server Reporting Services. For example, if you want to build something to automate invoice generation or create long lists of data for distribution, you could do that here.

Power BI Report Server on premises
> If, for security reasons, you cannot publish reports to the Power BI service, your IT team may put a version of that software on an internal server behind the company firewall using on-premises computing resources, as opposed to cloud resources. Power BI Report Server is not always in feature parity with the Power BI service. That's because Report Server is updated only three times a year (January, May, and September). It's also worth noting that if you are going to deploy reports to Report Server on prem, you will need to use a special version of Power BI Desktop that is in alignment with the version of Report Server installed.

Power BI Embedded
> Allows you to integrate Power BI reports and visuals into applications or websites. This has its own pricing and licensing structure.

Now that the whole family has been introduced, we'll shift focus to the two components pertinent to this book, Power BI Desktop and Power BI service.

Power BI Desktop

Power BI Desktop is software that allows you to connect, transform, and visualize data. Let's dig into some details. Power BI Desktop comprises its own components. The two that are most important to a Power BI beginner are the Power BI canvas and Power Query, so those are the two we're going to focus on. Essentially, this is where you'll spend the most time in your Power BI Desktop work.

The *Power BI canvas* is the place where you build visualizations. Think of the canvas as a PowerPoint slide for your data. Here you'll use drag-and-drop functionality to pull information into different visualizations to explore your data and garner insights. This is also where you'll apply formatting to visuals, add images and text boxes, and more.

Power Query is used to import and manipulate data, essentially shaping it. In Power BI, unlike Excel, for example, you do not edit *cells* of data; you manipulate *columns* of data by using its functions, wizards, and formulas. Power Query provides options for creating custom columns based on rules you design. It lets you combine multiple tables of data or add values from one table to another.

Everything in Power Query first begins with getting data from your sources, and Power Query supports a huge number of data sources. You want to connect to a database? SQL? Oracle? Teradata? Power Query has you covered. You want to connect to an Excel workbook to get a table? No problem. Comma-separated values (CSV)? Easy. Cloud sources? Also not a problem.

Microsoft has gone out of its way to create new connectors to data sources to show that Power BI is not just to be used with other Microsoft products but wherever your data lives. If you become sufficiently talented at M (the programming language of Power Query), you can even, in theory, create your own custom data connectors to data sources that aren't officially supported. Just note that this book isn't going to discuss M or advanced Data Analysis Expressions (DAX) topics or actual programming. We're here to help you as a Power BI beginner, and you'll do just fine without those.

The Power BI Service

Now we get to the good stuff that's going to move you from an ordinary person who just produces reports to a celebrity whose reports draw people from far and wide. The Power BI service, the online SaaS solution, allows users to share their reports from Power BI Desktop with other users in their organization.

Everyone has access to their own personal workspace for free. You get one personal workspace that is pregenerated when you log in for the first time, and it's like a private development space in the larger Power BI service environment. You technically can share things from this personal workspace, but it's not a best practice to do so, and anyone you share it with would still need the appropriate licensing to view it.

The right way to share reports with other users is to create a new workspace and invite them to that workspace. To be eligible to be invited to a workspace, a user must have a Power BI Pro license, or your organization must be using Power BI Premium dedicated capacity to share reports with users who do not have Power BI Pro licenses.

The Power BI service lets other end users explore reports you've created to get insights from your work. This exploration can take the form of dashboards of curated visuals you put together. Or it can be access to a report you've created with all its pages. Or it can even be the ability to ask natural language questions using the Q&A feature to get insights from the data.

The Power BI service also includes several other features, such as the ability to create special objects known as *dataflows*. These dataflows can be used to get information in the Power BI service outside of a database, while allowing end users to access that data and combine it with other data inside a Power BI Desktop model.

Developers can manage deployment pipelines for workspaces in the Power BI service, which lets you create and manage the development, test, and production workspaces. Deployment pipelines enable ongoing development work on Power BI projects, without impacting the user experience for items already being used by end users.

A new feature in the Power BI service gives users the ability to create goals. The goals are tracked using data in the Power BI service. Information on the goals can then be shared with appropriate users for quick, actionable insight.

In sum, the Power BI service is the critical glue that makes Power BI different from, say, simply sharing an Excel workbook around the office. It creates a shared space enabling people to see the same insights securely, while inviting them to explore shared data elements that can be curated for meeting the specific needs of each end user.

The Power Platform

Now let's take a step back and look at the big picture: what are the "Power" products within the Microsoft family? The Power Platform is a larger compilation of low- or no-code products that support one another, with Power BI as just one component. While we won't train you on these other items, it's good to know what else is out there in case you develop a need to integrate one of the products into your Power BI reports in the future:

Power Apps
> A low- or no-code development environment where you can develop your own applications to solve different business challenges

Power Automate
> A framework that allows end users to create "flows" that automate organizational processes

Power Virtual Agents
> A no-code tool that lets you build chatbots to engage with customers and employees

Each of the components can be used by Power BI to create insights to help push your work forward. Let's go through some examples of how each piece could work with Power BI.

In Power Apps, for instance, you could have an application that would allow a site inspector to take notes and upload that data to a SQL Server database. A Power BI report could also be connected to that SQL Server database, download that information that was uploaded by the Power App, and update the report based on the new data being added by the numerous inspectors in the field using Power Apps.

Let's say your boss, for whatever reason, wants to see a static version of a report every day. Well, you could manually go into the Power BI service and create an export, download it, write up an email, and click Send. Instead, a more efficient option would be to use Power Automate to create a flow that would automate the task for you, ensuring that at 8 a.m. sharp every day there's a nice PDF in your boss's inbox with the most up-to-date version of your Power BI report. If that doesn't get you points, I don't know *what* will.

When it comes to virtual agents (software that provides customer service to humans, mimicking a customer service representative), a large amount of data is collected in the process whenever end users interact with your chatbots. All that data is collected and stored, which means Power BI can generate reports about it. This creates an end-to-end reporting solution that allows your organization to get textual insights into what your consumers are really looking for from your organization. The end users can work with and see the actual data.

How Did We Get to Power BI?

Microsoft's history in business intelligence is long and storied. In many ways, Power BI is the most recent (and maybe final) chapter, representing the culmination of business intelligence capabilities developed in a series of components Microsoft built throughout the years. For you to get the most out of this product, it's worth discussing how Microsoft's business intelligence stack got to Power BI and what that journey means for you as an end user.

This section will provide you with valuable context: why was Power BI developed, why is it important, and what products are interrelated? Knowing this up front will help you the same way it helps when you do research about a company before you walk into a job interview. The clarity you gain will serve you well in the future.

SQL Server: Microsoft's Relational Database

In 1989, Microsoft released its first relational database in the form of SQL Server for OS/2. A *database* is a piece of software that contains and organizes large portions of data for different uses. While SQL Server was the first step (and a necessary one) for Microsoft to move into business intelligence, a database alone isn't sufficient to provide business intelligence.

SQL Server Analysis Services Multidimensional: One Small Step into BI

As processing power grew, new methods to process data became popular—for example, data cubes. In 1998, Microsoft released its first online analytical processing (OLAP) engine and called it OLAP Services, which would eventually become SQL Server Analysis Services. *OLAP Services* is a fancy way to say a cube-based way to interact with data for analysis. The cube approach dominated many enterprise BI environments for well over a decade.

SQL Server Reporting Services: Pixel-Perfect Reporting, Automated Reports, and More

Microsoft eventually needed to add a pixel-perfect reporting option to SQL Server. This was required because, as data use cases grew, the need to create reusable assets to an exact specification grew as well. For example, you want to make sure that every invoice you print is in exactly the same format every time.

In 2004, Microsoft released SQL Server Reporting Services as an add-on to SQL Server 2000, with its second version being released alongside SQL Server 2005. SQL Server Reporting Services had several features that were useful in an enterprise deployment, including pixel-perfect report generation, automated report distribution, and, in many deployments, the ability for end users to generate queries to the backend SQL Server database through a user interface.

Excel: A Self-Service BI Tool

Every piece of software mentioned so far is what we would define as *enterprise business intelligence* tools. These expensive tools required large teams to manage and deploy them.

If enterprise business intelligence is defined by its large deployments and high levels of investment, *self-service business intelligence* is the ability to use and manipulate data in such a way that you empower the end user to explore and analyze the data they have.

Microsoft's history in self-service business intelligence comes down to one core product that almost everyone has seen or touched once: Microsoft Excel. The first version of Excel came out for the Macintosh in 1985. At its core, Excel is a product that allows you to take data, pull it into a "flat" extract, and manipulate it or make impromptu calculations on it as needed. Excel empowered end users to take their data and get insights out of it. That's the premise of self-service business intelligence.

Power Pivot

In 2010 Microsoft released PowerPivot. PowerPivot was later renamed to add a space so it was two words, thereby matching the other product names in this new Power BI suite of tools. Originally an add-on for Excel, Power Pivot let end users get information from a myriad of sources and store that information in a relational OLAP (ROLAP) model inside the workbook. Power Pivot also shipped with Power Query. Power Query is an in-engine extract, transform, and load (ETL) tool that allows for data manipulation using the M language.

Important New Functionality That Leads to Power BI

Around this time, we began to see enterprise and self-service business intelligence start to flow together. In SQL Server 2012, Microsoft released a new feature with Analysis Services called the *tabular model*. Analysis Services could now support a method of data organization more like that of a classic data warehouse, as opposed to a cube structure that becomes increasingly difficult to manage over time and tends to be more confusing for end users. The difference was that to get performance gains in this tabular model, Microsoft developed its first columnar (column-based) data store technology. Eventually, this would become what we know as *VertiPaq* today, the in-memory columnar data store Analysis Services tabular model. So basically, with these improvements, performance became really fast.

Alongside this process, a new formula language called *DAX* was developed to support these tabular models that allowed for calculations across those columns of data to help make that data actionable.

The next version of Power Pivot released with Excel 2013 used this engine as the base for its work.

Power BI Desktop Is Born

On July 24, 2015, the first generally available version of Power BI Desktop was released to the world. Inside Power BI Desktop was an entire enterprise-level semantic (designed to be understood by people) modeling tool with the VertiPaq engine and the DAX formula language. It used Power Query to get information from a wide variety of sources and pull it into the engine, and it allowed for transformations that could shape that data for future analysis.

Figure 1-1 shows the timeline of the Microsoft business intelligence tracks and how they converge, highlighting some of the milestones over the last 30 years in both enterprise and self-service business intelligence.

No one will quiz you on this history, but hopefully it has given you the perspective to understand how we got here. I mean, sure...not all of us keep history books on Microsoft on our bookshelves, but not all of us have secret shrines to Satya Nadella either. It's a life choice.

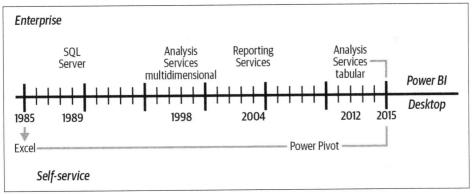

Figure 1-1. This Power BI timeline shows the evolution of business intelligence from Excel to present-day Power BI Desktop

Power BI Desktop Under the Hood

Power BI Desktop works because under the hood it has two powerful engines. These are what make the whole thing work on a technical level. There's the formula engine, which takes data requests, processes them, and generates a query plan for execution. Then there's the storage engine, which stores the data of the data model and pulls the data requested by the formula engine to satisfy a query's demand.

Another way to look at it is to think of the formula engine as the brain. It figures out the best way to approach a problem and sends the appropriate work order to the right parts of the body to get it done. The storage engine is the body that receives those commands and does the work of getting all the data together.

VertiPaq: The Storage Engine

Let's meet the storage engine of SQL Server Analysis Services tabular models, called VertiPaq. This enterprise-level semantic modeling tool is included with every copy of Power BI Desktop. When you pull data into Power BI Desktop, the VertiPaq engine reads the data source post-transformation and puts the data into a columnar structure. This division of the data allows for faster queries via selective column selection and data compression as entire columns get compressed. This compression of the data significantly cuts the file size compared to what it would be otherwise. It then puts the entirety of the data model in local memory. This view can be refreshed from the original data sources.

Now, before you get excited and run out to celebrate, know that this data storage engine comes with a significant hurdle for users coming from, say, Excel. You cannot modify individual cells of data. As the data is converted into columns for storage and indexed and then compressed, the data inside the model becomes effectively immutable. You can add calculated columns and measures, but the underlying data doesn't change. If you want to change the data, you must either go back to the transformation step of the data (say, in Power Query) or go back to the data source and make your edits there, and then refresh your data.

DAX: The Formula Engine

Also, let's discuss the formula engine and its language, DAX. DAX is a formula language used in Analysis Services Tabular, Power BI, and Power Pivot. When you want to access the data in your data model, DAX is how it's done. This is done in the same way as someone would write SQL to get data from a database. Power BI users will most commonly use DAX to create measures and calculated columns. The wonderful thing about Power BI is that for simple drag-and-drop functionality, or when visuals get created, Power BI generates the DAX for you and passes it to the internal engine to have its query plan generated and executed.

Nothing you do in Power BI is done without DAX. You may not see it, but it's always there, playing the pivotal role of figuring out how best to get the information from your data model to satisfy your request.

What Makes Power BI Different from Its Competitors?

Honestly, there has never been a better time to be a data analyst than today. Many of the tools in the marketplace have a variety of strengths and weaknesses, and Power BI is no exception. In fact, just to see how many competitors there are in this marketplace, let's take a quick look at Figure 1-2, which shows Gartner's Magic Quadrant for Analytics and Business Intelligence Platforms for 2021.

Now, whatever you think about the position of the competitors on the analysis, the sheer number of them can be enough to make your head spin. Each competitor has a reason they're in the market today. Notice, though, that the leader's quadrant contains only three players: Qlik, Tableau, and Microsoft.

Figure 1-2. Gartner's Magic Quadrant for Analytics and Business Intelligence Platforms

The real source of differentiation between Microsoft and its competitors in this space is the ability to execute on its plan for its software. Microsoft has a more than 30-year history in business intelligence, and SQL Server is itself now over 30 years old. Microsoft has been in this game a very long time and has the highest number of supporting technologies to its business intelligence platform, as compared to the others.

All these major competitors offer products that allow you to take data and turn it into great data visualizations that help you learn something you didn't know from your data. I will forever be jealous of Tableau's capability to click and drag for groupings, for instance.

Regardless of Tableau's dazzle, Power BI offers a tool for data ingestion that is unequaled in terms of ease of use for nontechnical resources in Power Query. It also has one of the strongest, if not *the* strongest, analysis engines on the planet today in the form of Analysis Services Tabular. These tools have accelerated the rate of data democratization inside many organizations. Power BI has created citizen data analysts around the world who use data to do transformative work. Indeed, by putting in the effort to read and digest this book, you're taking the steps necessary to join that community!

Here are some examples. The world's leading conservation organization, the World Wide Fund for Nature, uses Power BI to share impact effects with donors. Engineers at Cummins use Power BI to do advanced capacity planning to get engines out the door more quickly. Humana leverages Power BI to centralize and visualize data against more than 45 unique data sources across its enterprise, using Power BI as a consolidation platform for end users. King's College London uses Power BI's artificial intelligence (AI) visuals to identify key factors that could indicate shifts in student performance, allowing for targeted outreach to maximize the opportunities for student success. These are just some of the varied use cases happening today on this platform.

Power BI has decades of Analysis Services experience behind it, with a frontend that can now match its promise. In addition, Microsoft releases updates for Power BI Desktop every single month with new features, connectors, and visualizations. Microsoft is committed to the Power Platform, and it's safe to say Microsoft will be here for the long haul. When 97% of the Fortune 500 agree on something, there's probably a good reason.

Conclusion

Power BI at its core is more than just a desktop authorship tool. It's an entire platform that Microsoft has been working toward for the better part of three decades. It has the unique strength of having two of the most enterprise-tested analysis engines in the world, VertiPaq and DAX. It also has a great tool to allow nontechnical users to get disparate data together and begin real analysis on that data with Power Query.

Power BI Desktop is now an enterprise-level solution that is used by the world's largest companies, nonprofits, and even small businesses to help get insights from their data that would have previously been impossible.

With an understanding of what Power BI is, we are ready to finally open the software with a clear vision about what we'll do with it. That begins with the Report view, so get a soda, pet your dog, and let's dive in. This next chapter will cover the user interface and how to use it.

CHAPTER 2

The Report and Data Views

Power BI Desktop is a robust data visualization tool that allows you to take your data and create visualized insights from it in a variety of ways. In this chapter, we'll go over the basics of the Power BI Desktop interface, specifically looking at the Report and Data views.

This will be a detailed dive into the User Interface, so stay with me. Parts of this chapter might be a bit dry since I'm going to concentrate on what the UI does, not necessarily on how we'll use it.

A majority of our focus will be on the Report view because that's where you'll be working the most. Plus, the Report view has the largest number of elements to interact with. The two most important things you need to know about within the UI are the functions of the Home tab of the ribbon and the Visualizations pane, so keep that in mind as you read.

Microsoft said its goal for Power BI Desktop was to make it "PowerPoint for your data." As of the writing of this book, you can see that Power BI has adopted many design principles from other tools in the Microsoft Office family, PowerPoint included.

If you've used any other Microsoft Office product since 2010, you've seen some version of the ribbon UI in Word, Excel, PowerPoint, and other products. Having that familiarity with the interface gives you an advantage, but the Power BI user interface does have some quirks. Now and then, you'll see that Power BI will add and remove items from the ribbon based on item selection context, which can feel awkward at first.

Let's look at how Power BI integrates the ribbon and show you the first thing you'll see when you open Power BI Desktop. See Figure 2-1.

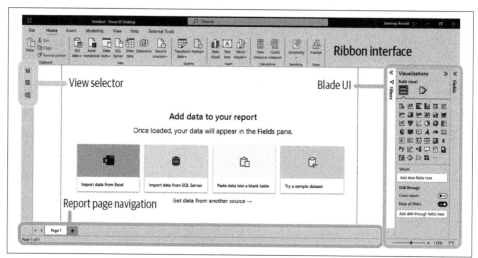

Figure 2-1. This is the first thing you see when you open Power BI Desktop

Looking at the view selector in Figure 2-1, we see three possible views: the Report view, the Data view, and the Model view.

Report View: Home Section of the Ribbon

Power BI defaults to the Report view when you open it. You can see a classic ribbon interface at the top that allows you to search for actions you might take. On the right, you'll see the pane portion of the UI. This part is very similar to what Microsoft did with the original Xbox 360 interface.

You can add different panes to see by using the View portion of the ribbon. You can also take panes that are currently visible and minimize them, as you can see with the Filters and Fields panes in Figure 2-1 where the Visualizations pane is open.

At the bottom, you'll see the Report Page Navigation options. You can click individual report pages or, if your report is large, you can use the arrows to scroll across your list of pages, very similar to how you would explore worksheets in Excel. Finally, on the left, you'll see the three icons that indicate the view selector. The views in order from top to bottom are Report, Data, and Model. The ribbon menu changes based on which view you are in.

Starting with the ribbon interface, the default view is the Home tab, as seen in Figure 2-2. The Home tab goes by a few names, including Home view, Home ribbon, and Home section. I'll refer to its parts (Home, Insert, Modeling) as *tabs* moving forward.

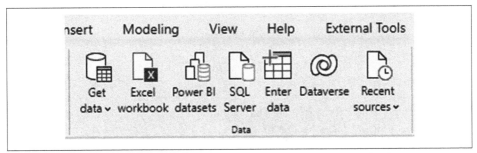

Figure 2-2. The Home tab, also called the Home ribbon, Home view, or Home section, is Power BI Desktop's default view

All of the tabs, or main ribbon sections, in Figure 2-2 are divided into *subsections* separated by a faint vertical line. The names of the subsections are on the bottom row of the ribbon. In Figure 2-2, the subsections are Clipboard, Data, Queries, Insert, Calculations, Sensitivity, and Share. So when I refer to a "subsection" of a tab moving forward, look down at that bottom row to see what I'm referring to.

(I realize that if you've been alive for the last couple of decades and used any Microsoft Office product, you already know this, but I just want to make sure we're aligned on what I mean when I refer to a "subsection" of a tab.) After I identify the tab and the subsection, I'll get into the buttons.

The Clipboard Subsection

So let's get back to the Home tab. You'll first see the Clipboard subsection with items for your standard Cut, Copy, and Paste functionalities. You can use Format Painter to apply one visual's formatting to another, just as you would if you were using format painting in Excel or PowerPoint.

The Data Subsection

In the next subsection, the Data subsection, you'll see several fast options to quickly connect to different data sources. We can see these more clearly in Figure 2-3.

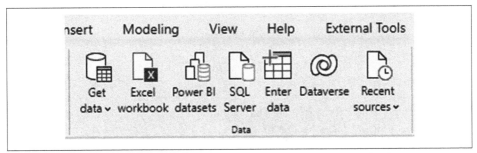

Figure 2-3. The Data subsection allows you to choose where you get the data

Starting on the left, you see the "Get data" button, which has an icon and a drop-down arrow. If you click the icon, you'll see a new menu appear with the entire list of possible data connectors in Power BI, as shown in Figure 2-4.

Figure 2-4. Here's a look at the full Get Data window for when you need the whole enchilada, meaning the entire list of data connectors

If you click the drop-down button, you'll see a smaller, truncated list of more commonly used data sources. This can be very convenient when you don't need to access the full list of connectors. The truncated list is shown in Figure 2-5.

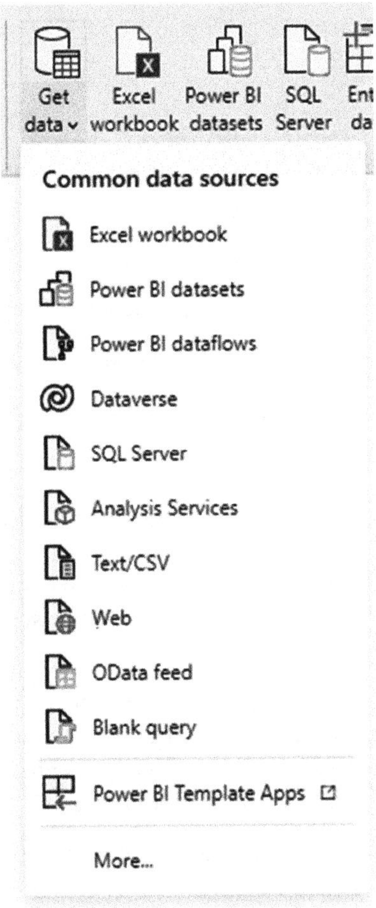

Figure 2-5. The quick data selection list is a shorter list of data connectors, for when you're having a "classic" for lunch

The "Excel workbook" button will immediately open an Explorer window to navigate to your Excel file. Click the "Power BI datasets" button, and a window will appear so you can select a dataset that is already published in the Power BI service to connect to via a "live connection." For reference, see the window in the example in Figure 2-6.

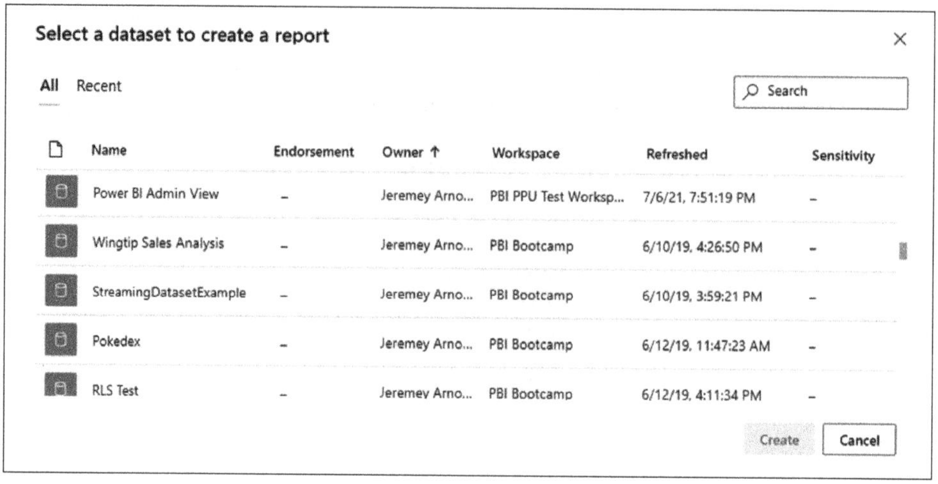

	Name	Endorsement	Owner ↑	Workspace	Refreshed	Sensitivity
	Power BI Admin View	–	Jeremey Arno...	PBI PPU Test Worksp...	7/6/21, 7:51:19 PM	–
	Wingtip Sales Analysis	–	Jeremey Arno...	PBI Bootcamp	6/10/19, 4:26:50 PM	–
	StreamingDatasetExample	–	Jeremey Arno...	PBI Bootcamp	6/10/19, 3:59:21 PM	–
	Pokedex	–	Jeremey Arno...	PBI Bootcamp	6/12/19, 11:47:23 AM	–
	RLS Test	–	Jeremey Arno...	PBI Bootcamp	6/12/19, 4:11:34 PM	–

Figure 2-6. Connecting to a dataset already in the Power BI service

If you click the SQL Server button, a pop-up menu will appear for you to enter the server's name or address, along with an optional database name. The server will ask for your credentials when you try to connect.

You'll also see an option for selecting Import or DirectQuery. In Import mode, you download the data into your local data model. In DirectQuery mode, Power BI generates queries against the database and then, when that data is returned, does whatever is needed with the data. That window is shown in Figure 2-7.

There is also an "Advanced options" button you can click that will allow you to add a command timeout in minutes, pass a custom SQL statement, include relationship columns, navigate using full hierarchies, and enable SQL Server failover support.

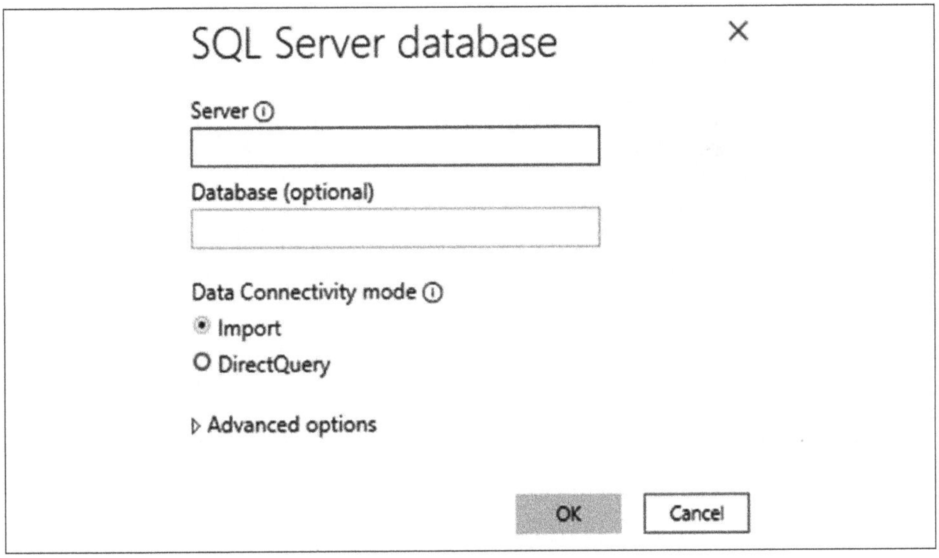

Figure 2-7. Connecting to your friendly neighborhood SQL Server

The "Enter data" button (way back in Figure 2-3) will give you a0n interface that should feel familiar if you use Excel, as it opens a table-like structure where you can add columns, name them, and put data into cells, as shown in Figure 2-8. It's important to note that this interface has no formula function. It's only for simple data entry. You can copy and paste information into this window, as well, but be careful before going copy-paste crazy.

This window can be useful for testing or if you have a lookup table that you want to generate for your model. But I recommend that you do not put large amounts of information into this type of table structure because it has to be manually managed and has a maximum capacity of 3,000 cells' worth of data.

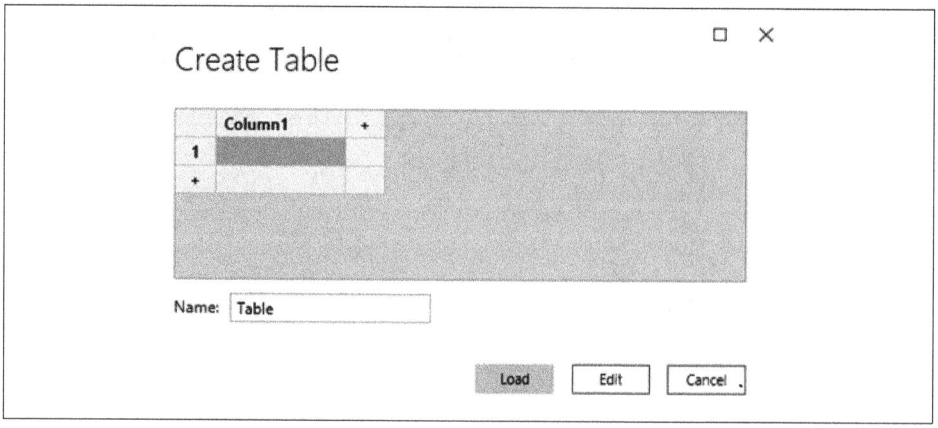

Figure 2-8. A simple data entry window, for when you need a little extra something you don't have elsewhere

The Dataverse button seen back in Figure 2-3 will generate a pop-up for entering your environment domain information alongside a prompt. If you're familiar with Microsoft Dynamics, you might have heard this referred to previously as the Common Data Model. The window for providing your Dataverse information is shown in Figure 2-9.

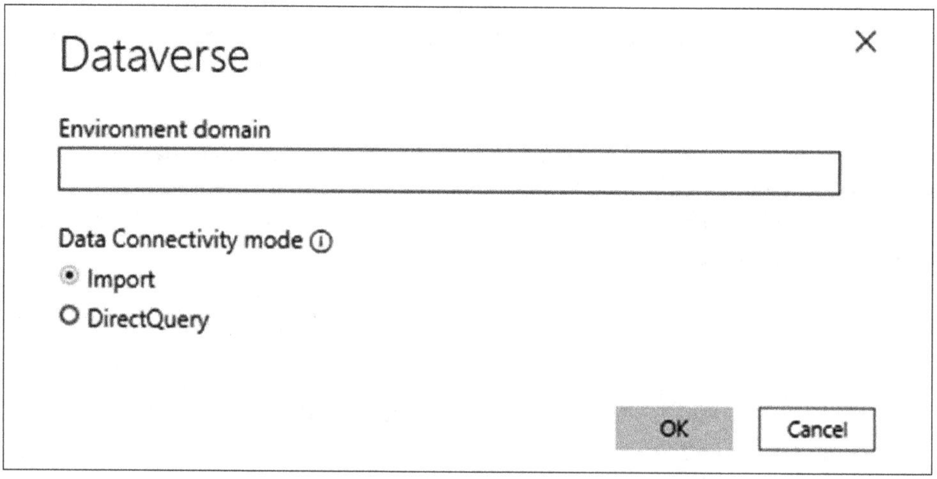

Figure 2-9. If you are in the Dynamics 365 universe, you'll probably connect to Microsoft Dataverse

The "Recent sources" button (Figure 2-3) will open a drop-down menu of your most recent sources so that if you must connect to a data source again, it's conveniently already there for you. You can click More from the drop-down to get an even longer list of recent data sources. Figure 2-10 shows some of my mos000t recent data sources in Power BI.

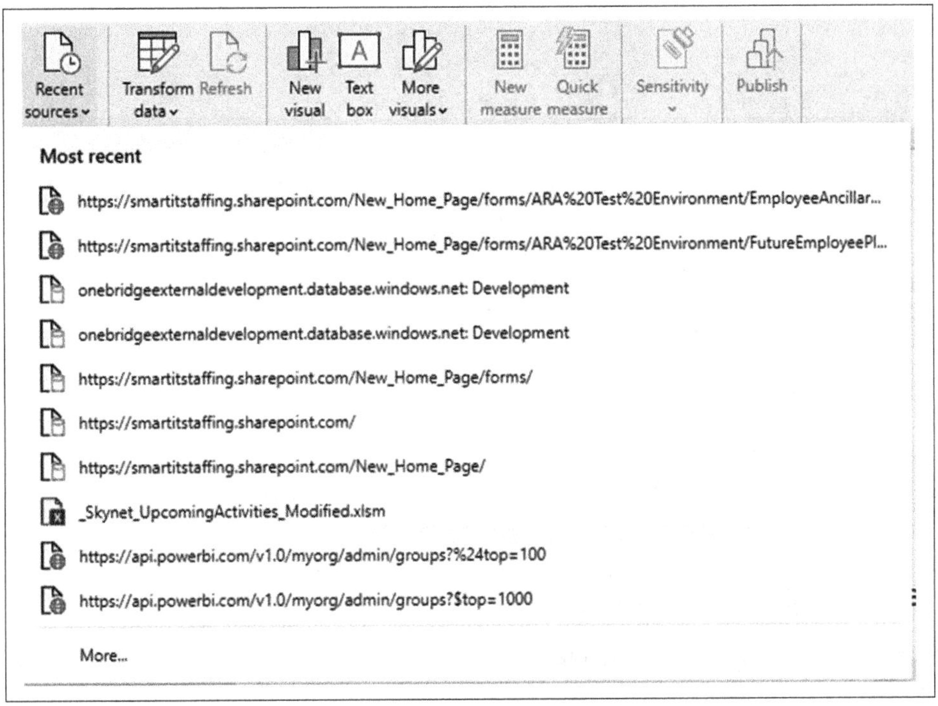

Figure 2-10. My "Recent sources list" (ignore Skynet...)

The Queries Subsection

Moving 00on to the Queries subsection, you'll see two buttons: "Transform data" and Refresh. Refresh is grayed out in Figure 2-11 because I have no data in my model to refresh. However, when that button is available and clicked, it will do a complete refresh of all data sources in your data model.

"Transform data" has two separate functions, depending on whether you click the its icon or its drop-down arrow. If you click the icon, it takes you straight to the Power Query interface, which we'll discuss in more detail in Chapter 3.

If you click the drop-down arrow, you'll get a drop-down menu with a couple of options. "Data source settings" takes you to a pop-up to modify those settings for things like credentials or locations of files and the like. If you have parameters and variables, they can be modified here as well.

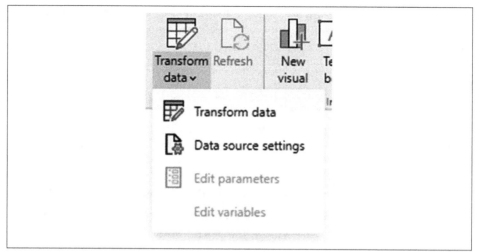

Figure 2-11. "Transform data" options

The Insert Subsection

Next is the Insert tab, which has three options. You can insert a new visual onto your report page, insert a text box, or add more visualizations to your list of visualizations in the Visualizations pane.

If you click "New visual," a visual will be put onto your canvas. The default visual that will be placed on the canvas is the stacked column chart.

The "Text box" button will put a text box onto your canvas in the same way it would appear in PowerPoint.

The "More visuals" button, when clicked, will look like Figure 2-12. If you select "From my files," you'll be directed to an Explorer window, where you can select a visual to add from a file on your local machine. These files are usually in PBVIZ format, though in recent years Microsoft has really pushed AppSource as the preferred method to get custom visuals.

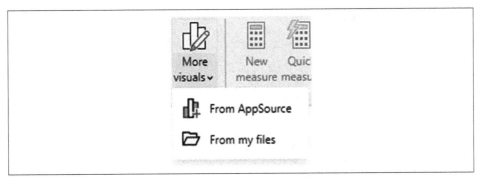

Figure 2-12. Adding visuals from two possible sources

If you select From AppSource, you'll see the window shown in Figure 2-13. Here you can select a third-party visualization to add to your list of visualizations.

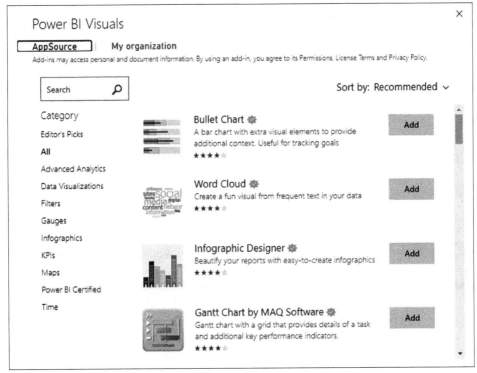

Figure 2-13. Power BI AppSource has a wealth of additional visualizations you can select for your reports

The Calculations Subsection

Under Calculations, you have" New measure" and "Quick measure" options.

Measures are calculations across your data using DAX. We will discuss measures in more detail later in this book, but for now, if you click "New measure," you'll see a formula bar appear below the ribbon, where you can put in the DAX for your measure. This is like the formula bar you might use in Excel.

Clicking the "Quick measure" button opens a pop-up box that helps you create a measure by using a wizard with several predefined calculations. You can see both the formula bar and pop-up in Figure 2-14. Here's a helpful tip: Microsoft adds new quick measures in some releases, so it's always worth going back after an update to see if new quick measures have been added.

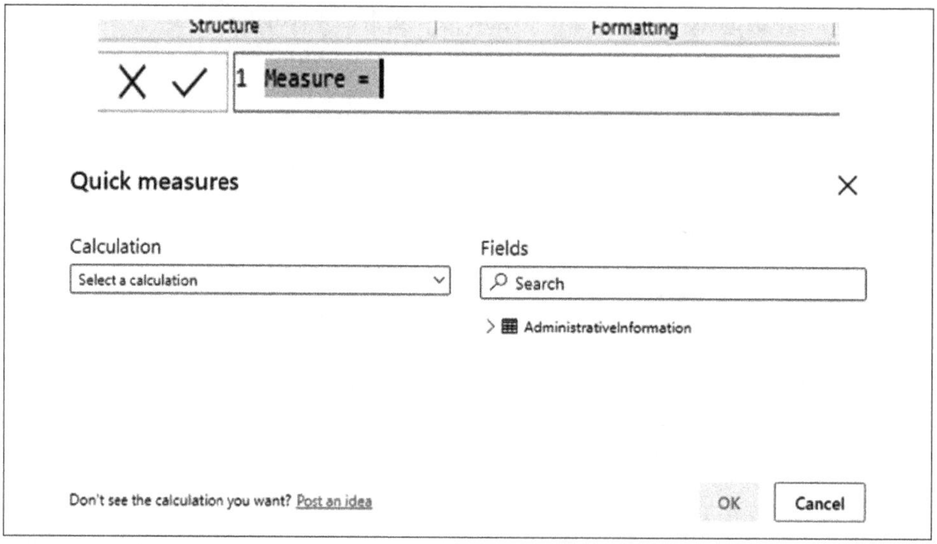

Figure 2-14. The DAX formula bar and "Quick measures" menu. You will use these, I promise.

The Final Subsections: Sensitivity and Share

The last two buttons on the Home tab deal with sensitivity labels and the capability to publish your report to the service. I'll discuss more about publishing and sharing reports in the Power BI service in Chapter 8.

Report View: The Insert Tab

Next on the ribbon under Report view, we move to the Insert tab shown in Figure 2-15.

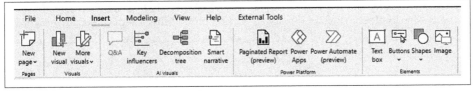

Figure 2-15. The Insert tab in the ribbon

The Pages Subsection

In the Pages subsection, the "New page" button will create a drop-down menu no matter which portion you click. That menu gives you two options: "Blank page" and "Duplicate page."

"Blank page" creates a new page in your report farthest to the right of all your other report pages. "Duplicate page" will make a copy of your current report page exactly as it is currently configured, with all visuals on the canvas, and you'll find that new copy farthest to the right of all the other pages in the report.

The Visuals Subsection

The Visuals subsection has two of the exact same buttons that we saw in the Home tab: the "New visual" and "More visuals" buttons. Their functionality is exactly the same too. They are duplicated here as a matter of convenience, so if you're looking for other specific items in this subsection of the ribbon, which revolves around putting things onto the canvas, you can also do it from here.

The AI Visuals Subsection

The next subsection in the Insert tab deals with AI visuals, shown in Figure 2-15. At the time of this writing, there are four of these AI-powered visuals in general availability. If you click any of them, that puts a blank version of that visual onto the canvas as far to the top and left-hand corner as possible. We'll discuss these visuals in more detail in Chapter 7, where we'll provide a complete rundown of all the visuals that are available in Power BI out of the box.

What's important here is that these visuals in particular offer unique functionality in terms of analytics capability. Microsoft is keen to demonstrate its AI prowess in as many Power Platform products as possible, and Power BI is no exception. I expect more AI-powered visuals to come to general availability down the road.

The Power Platform Subsection

The next subsection, Power Platform, deals with items that are technically visuals, but they are fundamentally different from every other visual in the platform.

Power Platform visuals offer the ability to interact with and engage the other portions of the Power Platform that we discussed earlier, embedding them into your Power BI report. They are very powerful and help demonstrate the Power Platform's holistic value inside an organization.

The Elements Subsection

The final subsection of the Insert tab, Elements, deals with report elements. These are items that aren't necessarily interactive like Power BI visuals, but they can help enhance your report or give it extra clarity. Elements choices include the Text box, Buttons, Shapes, and Image controls.

"Text box" in Power BI does the exact same thing it does in PowerPoint. It puts an editable text box onto the canvas, along with a basic formatting tool for your text. This tool allows you to change the font, font size, text color, bolding, italicizing, underlining, and text alignment, and to add hyperlinks to web pages outside of your report.

Other elements on the "Text box" can be edited in the "Format text box" pane that appears when a text box is selected. See an example of what that looks like on the canvas in Figure 2-16.

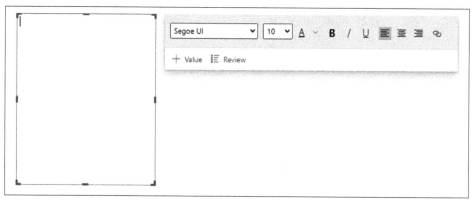

Figure 2-16. The "Text box" interface lets you apply all kinds of formatting options

Click the Buttons element to get a list of options that can help with report navigation or provide additional information. There are quite a few. Figure 2-17 shows the whole list, so you can start thinking about how you might use these in your future reports.

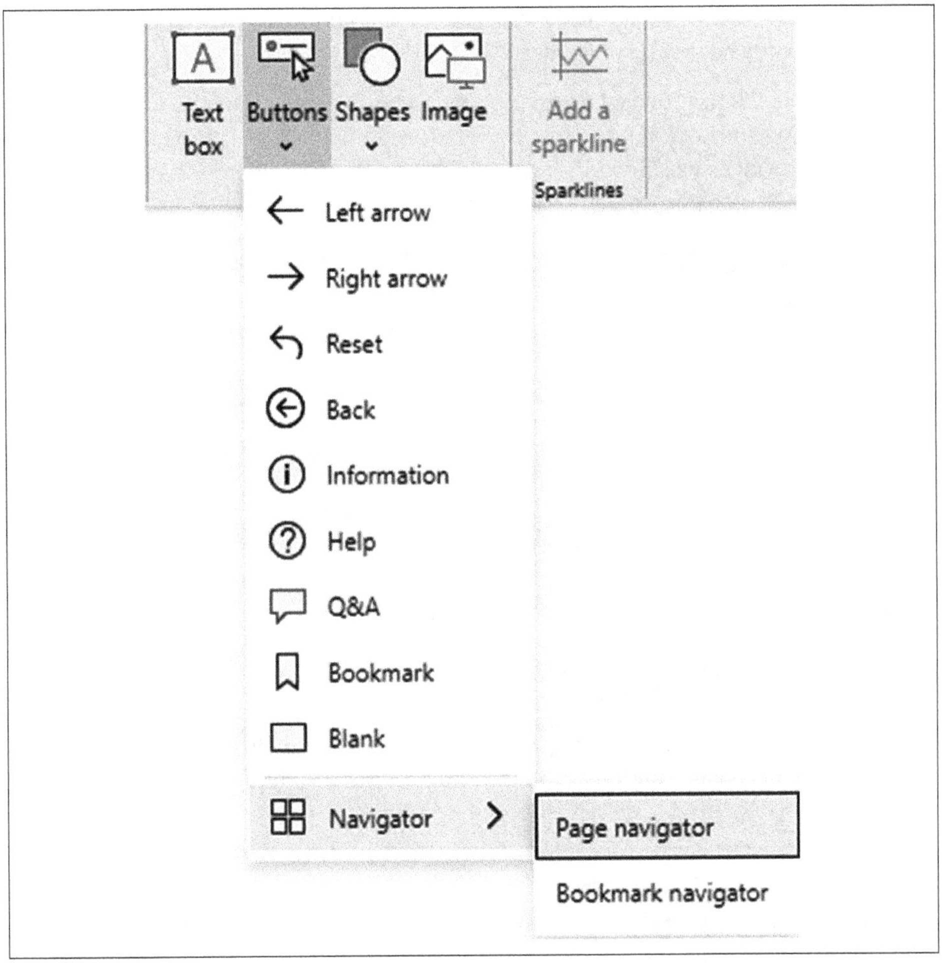

Figure 2-17. Buttons...buttons as far as the eye can see

It's important to note that for all these buttons, except Q&A, Bookmark, and the Navigator options, placing the button on your canvas doesn't do anything until you give Power BI the context for how that button should be used. When you put one of these buttons on your canvas, you'll see a "Format button" pane appear on the right, and it will contain visual formatting options, noting what action that button should do.

The Q&A and Bookmark buttons have default actions already set to the Q&A and Bookmark functions, respectively. However, you can still change these actions if you feel your report could use that button in a different context.

The Shapes button will show you a wide list of shapes that you can put into a report. The shape, when selected, will appear on your canvas already filled with a default color based on your theme. You can change it from there by manipulating the size of the visual on the canvas. The shape can also be manipulated when selected for formatting, as shapes have their own special pane.

Finally, if you click the Image button, an Explorer window will pop up, allowing you to select an image to bring into your Power BI report. Power BI can add in pictures from several formats, as shown in Figure 2-18. (As an aside, there is a correct way to pronounce GIF…don't be on the wrong side.)

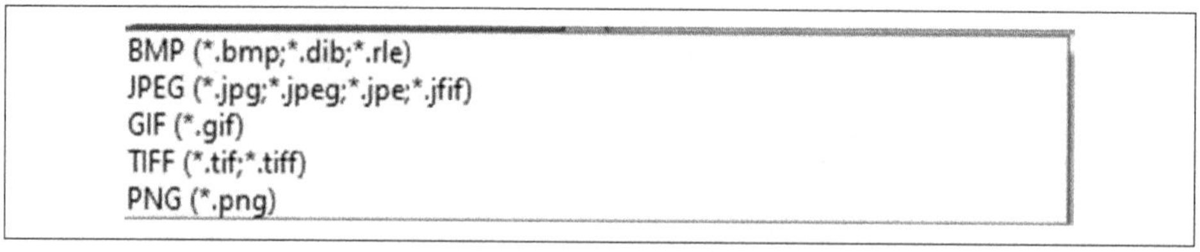

```
BMP (*.bmp;*.dib;*.rle)
JPEG (*.jpg;*.jpeg;*.jpe;*.jfif)
GIF (*.gif)
TIFF (*.tif;*.tiff)
PNG (*.png)
```

Figure 2-18. Seriously, there's an image format for just about everybody

Once your image is on your report page (as with every other item available in the Elements subsection of the ribbon), when selected, it will have its own special formatting pane appear on the right side. The shape can, like all other Power BI elements, have its size modified in the report by clicking and dragging the box to the size desired.

Report View: The Modeling Tab

The third part of the ribbon in the Report view is the Modeling tab. Here you have more data management options from the Report view. There is a lot of magic in Figure 2-19.

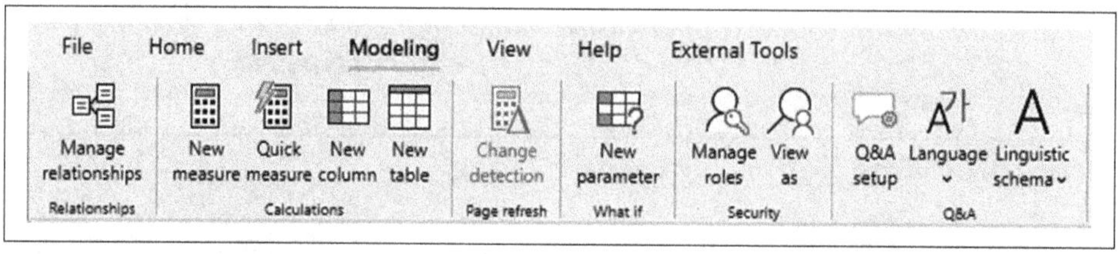

Figure 2-19. Modeling your data is critical to being successful in Power BI

The Relationships Subsection

First we see "Manage relationships." This button opens a window where you can see all the relationships in your model, and you can add or make edits to existing relationships from here.

By default, Power BI will try to autodetect relationships based on column names. This can be useful for getting an initial set of relationships together for your data model, but it might not always be the way you want the model set up. It's important to note that this button is grayed out if you have fewer than two tables in your data model.

We will go into more detail on relationships in the next chapter, when we discuss the Model view.

The Calculations Subsection

The next area involves Calculations. The "New measure" and "Quick measure" buttons function exactly as described earlier for the Home tab.

The other two items are prompts that will bring up the inline DAX editor that we showed earlier so that you can create either DAX calculated columns from the "New column" button or DAX calculated tables from the "New table" button.

Please be aware of an inconvenient quirk with the "New measure" button. If you don't have a table highlighted in the Fields pane before selecting this button, Power BI assumes that the measure is going to go into the first table that it sees in that pane. In theory, these objects can be moved by dragging and dropping them in the Fields pane to another table, but be aware of that behavior.

The Page Refresh Subsection

The "Page refresh" subsection has a "Change detection" button that is relevant only in DirectQuery scenarios, as discussed briefly earlier in the chapter. You can determine whether you want your pages to refresh when there's a detected change in the data or on a fixed refresh interval. You can simulate this function in Power BI Desktop using this feature.

The What If Subsection

"What if" simply lets you create what-if parameters. They will be discussed in further detail in Chapter 7.

The Security Subsection

The Security subsection has two buttons that are very important. The "Manage roles" and "View as" buttons are how we do row-level security (RLS) in Power BI.

RLS is a feature enabling us to control the way people see the data in our model, based on roles that are formulaically constructed using DAX. Think of this as making sure that people can see the data only in a way that's filtered for their specific context and security constraints. For instance, if we had a report published for multiple college classes, we could create simple DAX statements that describe how we want the data filtered and then, as shown in Chapter 9, assign users to those roles so the data is then filtered in the way we want for them. We can see an example of this in Figure 2-20, where I create a role for spring 2021 students with a very simple statement to define a filter condition.

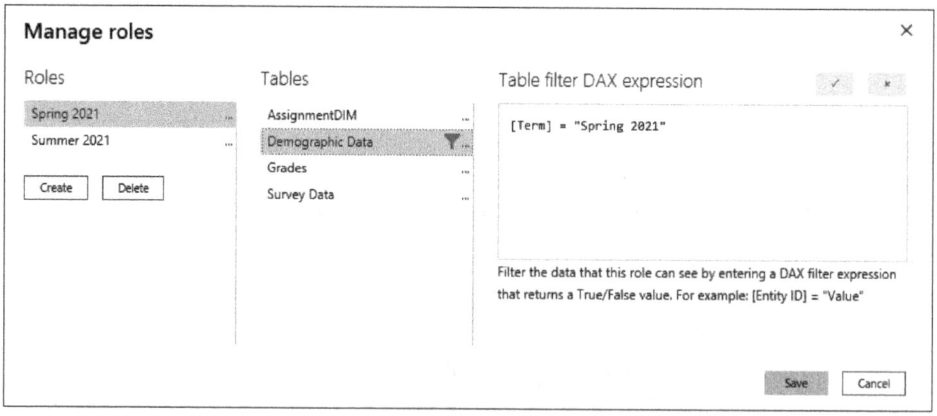

Figure 2-20. In this simple RLS example, users assigned to the Spring 2021 role would see only data for which the Term field in the Demographic Data table is equal to Spring 2021

The Q&A Subsection

Finally, we have the Q&A subsection. The "Q&A setup" button brings up a large wizard that shows how you can fine-tune the Q&A engine to adapt to more natural language around your users. See Figure 2-21. You can use this to teach the engine synonyms so that when you ask a question with a certain word, the Power BI engine knows what that word means in the context of your data model.

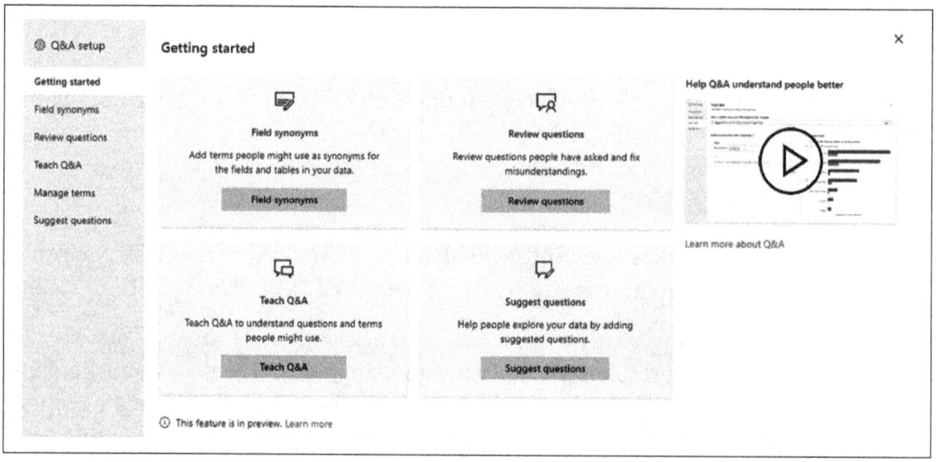

Figure 2-21. The Natural Language Wizard

Select the Language button to get a list of eligible languages for Q&A. I expect the list of languages to grow in the future.

Lastly, the "Linguistic schema" button has a drop-down that allows you to import or export a linguistic schema file. If you want to learn more about this subject, I suggest you go to "Editing Q&A Linguistic Schemas" (*https://oreil.ly/7ao9b*) and download the example linguistic schema file and example PBIX file.

Report View: The View Tab

The next major part of the ribbon is the View tab, shown in Figure 2-22. This tab is important because it allows you to set themes, set up different page views to see how your users might see your report, and more. Want some PowerPoint in your Power BI? This is where to make some of that happen.

Figure 2-22. Put some PowerPoint in your Power BI by using the View tab

The Themes Subsection

The Themes subsection works the same way it does in PowerPoint. You can work from default themes, or you can click the drop-down menu on the right to get more themes to choose from, browse for other themes, see the theme gallery, or customize your current theme and save those changes. There are many themes, so feel free to experiment!

The Scale to Fit Subsection

In "Scale to fit," the "Page view" button gives you the option to your canvas to fit the page, fit to width, or show its actual size. This goes hand in hand with the Mobile subsection's "Mobile layout" button, which will change your report canvas to a size and shape suitable for reports being displayed on a mobile device.

Mobile report development is quite a bit different from standard report development in terms of what you must think about, since you have more limited real estate.

The Page Options Subsection

In the "Page options" subsection, you have three buttons to select from. You can show the gridlines, have items snap to the grid, and lock objects.

Gridlines are helpful in giving you guiding references for where your items are in respect to other items.

"Snap to grid" has a function only while in Mobile layout and will force all visuals to fit neatly into a given pixel density.

"Lock objects" prevents items on a page from being moved around.

The Show Panes Subsection

The "Show panes" subsection is the last one on the View tab. This subsection is related to the different panes you can have added or removed at any time from that portion of the UI.

We will detail these functions' UIs later in this chapter, but as a general overview, the Filters pane allows you to modify filters at a visual, page, or report level.

Bookmarks allows you to set a report page to a certain series of events and then return to that state at a later point, like a web bookmark.

The Selection pane shows you all the objects on your canvas in each report page and can allow you to quickly select a specific object. You can also use this to group objects and determine their hierarchy of importance when they might overlap.

The Performance analyzer lets you see what's impacting your report page's performance and can allow you to extract machine-generated DAX.

The "Sync slicers" pane allows you to determine which slicers, if any, should be synced across report pages, enabling a way to keep comparisons the same across different report pages.

Report View: Help Section

The Help tab on the ribbon will enable you to see which version of Power BI Desktop you're using and provide links to guided learning, training videos, documentation, and support links, as shown in Figure 2-23.

I'm going to skip to the Community subsection because the Info, Help, and Resources subsections are self-explanatory. Plus, the Community subsection is very powerful.

Under Community, you'll find links to the Power BI blog, ways to connect to the broader Power Platform community, specific documentation for developers (called "Power BI for developers"), the ability to submit an idea for Power BI Desktop, and a link to commonly used external tools.

I do want to highlight the submitting and voting on ideas because this is something that will help you. The Microsoft Power BI development team has said on multiple occasions that it listens to those ideas and pays attention to what is getting voted on. Almost every month or two, there's an update to the software, and the team discusses how popular a given idea was on Power BI Ideas (*https://ideas.powerbi.com*). So if you have an idea, this is the right forum for it.

Figure 2-23. We can do with a little help from our friends, and we get this on the Help tab

Report View: External Tools Section

Lastly, there's the External Tools tab on the ribbon. There are a ton of external tools, and they're not all equal. Just to give you an example, see Figure 2-24. We'll further explore some of the most important external tools in Chapter 10, but for now, just take a look at the variety.

Figure 2-24. That's a lot of external tools!

The Pane Interface of the Report View

Each section of the user interface has a unique set of panes that allows for different functionality. In the report view you can access seven panes, as shown in Figure 2-25..

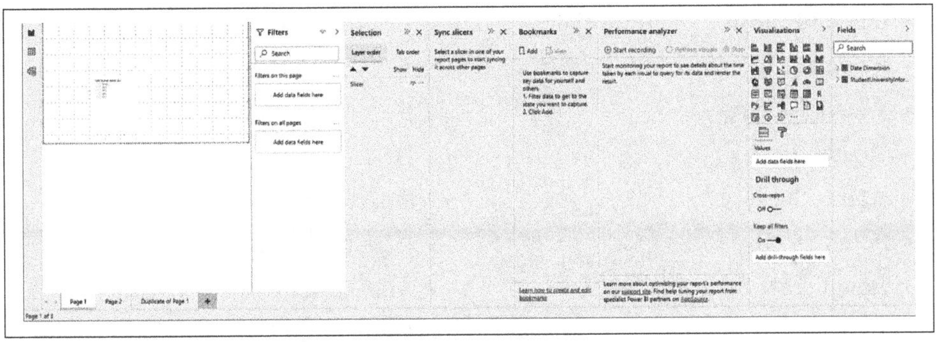

Figure 2-25. All the panes together. All together now!

As you can see, when all the panes are displayed fully, they don't leave you a lot of real estate to work with. However, only two are always visible: the Visualization and Fields panes. Further, the Filters pane is different in that it's more attached to the canvas than the other panes, since it dictates how items on the canvas behave.

Visualizations Pane

The Visualizations pane is where you choose visualizations to add to a report, add columns and measures to display in those visuals in the Values subsection, and more. Let's go through the visuals list first, and then to the next subsection. The visuals are listed in order from left to right, top to bottom:

- Stacked bar chart
- Stacked column chart
- Clustered bar chart
- Clustered column chart
- 100% stacked bar chart
- 100% stacked column chart
- Line chart
- Area chart
- Stacked area chart
- Line and stacked column chart
- Line and clustered column chart
- Ribbon chart
- Waterfall chart
- Funnel chart
- Scatter chart
- Pie chart
- Donut chart
- Treemap
- Map
- Filled map

- Shape map
- Azure map
- Gauge
- Card
- Multi-row card
- KPI
- Slicer
- Table
- Matrix
- R script visual
- Python script visual
- Key influencers
- Decomposition tree
- Q&A
- Smart narrative
- Paginated report
- ArcGIS Maps for Power BI
- Power Apps for Power BI
- Power Automate for Power BI

That's a very large number of visuals out of the box, and it can seem overwhelming. I promise it's not as bad as it looks, and some of them might be items you never use.

Be aware that if you have any custom visuals or imported visuals in your Power BI report, they will appear beneath this list, above the Fields and Format buttons that we will discuss next.

Between the visualization list and the Values subsection are two buttons. The left is for Fields, and the right is for Formatting. Each visual's subsection is going to look slightly different, as they accept different parameters. A column chart and a line chart might look similar, but a column and line chart are going to have multiple areas to put fields, for instance.

Likewise, the Format pane is also going to have different parameters based on the visual, as each visual has something unique about it to format. However, there are some constants. You'll also note that when you have a visual selected, a third option will appear in this area as well. That's the Analytics button. It's important to understand that this function works only with the visualizations built into Power BI by default, and even then, they aren't available for every visual. However, you can do things like set trend lines, constant lines, averages, etc.

What's important about this subsection is that you should feel free to explore the myriad of settings available. If you aren't sure, let Power BI do the work for you with its default settings. When you're ready to take a little more control, the Format and Analytics subsections give you the abilities you'll need.

The final area of the Visualizations pane is the "Drill through" subsection. This is a powerful feature that allows you to drill down from one subsection of your report to another, while keeping all the data elements filtered as you had them previously— enabling you to quickly develop a story with data that allows users to find specific examples that are relevant to their analysis.

Fields and Filters Panes

The Fields pane contains a list of all the tables, columns, and measures in your report. Beyond that, it will also contain any folders you might create, as well as any hierarchies or groups you may define in your data model. Adding these items to your visuals is as easy as clicking and dragging the column or measure to the appropriate area of the Visualizations pane or onto the visual itself on the canvas. You can also click the check box to have Power BI move the item into your selected visualization. Or if you don't have one, Power BI will put a visualization on the canvas for you with that chosen data element.

If you right-click a table in your model, you'll get a context list for adding a new measure, a new calculated column, a new quick measure, refreshing the data, editing the query for that table in Power Query, and more.

If you right-click a column in this area, you'll get a context list for checking it to your canvas, creating a hierarchy from that first column, adding a new measure or column, adding the column to your filters list, or adding it to drill through. You'll also have the option to hide it from sight in case you don't want that data element used at that time.

The Filters pane has three subsections. You've likely used filters already, but a *filter* is a function that sets a condition by which the data must be true in order to be displayed. For example, if I have a filter of an age bracket and select the grouping from 12 to 18 years old, that is all the data I would see. All other data would be ignored.

On the Filters pane, when you have a specific visual selected, it will allow you to apply filters to that specific visual.

"Filters on this page" filters all visuals on that specific report page.

"Filters on all pages" sets a filter condition for the entire report.

By default, any fields that are in a visual will also show up in the Filters pane in the "Filters on this visual" subsection and can be interacted with there.

You can set three common filter types in the Filters pane, each with its own behavior. The basic filtering displays all the values for the given column and allows you to select any number of those values to be true. It's very straightforward. The advanced filtering offers you a combination of two separate and unique conditions with logic available based on the type of data the column represents:

- Contains (text)
- Does not contain (text)
- Starts with (text)
- Does not start with (text)
- Is (all)
- Is not (all)
- Is blank (all)
- Is not blank (all)
- Is empty (text)

- Is not empty (text)
- Is after (date)
- Is on or after (date)
- Is before (date)
- Is on or before (date)
- Is less than (number)
- Is less than or equal to (number)
- Is greater than (number)
- Is greater than or equal to (number)

Most of these conditions are clear-cut, but it's important to remember that you must put the value into the subsection yourself, unlike with basic filtering, which allows you to see a selection of values. You can then select the button to make an and/or condition and set a second logic set. You don't need to set a second logic condition to use advanced filtering.

The third common filter type is a Top N–type filter. Here you can set the number of top or bottom values you want to display by a certain value in your model that can be, but don't have to be, in that visual.

A classic example of this would be to see your top 10 sales clients by state, country, revenue, or volume. You set the number of values to display and whether you want the top or bottom values for that specific field in the visual. You will note that Top N is not available when filtering for an entire page or report. Top N filtering works only when used at the visual level.

Dates also have two other possible types of filters that can be utilized: relative date and relative time.

Relative time will show only if the date field has a time component as well. These filter options allow you to set specific time intervals for a visual or for the report, like the last 10 days or the next week or the last year. Relative time allows you to get into this level of detail with hours and minutes.

A Quick Rundown of the Other Panes

Four panes are not visible by default, but you can turn them on in the View tab, and they'll appear in whatever order you add them. These are the Bookmarks, Selection, Performance analyzer, and Sync slicers panes (Figure 2-26).

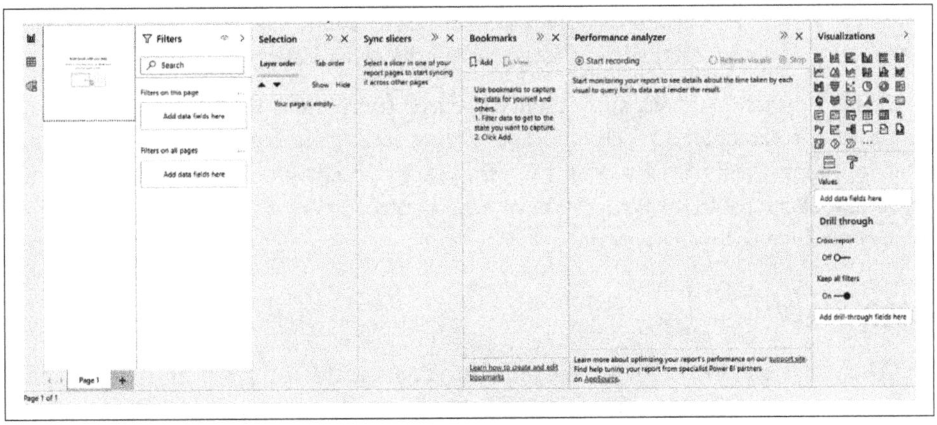

Figure 2-26. The Bookmarks, Selection, Performance analyzer, and Sync slicers panes

The Bookmarks pane allows you to save filters, drilling, and other conditions you may have set for a given report page, like a bookmark that you can return to. Let's say, for instance, we have an example of our report page that shows all the data, but we would like end users to be able to quickly change the report to a specific filtered view. We can use Bookmarks to toggle the conditions of the page from one point to another.

The Selection pane allows you to quickly manage visibility and layering order of objects in the report. Say you have a logo that you want to appear in a very specific location on the report at all times, but as you put visuals onto the canvas, the logo gets covered up by the visual's box, even if the portion of the box that's overlapping the logo is blank. Well, to fix that, you would want to bring the logo to the front, and you can do that and manage your entire layering order from this menu. You can also group objects to be treated and moved together.

The Performance analyzer helps you, when you're ready, to troubleshoot why something in a report might be taking longer to display than you think it should or why it loads slower than it perhaps did in the past. You can use the Performance analyzer to gather information around how many milliseconds it took to generate the DAX query, visualize the results, and other items, including the DAX that Power BI generated to create the visual. While machine-generated DAX isn't always the easiest to learn from as a beginner, when you have some DAX experience under your belt, it can be useful to know all the filter and row context to see how Power BI generates the appropriate code to power the visualization. Likewise, when your report is having issues, you can test different configurations to see if your report performance improves or degrades.

The last pane to discuss is the "Sync slicers" pane. When you put slicer visuals onto a report, they function only for that page. However, with the "Sync slicers" pane, you can select a slicer and add it to other pages and sync them—so that when the slicer is changed on one page, that slicer changes on all the other pages.

This can be great for exploratory analysis, when someone is looking at the data and they find, for example, a specific company they want to home in on. If they set that filter in one portion of the report, this will carry that slicer selection to all the other pages that also have that slicer. You even have control to say it should sync on Page A, but not on Page B, for instance.

Data View

The Data view allows you to see the table-level data inside your report. It will display the columns in your report in their ordinal order instead of their alphabetical order. The *ordinal order* is the order of the columns from the data source or, in our case, the order of the columns as they appear in Power Query before being loaded into our data model. Let's take a look at my sample Date Dimension table to see what an entire table looks like in the Data view in Figure 2-27.

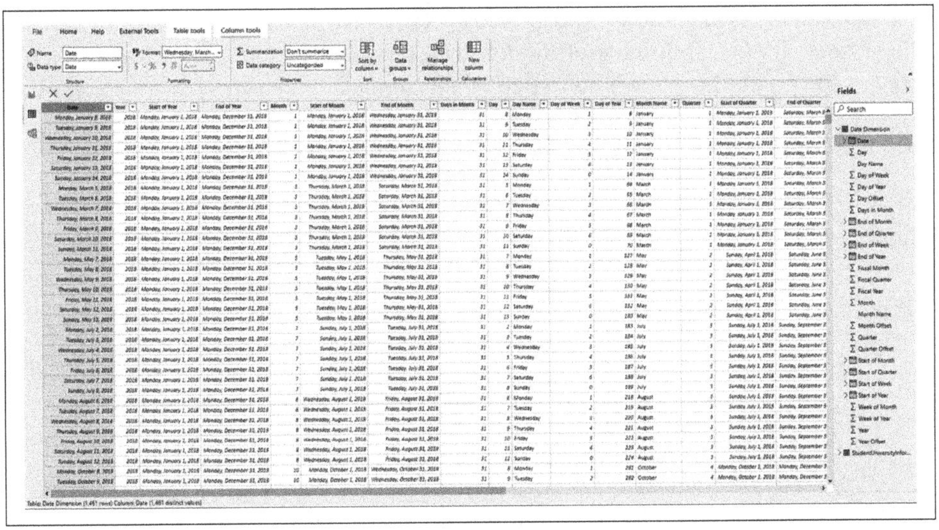

Figure 2-27. An example table in the Data view

First, you'll note two new subsections of the ribbon to interact with. The "Table tools" tab of the ribbon will show up when you have any table or column selected in the Fields pane. The "Column tools" tab will appear only when a specific column is selected. These tabs are completely contextual. Let's see that by zooming into Figure 2-28.

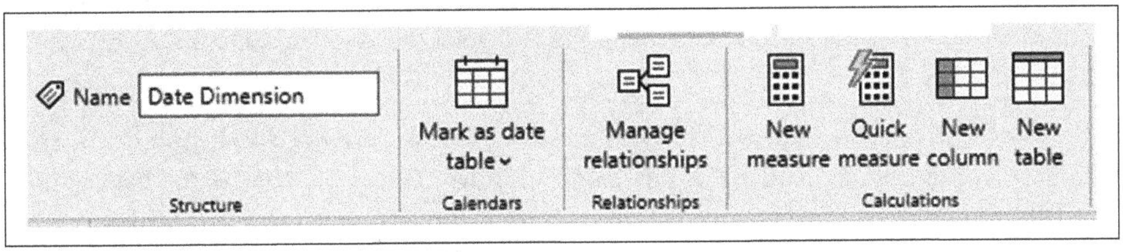

Figure 2-28. New view, new ribbon options

The Table Tools subsection allows you to change the table name or mark it as a date table, or we can look at our relationships here in the same way we did from the ribbon as discussed previously. In addition, we have our calculation options for creating measures and tables. Not too much here is new, and this view also shows up in the Report view when you have a table or column selected.

The one thing that is unique here that's worth discussing is the "Mark as date table" function. By default, behind the scenes, Power BI creates a date table for every instance of a date field in your data model that contains all the dates between the first and last date for that field. It does this so it can put together date hierarchy functionality and some other necessary functions behind the scenes.

In a small model, this isn't a big deal. However, when you start to get large models with dozens or even hundreds of hidden date tables, your model can start to grow very quickly. Power BI allows you to bypass this process by setting a date table in your model to serve that purpose for all those other dates. Since I have a Date Dimension table, I'm going to do exactly that.

When I have a column selected, I can also see the "Column tools" tab, as seen in Figure 2-29.

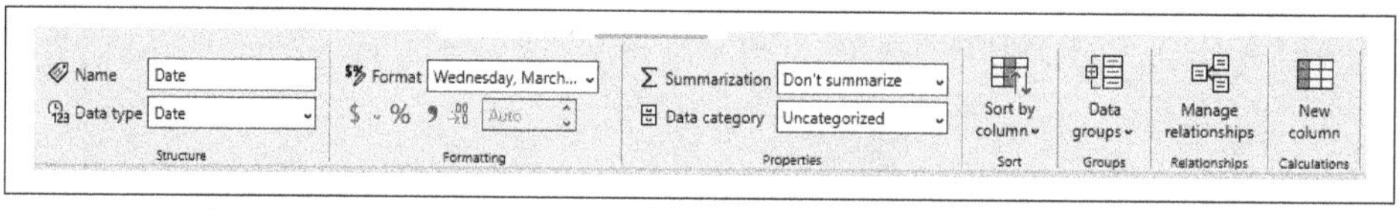

Figure 2-29. "Column tools" tab

Starting on the left, I can see the name of the column and its data type. In this case, I'm looking at the Date column, and it has the Date data type that is different from the Date/Time data type. I can select how I want the data to be formatted when it is brought into a visual. Given that it is a date, I can select a drop-down and see a variety of options.

If I have a column with numbers selected, I can choose to show the value as currency, a decimal number, whole number, percentage, or in scientific notation. The General option will default to the way the data is stored in the data model. There are grayed-out options for currency, percentage, showing commas in values, and setting the number of decimal places for a value since the selected data in Figure 2-29 is not a numeric data type.

Next, in the Properties subsection, you can set the properties of that column for its default summarization and how Power BI should categorize that data. By default, nonnumeric columns are not summarized. However, you can set a default summarization for any column or count or count (distinct). The default summarization for numerical columns is set to sum; however, this doesn't always make sense. The default summarization options are sum, average, minimum, maximum, count, and count (distinct). You can always set any column to have no default summarization by setting it to "Don't summarize."

The Data category is a description of the context for that data. By default, most columns are not assigned a data category and are left uncategorized. For numbers, there aren't very many options, unless you want to set a numerical value to be recognized as, say, a postal code or a barcode value. Dates do not have any data category options. Text, however, has a great number of options, and having these selected for appropriate columns can make working with that data in certain visualizations much easier. These options are Address, Place, City, County, State or Province, Postal code, Country, Continent, Latitude, Longitude, Web URL, Image URL, and Barcode.

The next subsection is "Sort by column." This is hidden away, but it's a jewel of a setting. This allows you to set a rule for a column in terms of how it automatically sorts itself when put into a visual. I have some example data for a fake university, Cool School University. This data is specifically for ISOM (Information Systems Management) 210 Introduction to Data Visualization. What if I want to sort one column by another value? Like sort last names by their Student ID number? That's what "Sort by column" allows you to do.

Data groups allow you to put combinations or bins of data together for quick analysis. Some obvious examples of this are age brackets or ethnographic groupings. However, you can probably come up with a ton of ways to create groups. Have a complicated product list? Group them into more manageable ones. Want to separate a certain patient condition from others as a control group? Group them specifically.

Conclusion

Hopefully, in this chapter you've gained a better understanding of the UI for the Report and Data tabs by using the ribbon and the panes in that interface. We've seen there are a ton of ways to interact with our data in the Data view that will be helpful to us later. However, we must get data into our Power BI file before we do anything else. To that end, in the next chapter we'll discuss bringing data into our model and how we use the Model view.

CHAPTER 3

Importing and Modeling Our Data

In the previous chapter, we went into detail to help you understand the UI functions of the Report and Data views. This chapter deals with the UI of Power Query and the Model view. By the end of this chapter, we'll have imported the mockup class data into a Power BI Desktop file and used that data to demonstrate some of the basic capabilities of Power Query for data manipulation and shaping.

In our discussion of the Model view, we'll demonstrate what relationships are in a data model and what they do. Finally, we'll go through the data and actively try things with it. If you're a hands-on learner, I highly recommend you take the sample data and follow along with me to try to replicate the steps and results.

Getting Our Data

For the purpose of this exercise, I'll be working from three Microsoft Excel files that can be downloaded from *https://oreil.ly/MS-power-BI-files*. We'll place ourselves in the shoes of a data visualization course instructor at Cool School University. We have files representing the information the school has given us, the information we've acquired ourselves from our pupils, and the students' grades on their assignments.

Starting from the Home tab on the ribbon in the Report view, let's use the Excel workbook shortcut and bring in our first file, called *School Supplied Data*. When we click the "Excel workbook" button, Power BI brings up an Explorer window to navigate to the Excel file. Select the file and click Open.

A Navigator window pops up that will generally look like the one in Figure 3-1. I say "generally" because when you're using a database as a data source, you'll probably see a larger number of selectable data elements based on your access level to the database. When connecting to an Excel workbook, you should see all the worksheets in the workbook. When you select a data element, in our case Sheet 1, from the drop-down menu, a preview of the data will be displayed, as shown in Figure 3-2. Notice that I clicked the square next to Sheet 1, effectively selecting it for import. Just so you know, you don't need to have the checkbox selected to see the preview.

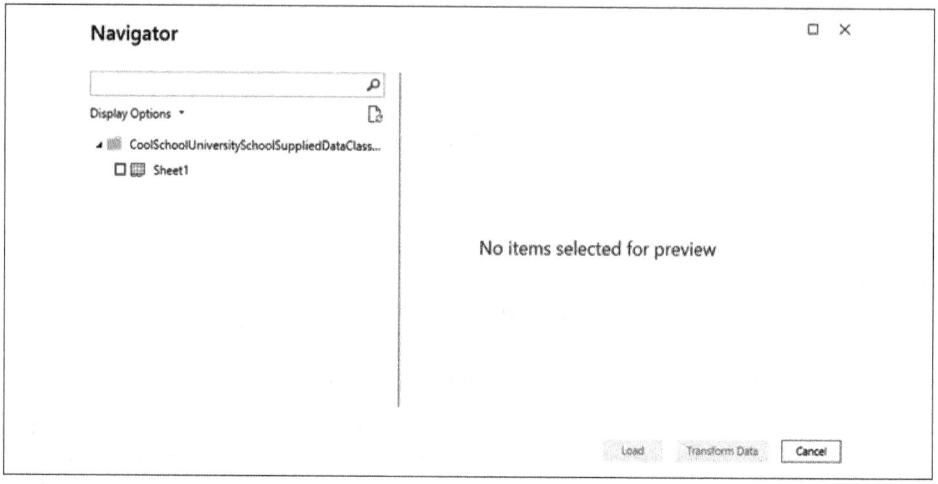

Navigator

Display Options ▾

▲ CoolSchoolUniversitySchoolSuppliedDataClass...
    ☐ Sheet1

No items selected for preview

Load   Transform Data   Cancel

Figure 3-1. The Navigator window should pop up as soon as you open the School Supplied Data file

From here, I want to bring your attention to the bottom-right corner, where you can see that the Load and Transform Data buttons are no longer grayed out. This happens after a data element is selected by clicking the checkmark box. While this file has only one worksheet, if the file did have multiple worksheets, we could select multiple worksheets at the same time for importing. However, as I once learned from two wise bald men who conveniently live in cubes, always select Transform Data. Clicking Load will take the data exactly as the preview sees it and load it into the data model. Nothing prevents us from going back into Power Query later and manipulating the table, but once we choose Load, every other process stops for Power BI to bring in that data and put it into VertiPaq's storage.

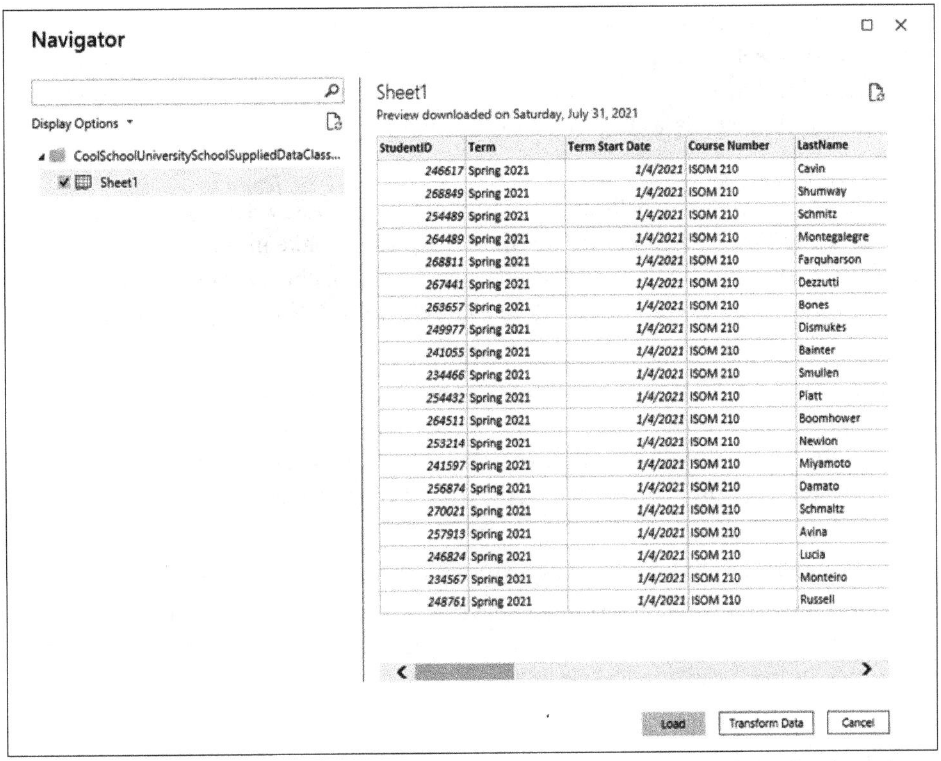

Figure 3-2. You'll see a data preview when you select a data element from the drop-down menu

My general rule of thumb is it never hurts to take an extra second, click Transform Data, and double-check in Power Query that the data is shaped and typed the way you intend. Let's see what happens when we click Transform Data in Figure 3-3.

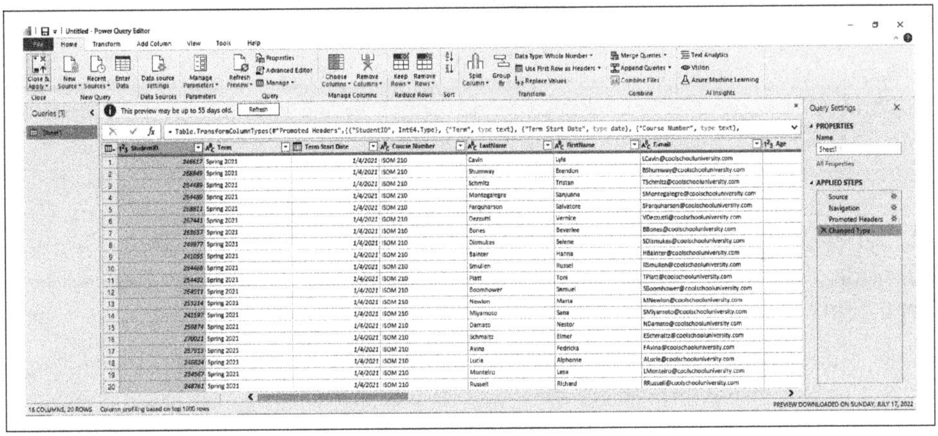

Figure 3-3. Power Query is where we will shape our data to fit our needs

A new pop-up window appears. It shows a lot of stuff: our prospective table (currently titled Sheet 1), a preview of the data, a whole ton of data transformation options, and the currently applied transformation steps to what Power BI is now calling a query. A *query* is a data element that is going to be imported into our data model.

Before we go into all the bells and whistles of Power Query, let's get our other two Excel files into Power Query and give them names that make more sense than Sheet 1 and Sheet 2. Without leaving the Power Query window, choose New Source → Excel Workbook and add *GatheredStudentInformation*. Done? Now repeat that to get our grades for the semester.

It's worth noting that when you add data sources from inside Power Query, the Navigator window will not show you the Load and Transform Data options. There's just a single yellow OK button and a Cancel button. Not to worry; when you click OK in the Navigator window from Power Query, it acts as though you chose Transform Data.

At this point, you've probably noticed that the *Grades* file is different from the first two! Sorry, I had to sneak in a bit of a curveball here. This file does, in fact, have two worksheets. We know from our earlier discussion that we can bring in both worksheets by selecting both and clicking OK.

But look at the GradeScores data preview, and you'll notice it has extra columns that are not named and are null. I intentionally messed with this file a bit so I could show you the Suggested Tables feature. In the Navigator window, you'll see a Suggested Tables drop-down. If you select it and preview the data, you'll see it looks correct without the extra null columns. Let's select the AssignmentDIM from the top and Table 1 from the bottom and bring those both in. If you can figure out what I did to mess up the Excel sheet, I'll give you 15 points. Unfortunately, much like the originally British and then American comedy show, *Whose Line Is It Anyway?*, the points are fake and don't matter.

Now, before we wrap up this section, let's rename the queries so they make sense. The AssignmentDIM kept its worksheet name, which is helpful, but we still need to rename the others. Remember the survey data came from the *GatheredStudentInformation* file and the school-supplied demographic data came from the *SchoolSuppliedDataClassStart* file. Rename those by either right-clicking the table in the Query view and selecting Rename, or adjusting the name from the properties window on the right side of Power Query with the query selected. Let's rename these "Demographic Data," "Survey Data," and "Grades."

If you did everything correctly, Power Query should look like Figure 3-4. If not, I suggest right-clicking each object, choosing Delete, and starting over to see if you can figure out where you went wrong. When you have it all together, click the Close &

Apply button to load the data. To come back to the Power Query window from the Report view, in the Home tab, click the Transform Data button. Once Close & Apply is hit, the data will get loaded and then compressed into the storage engine.

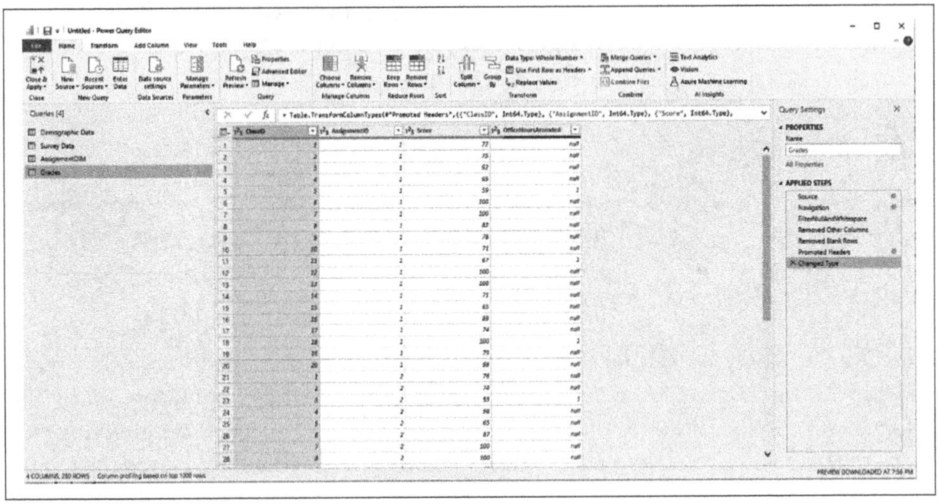

Figure 3-4. If you're following along at home, you should be here

The Power Query Ribbon

Now we've imported our data into Power Query, and just by clicking around the ribbon, you'll see there are many ways to transform your data. For this introduction, I'll be focusing on the Home, Transform, and Add Column areas of the ribbon of Power Query. If there is a data transformation you want to do, but you can't find it in the ribbon, you may be able to perform that via manual coding. That is beyond the scope of this exercise, but if you want to learn more about M, the Power Query language, you'll find Microsoft's documentation on the language at "Power Query M Formula Language" (*https://oreil.ly/kHmSs*).

Finally, before I move on, in the following section you'll note references to selected columns. You can select a column by clicking the column title. As you can see in Figure 3-4, I have the ClassID column selected. When you want to select multiple columns, you can select a column and hold down Shift and click to another column. This will select all the columns between those two columns. To choose columns individually, press Ctrl and click to select multiple individual columns.

The Home Tab

The Home tab in Power Query is, for the most part, straightforward. Looking at Figure 3-5, we can see all the icons in their groups, and we'll walk through them and give you some examples of their use cases.

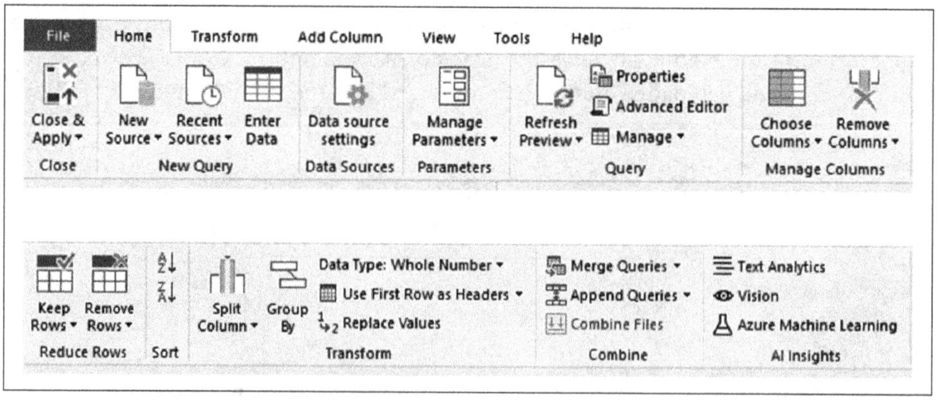

Figure 3-5. The Home tab is where the heart is…or would it be brain?

The Close & Apply button takes all the modifications you've made until that point and applies all the changes, refreshing any data elements that were impacted by the changes. If you click the drop-down arrow, you'll see a drop-down menu giving you three options: (1) Close & Apply; (2) Apply, which, as you might expect, applies changes but doesn't close Power Query; and (3) Leave, which does not apply any changes. If you choose to leave, Power BI Desktop will warn you that you have unapplied changes.

The New Query section allows us to bring in new data with the New Source button. Clicking its icon brings up the whole data source selection menu, whereas clicking the drop-down arrow generates a drop-down menu of the most common data.

The Recent Sources button allows you to quickly connect to any data source you have worked with recently, not just in your current Power BI Desktop file. This can be useful if you are doing testing and want to generate a second file and make quick connections, or if you are working on a new model and want to add onto it with something you've worked with previously.

Enter Data will bring up a rudimentary table structure where you can manually insert data and create column names. I don't recommend using Enter Data extensively, but it can be useful if you have disparate data sources to make a mapping table or a quick extra dimension that may not exist elsewhere in your data. While the interface for Enter Data may look very Excel like, it has no formula support and no data validation rules. It's just rows and columns, and the more data you put into it, the more you must manually manage. That's why I generally caution about using Enter Data if it all possible, but it's there if you need it.

The "Data source settings" button will bring up a window like the one shown in Figure 3-6. From here, you can change sources, export a PBIDS file (which you can imagine is basically a Power BI Desktop shortcut for that data source that you can open in a different Power BI file), edit permissions, and clear permissions.

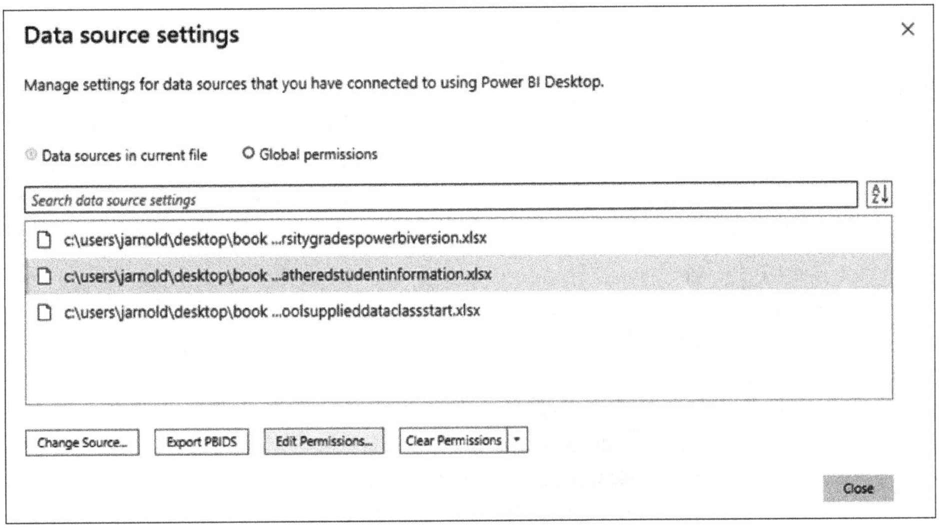

Figure 3-6. "Data source settings"—this area doesn't seem that important, until it is

Manage Parameters allows you to create, view, and edit all your existing parameters. *Parameters* in Power Query are values that can be called in specific contexts to change the way certain data is interacted with. Parameters have a multitude of applications that we will discuss later, in conjunction with what-if analyses, parameter rules in deployment pipelines, and more. For now, just recognize that there's power in parameters, and we'll return to this later.

The Query section of the Home tab allows you to refresh the preview, see the properties, open the Advanced Editor, or manage a query, the meaning of which isn't necessarily obvious.

The Refresh Preview button takes the query you currently have highlighted and gets an updated preview of the data for you to reference as you're working. This can be helpful when you have datasets that update frequently and you want to confirm that you are still getting your intended transformation behavior while that data is changing. You can also click the drop-down arrow to choose to refresh the preview of all the queries in your model currently.

The Properties button opens a dialog box that shows you the name of the query, the description of the query, and two selections to "Enable load to report" and to "Include in report refresh"; by default, these are always selected. There is nothing in the description window until it's added, so describing a query can be helpful.

When "Enable load to report" is turned off, that will treat the entire table as if it does not exist, and all visuals that rely on that table will break. Think of this sort of like a soft delete of a table from your data model. It's still here in Power Query if you want to reenable it, but otherwise Power BI treats it like it doesn't exist.

The "Include in report" refresh function is not quite as intuitive as it should be. If "Enable load" is turned off, you cannot include that table in the report's refresh. When this is disabled, it leaves the data as it currently exists in the model but does not update that query when data refreshes occur. I generally use this when a table is very large and I want to test some other changes in a data refresh without reloading the largest table. In other use cases, people will keep certain data at a point in time for auditing purposes and such.

The Advanced Editor is where you can see the actual M that is generated by every transformation you make! I personally think it's neat that there's a way to see the code generated when you make a change, particularly if you have any interest in learning the language yourself. M as a language, in my opinion, is easy to pick up but difficult to master. If you want to try modifying the M directly from the editor here, make a copy of your currently functioning code in a text file or other backup before making changes. The reason is that whatever changes you make and then click Done, that's what you'll get, whether your code is functional or not. A good rule of thumb is, as always in programming, make sure you have a backup!

Finally, the Manage button is poorly named. When you click this button, you'll see three options: Delete, Duplicate, and Reference.

Duplicating a query takes the query as it currently exists and duplicates it. This is straightforward and does, in fact, mean you are storing that data twice.

Reference does something a bit different. It makes a new query that looks at first like a duplicate, but it's not. It takes whatever query it is referencing, in whatever its final shape is, and allows you to work from there. If you should make changes to the parent query, the referenced query will change as well, and that could cause errors in that query, so be careful.

The Manage Columns area has two buttons: Choose Columns and Remove Columns. Both get you to the same place, but in different ways.

Clicking the Choose Columns icon will bring up a dialog box where you can choose which columns you want to keep in the query, discarding the others. Clicking the Choose Columns drop-down arrow allows you to go to the Choose Columns dialog box just mentioned or to go to a specific column in the query. This second feature can be useful when you have many columns in a query and aren't sure where it is in the column order.

Clicking the Remove Columns icon just removes the column. It does not give you a dialog box. It takes whatever columns are selected and throws them into the abyss. Clicking the Remove Columns drop-down arrow opens a menu offering a second option, to Remove Other Columns. This takes all the columns you don't have selected and throws them out.

The Reduce Rows section has two areas: Keep Rows and Remove Rows. Each has its own unique use cases around the top X number of rows or rows between numbers X and Y. One thing I do want to warn you about in this area is the ability to remove duplicates as shown in the Remove Rows section. It is important to know that it removes duplicates based on the columns you have selected. So, if you have only one column selected and remove duplicates, you might lose data that you originally intended to keep. The Sort section allows you to highlight a column and then sort in ascending or descending order. This does not work when multiple columns are selected.

Next, we get to the Transform section, which gives you some basic transformation options. Split Columns allows you to take a column you've selected and split it into multiple columns based on a delimiter of your choosing. A classic use case of this is a single-name column that has a first and last name, but you need them separated.

Group By allows you to create some sort of aggregation across your current query. This can be useful when, say, you have a large amount of data and you want to do some sort of preaggregation to reduce the number of rows. In Figure 3-7, you can see an example group using our grades data to get the average score per assignment.

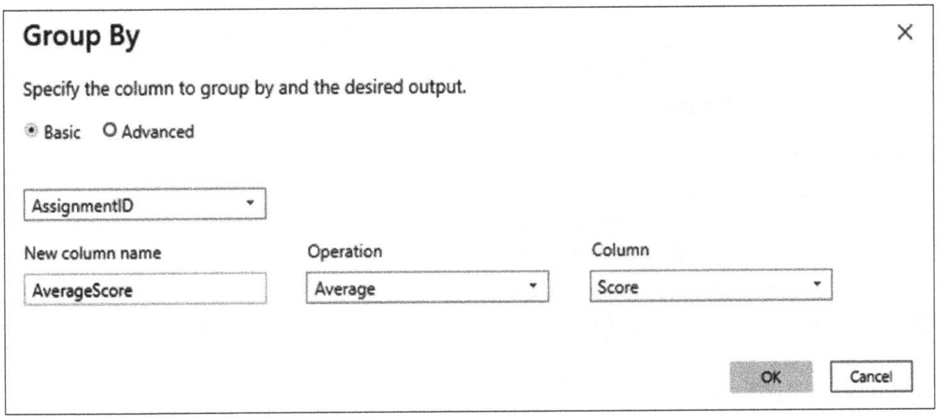

Figure 3-7. Group By enables us to aggregate data with a variety of operations

We can use the Data Type button to change the data type of a column that we have selected. There are many different data types, and Power BI will try to autodetect them when data is first brought in to Power Query. Power BI actually does a good job at detecting data types, but sometimes it's not perfect, so if you need to make a manual adjustment, you'll do that here. Coincidentally, you can see a column's data type by the icon in the column header, as well as a quick check.

Use First Row as Headers is pretty self-explanatory, and Power BI will often try to detect whether the first row comprises column headers, depending on the data source. If you click the arrow next to the Use First Row as Headers button, you will also see an option to make your headers the first row instead, the inverse operation.

Replace Values allows you to find and replace values in a given column. A common use case here would be to either treat zeros as nulls or nulls as zeros, depending on your analysis. It's important to note that you cannot edit individual cells because cells are not a concept that is known to Power Query; it understands only columns.

The Combine section allows us to merge queries, append queries, and combine files. Merge Queries works like a SQL JOIN statement. Say you have Column A in Table A and Column A in Table B, and you want to add Column N from Table B to Table A. A JOIN statement says that where the value in Table A's Column A and Table B's Column A are equal, give me the Column N value and add it. We're doing the same thing here.

The intended use of Append Queries is to take multiple queries where the data is the same shape and format and to consolidate them into one longer query, more like a UNION statement from SQL.

Combine Files allows you to get ahead of the issue in Append Queries by precombining multiple files into a single view. If you should have columns that are unique to each table, this option will smash all of that together to get a single result encompassing all the columns and values between the two tables, so be careful when appending tables that you are getting your intended result.

Finally, the AI Insights section has items that your organization may use that allow you to connect to Azure AI services. Understand that these features require Power BI Premium to be used if they're going to be refreshed. It's quite probable your organization does not have these resources, so I'm not going to spend time on this except to say that they're there. Ask your Azure Administrator if the organization does use Azure Machine Learning studio or Cognitive Services to learn more.

The Transform Tab

The Transform tab contains some extra options for transforming your data beyond what we saw in the Transform section of the Home tab. However, just as we saw in the previous chapter, Microsoft does put some redundancy into the ribbon here, and I'll call out those situations specifically. But first let's take a look at Figure 3-8 to see the whole Transform tab.

First, in the Table section, we see Group By and Use First Row as Headers. These are self-explanatory.

Transpose takes your columns and makes them rows. Reverse Rows takes the order of your data by row and flips it so that the last record is first and the first record is last. Count Rows will show you how many rows you have in that query.

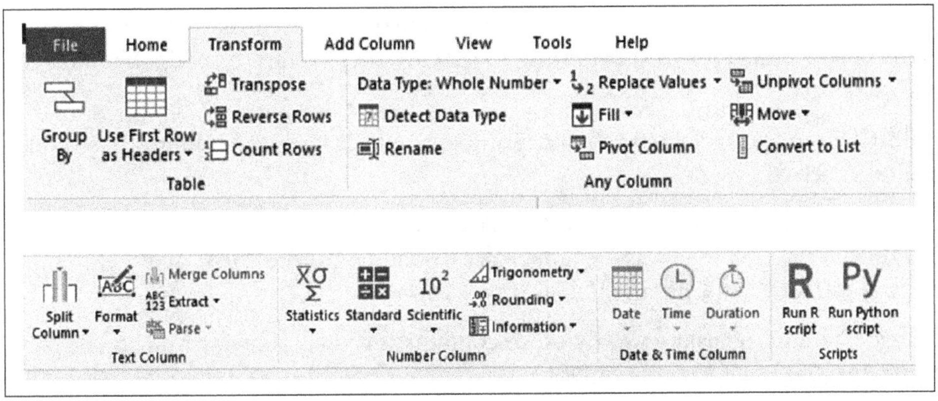

Figure 3-8. Transforming your data to more than meets the eye

The Any Column section provides the ability to edit a column's data type, as we saw previously. You can also replace values as discussed previously.

Unpivot Columns takes columns of data you select and reshapes the data into an "attributes" column and a "values" column. At times you may want to reshape your data in this way, like when you want to consolidate many columns into a smaller number of columns with a higher number of records.

The Detect Data Type button will go through each column and attempt to assign it an appropriate data type based on its preview of the data. Power BI will often do this automatically in the first pull of the data into Power Query, but you can have it do this again if you make a number of transformation changes that might change the data types of multiple columns.

The Fill button allows you to, either from the top or bottom, fill in missing values with a value based on other values in the column. I'll be completely honest, I've never once actually used this feature.

The Move button allows you to move the location of a column in a table. You can move it left, right, to the beginning, or to the end. You can do this with multiple columns selected.

Rename allows you to rename a chosen column.

Pivot Column allows you to take the values of a column, turn those values into columns, and recalculate values across the new combination. This can be useful when you have attributes in one column and values in another, and you want to see the values with the attributes as columns.

Convert to List is a unique function. It takes one column and turns it into a special type of table in Power Query called a *list*. Lists can be passed sort of like parameters to special custom functions. We're not going to worry too much about lists in this book.

The Text Column section is a bit strangely named because you can use these functions on more than just text columns. Thankfully, they are pretty straightforward for the most part.

Split Column allows you to take a column and split it into two columns based on a delimiter selection.

Format does not allow you to edit the data type. It does allow you to do things like making all the data lowercase or uppercase or adding prefixes or suffixes. Using this feature will turn that column into a text type column.

Merge Columns smashes two or more columns together, allowing you to choose a separator.

Extract allows you to modify a column or columns to keep specific characters in a column. I don't use this one very often, but when I have, I used it mostly to remove non-Unicode characters.

Parse does something different compared to everything else here. Parse takes a JSON or XML file, semistructured data, and puts it into a more classically structured format for analysis. We aren't using any JSON or XML files in our examples, but if you were working with NoSQL databases or getting results from API calls, you might need to parse that data before you could do analysis on it, and this parse function does that.

The Number Column functions can allow you to get statistics on a column as a separate value, perform standard calculations against a column to edit its values, apply scientific calculations against a column, perform trig functions against a column, round a column, or find whether a value is even or odd or its sign. With the exception of the statistics function, I recommend duplicating a column before applying any modifications to the data; then you can have both the original clean value and the modified value.

The Date & Time Column area functions in the same way as the Number Column, with numerous date and time transformations.

The final section in the Transform tab is the Scripts section, which offers the ability to run both R and Python scripts against your data. To use these functions, you must have R or Python installed, and Power BI has to know where your installation of those language libraries are. If you're more comfortable working with data frames in R or Python and would rather perform transformations there and use that as a single step, you can. You can also do pre-prep of the work in Power Query, apply a script task, and then make further modifications in Power Query. You can mix and match these functions, and if you wanted to use both, you could. Learning R and Python is beyond the scope of this book, but if you are going to pursue a career in data analytics, both of these languages could prove very useful to you.

The Add Column Tab

The first thing to note in the Add Column tab is that except for the General section, we have seen all the other functions in other places in the ribbon to this point. However, the General section contains so much that it still merits a section of its own. Looking at Figure 3-9 will make it a little clearer.

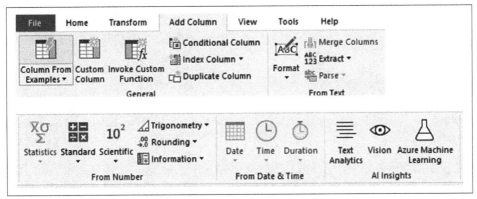

Figure 3-9. The Power BI ribbon will often have multiple places to find certain functionality, but at least they're topical

Column from Examples is actual, factual, black magic. You can select a column or columns to get pieces of data from. Then you'll have to give some examples of what the response would be, and Power BI will attempt to autofill the column as you provide examples to work from. In our Grades query, for example, I'm going to add a column from examples that will say if the OfficeHoursAttended column is null, then no, but otherwise, yes. We can see this in Figure 3-10, and you also have the bonus of seeing the logic it put together in M, which can be another way to see how the language handles different things.

Custom Column will bring up a dialog box where you can create a custom column using M. This can be useful if you have transformations that you want to do that maybe aren't supported by the UI or that you could do more efficiently via code. The dialog box will at least tell you if there is a syntax error in the code, but if you're just learning M, the errors aren't always super helpful.

Invoke Custom Function is an incredibly powerful tool that allows you to take a function and iterate over that function for a given column, finding a specific value and then applying some sort of logic. A simple example is creating a function that would make a new column and then take the value of one column and multiply it by another to get a third value that would be placed in this new column. Did you follow that logic? This is a very powerful tool, but it can also be hard to wrap your head around what it does the first time you work through it.

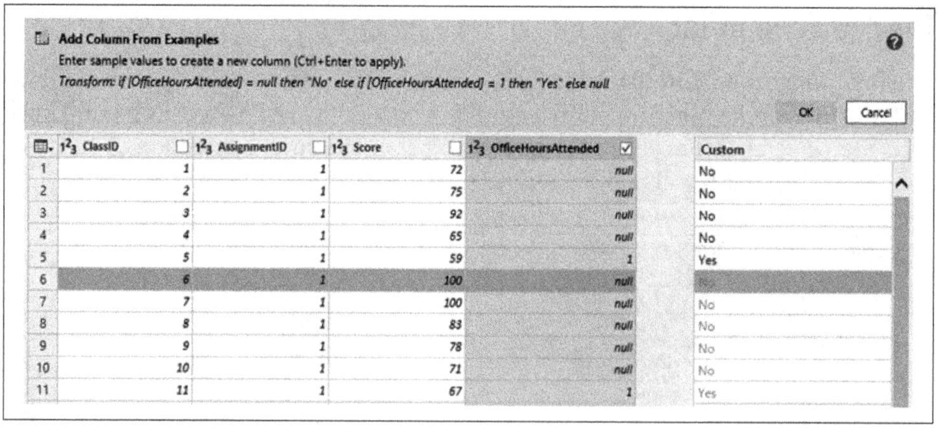

Figure 3-10. A couple of examples of what I want, sprinkle in some AI, and voila, fresh column!

Conditional Column allows you to create a column along the lines of an if-then-else statement. If Column X is less than Column Y, then Yes, else No. You can also have multiple clauses for more complicated or iterative if functions. If you're familiar with SQL, think of this much like a case when statement. Figure 3-11 shows the dialog box for adding a conditional column.

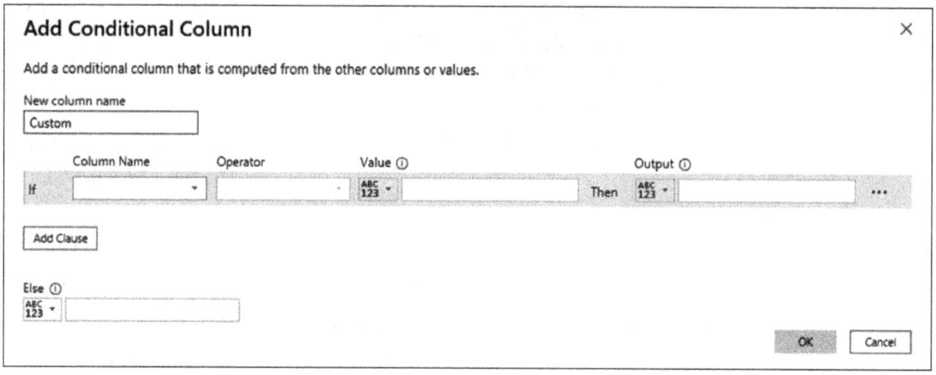

Figure 3-11. Sometimes we just need an if statement

Index Column creates a column that will start from 0 or 1 and create a unique list of values, usually corresponding to the row number. The most important thing about an index column is that it is completely unique and can be used as an impromptu key value if necessary, possibly merging that column with others to pass the index or key value to other tables for the purpose of creating relationships. Ideally, your data already has keys in place, and an index isn't necessary. But if you do need to create an index, it's very simple.

Duplicate Column takes the current column and makes a copy of it. That's it. No witty commentary on that one. It's just copy and paste.

Finally, I want to mention the View tab. The items on the View tab allow you to do some small customizations to the way you interact with Power Query. I want to highlight in the Data Preview section the Column quality, Column distribution, and Column profile checkboxes, as they'll allow you to see more detail around your data at the columnar level. This includes a percentage breakdown of valid, error, and empty values in a column, the numerical distribution of values in a column, and a distribution of data including the number of unique values in a column.

When you're done with all of your changes and you're ready to load your data with your changes, click that Close & Apply button. This will close your Power Query window and bring you back to the Power BI Desktop canvas.

The Model View

Returning back to Power BI, let's take a look at that third view in Power BI Desktop, the Model view. Why do relationships matter? What do they actually accomplish? Can I just ignore relationships and make one big table that can solve world hunger? We'll address these ideas in this section.

Let's take a quick look at the Model view of our current file in Figure 3-12.

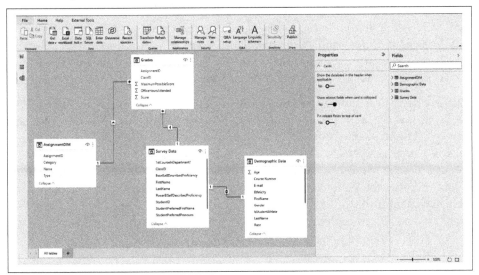

Figure 3-12. That's it, our data model

By default, Power BI will try to detect relationships when importing data and when the data is put together in such a way that Power BI will detect the relationships correctly. Unfortunately, it doesn't always do a good job of this. As a result, you should always double-check your relationships after you import data to make sure your model is constructed as you intended. Your model after your first import may not look like Figure 3-12 when Power BI first attempts to detect relationships and, as we will see here and in Chapter 6, the forms our relationships take really matters!

What Is a Relationship?

A *relationship* is, in the simplest terms, a way to tell Power BI which tables are connected and how. A relationship should be constructed so that the values in one column in one table match those values in another table, such that if we tried to query them, we could get back sensible results. A relationship is a combination of a few things—columns, direction, and cardinality. If we hover over the lines in our data model, they will glow yellow, and if we double-click that, we can see the relationship dialog box as shown in Figure 3-13. In this case, I'm demonstrating the relationship between AssignmentDIM and Grades.

Let's walk through this dialog box and talk about what we have. First, we see two tables are selected. In this case, because we chose the relationship from the Model view, it prepopulated the tables in question. You can see each table has one highlighted column. This is the column that forms the basis of the relationship.

Here we're telling Power BI the following: "When you have to run a query and pull data from both Grades and AssignmentDIM, you can join them on this column." This is critical in any database system, and Power BI isn't any different. Something that is different, though, is that I can't select multiple columns to have a relationship.

"But Jeremey!" I can already hear some of you yelling at the page, "I can write a SQL statement that has multiple join conditions between two tables!" Yes. Yes, you can. However, Power BI does not run SQL when it queries its internal database: it runs DAX. If you need to create a relationship between two tables with multiple columns, my suggestion is to create a column with a composite value of the columns you want to join in both tables and create your single relationship then, with your new concatenated column.

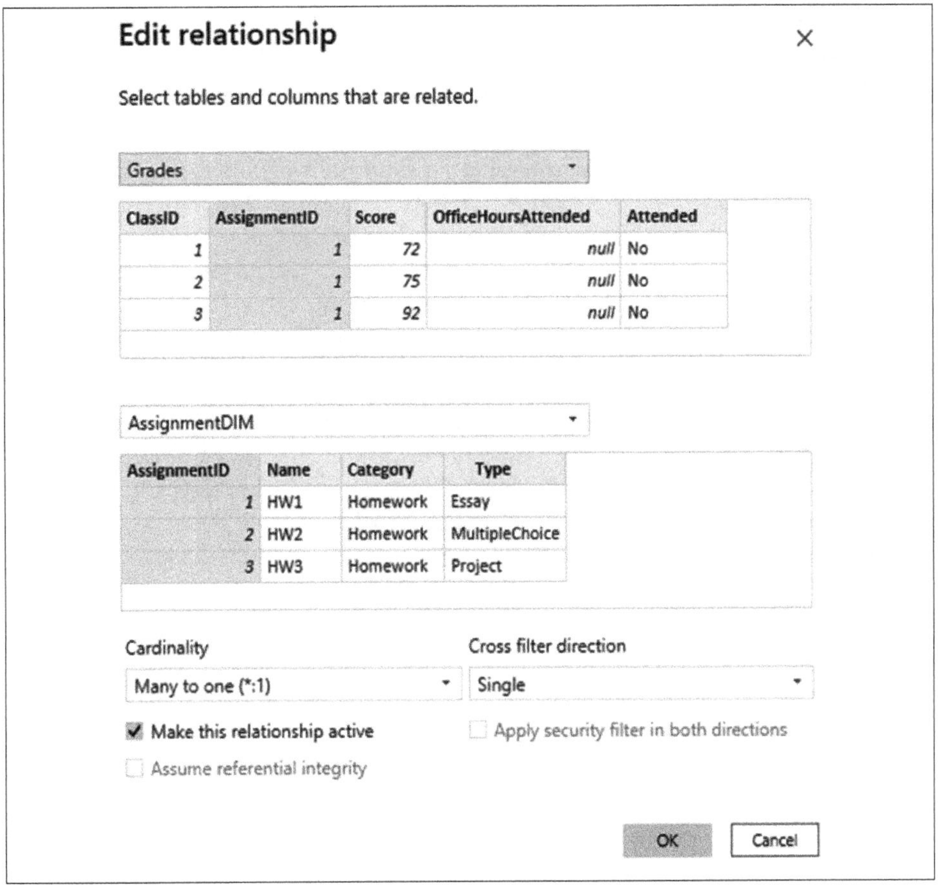

Edit relationship

Select tables and columns that are related.

Grades ▾

ClassID	AssignmentID	Score	OfficeHoursAttended	Attended
1	1	72	null	No
2	1	75	null	No
3	1	92	null	No

AssignmentDIM ▾

AssignmentID	Name	Category	Type
1	HW1	Homework	Essay
2	HW2	Homework	MultipleChoice
3	HW3	Homework	Project

Cardinality

Many to one (*:1) ▾

☑ Make this relationship active

☐ Assume referential integrity

Cross filter direction

Single ▾

☐ Apply security filter in both directions

OK   Cancel

Figure 3-13. It's not coincidental: relationships are fundamental

Next, let's talk about cardinality and direction. These two things go hand in hand. We can create three types of relationships in Power BI: one-to-one relationships, one-to-many relationships, and many-to-many relationships.

I don't like many-to-many relationships. The best practice when building a data model avoids many-to-many relationships wherever possible because they're not performant and can sometimes give you strange results compared to your expectations. Many-to-many relationships are more akin to a FULL OUTER JOIN, for you SQL people. You can quickly identify a relationship is many-to-many by looking at the line connecting the two tables and seeing if there are stars on both ends of the line.

In a one-to-one relationship, all the values in Column A of Table A are unique, and all the values in Column A of Table B are unique. You can quickly identify a one-to-one relationship by seeing the number 1 on both ends of the line connecting two tables.

In a one-to-many relationship, all the values in Column A of Table A are unique, but the values in Column A of Table B aren't unique. You can quickly recognize this type of relationship in your model by seeing that one end of the line will have a 1, and the other end of the line will have a star in the Model view. The benefit of both of these types of relationships is that I'm looking for one value and comparing those values in the other column, as opposed to looking for every copy of that value and comparing it to every other copy of that value.

When we discuss the direction of a relationship, we are discussing which table can filter the other. Can they filter both ways or just one? A one-to-one relationship by default has a filter direction of both. This can be seen in the middle of the line connecting two tables by having arrows pointing both directions. A many-to-many relationship can have only a filter direction of both. A one-to-many relationship defaults to a single filter direction, going from the table with the unique value to the table with the nonunique values. A single directional relationship can be identified because one arrow will be pointing toward the table that is being filtered.

Let's demonstrate a couple of examples to show what happens. First, I'm going to display a table that contains values from these two tables without any relationship at all, and then with the relationship in place, and then demonstrate how the direction functions. Figure 3-14 shows what happens with no relationship.

AssignmentID	Average of Score
1	77.07
2	77.07
3	77.07
4	77.07
5	77.07
6	77.07
7	77.07
8	77.07
9	77.07
10	77.07
11	77.07
12	77.07
13	77.07
14	77.07
Total	**77.07**

Figure 3-14. You're no expert yet, but you know that isn't right, and the relationship is why

Here, in Figure 3-14, I've taken the assignment ID code from the AssignmentDIM table and added the average of the score on those assignments. That 77.07 value is the average of the score across everything, but isn't the average score per assignment. Without any relationship, Power BI doesn't know how to generate a query that gets what I'm looking for.

Now let's add the relationship back in and see what we get in Figure 3-15.

AssignmentID	Average of Score
1	81.95
2	79.60
3	82.30
4	79.60
5	78.20
6	80.50
7	78.25
8	81.50
9	79.45
10	79.60
11	77.90
12	80.60
13	78.55
14	41.00
Total	**77.07**

Figure 3-15. That makes more sense, a lot more sense, because the relationship makes the internal queries functional

You'll notice that the total average is still correct; that value doesn't require any inter-action with the assignment ID. However, for each individual AssignmentID, I can create a query that basically says, "Where AssignmentID = 1, ignore all the other val-ues in the Grades table where the AssignmentID isn't 1, and then calculate the aver-age score for just that AssignmentID, and then do that again for each AssignmentID." Relationships make this possible.

Now let's talk about filter directions. In Figure 3-16, I have a slicer (a type of visual that filters other visuals on the canvas by applying a set value or values to the other visualizations, like a WHERE clause in SQL) on score, and I'd like to see which assignment IDs had that score in it.

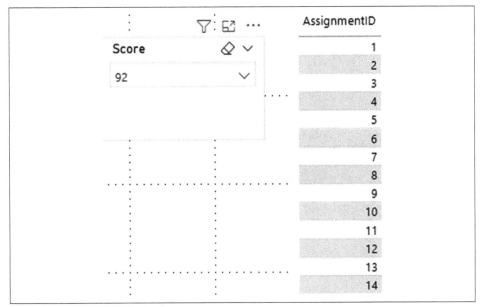

Figure 3-16. Useless filter is useless. Cardinality and relationship direction matter!

Remember, our data model has a one-to-many relationship between AssignmentDIM and Grades, and it filters in only a single direction, from the one in the AssignmentDIM to the many in the Grades table. So, the score from grades cannot filter AssignmentDIM.

Now, let's flip this the other way and put assignment ID on the slicer and the list of scores in the table, and see what we get in Figure 3-17. Then, in Figure 3-18, we can see what happens when the directional filter is set to both.

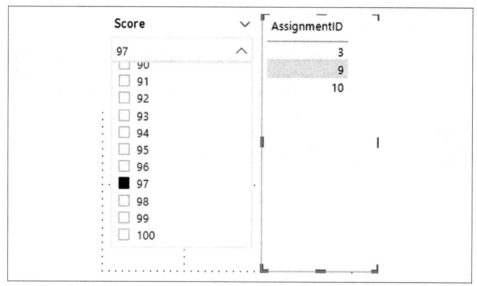

Figure 3-17. Useful filter is useful!

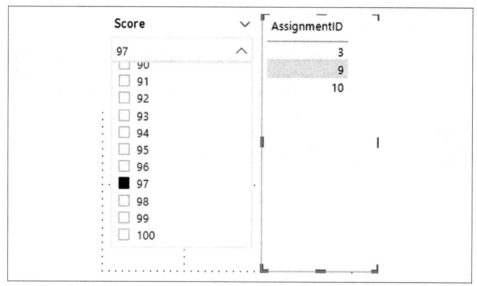

Figure 3-18. Bidirectional filtering

I can hear those cries from the ether again, "But Jeremey, if bidirectional filtering does that, why don't we just make that the default all the time?" The short answer is that it's not as performant, and you can create relationships where *ambiguity* can happen, which prevents other relationships from being used. Generally, the best data modeling practice would be a *star schema*, where you have a table containing your facts and then other smaller tables surrounding it, like a star that filters that table.

OK, well, what about that single table that solves world hunger? Wouldn't that be fine? Well, the short answer is no. A large single table doesn't leverage the benefits of a dimensional model approach, which has several data governance and ease-of-use benefits. Also, a single large table can quickly become unwieldy, as you create many complex edits in Power Query to facilitate the creation of that single table. It really is easier to deal with a table with 5 columns and a table with 10 columns compared to a single table with 15 columns.

In addition, single tables are more prone to breaking over single issues, as opposed to a multitable approach with multiple simpler items. If you are looking for the quick version of a good data model, it's a table that contains your facts, surrounded by tables that can filter those facts with multiple one-to-many relationships. If you're doing that, you'll be in good shape.

The Properties Pane

The Properties pane in the Model view is very contextual. You'll always find the Properties pane on the right side. Whatever data element you've selected will change the Properties pane to be relevant to the type of data object you've selected.

When a table is selected, you can see the Name, Description, Synonyms, Row label, Key column, the Is hidden flag, and the Is featured table flag. In the Advanced section, this pane will show the Storage mode. The Storage mode can be Import, DirectQuery, or Dual. Note that once something is in Import mode, it can't be changed. See an example of the Properties pane in action in Figure 3-19.

The Name field is straightforward. The Description will be blank and can be worth filling in with a summary of that table's contents or its purpose in your data model. The Synonyms are listed for the purpose of the Q&A feature, which we have touched on a little bit but will discuss in more detail later in the book. The Row label allows you to identify a column to serve as the assumed column when doing Q&A with a specific table.

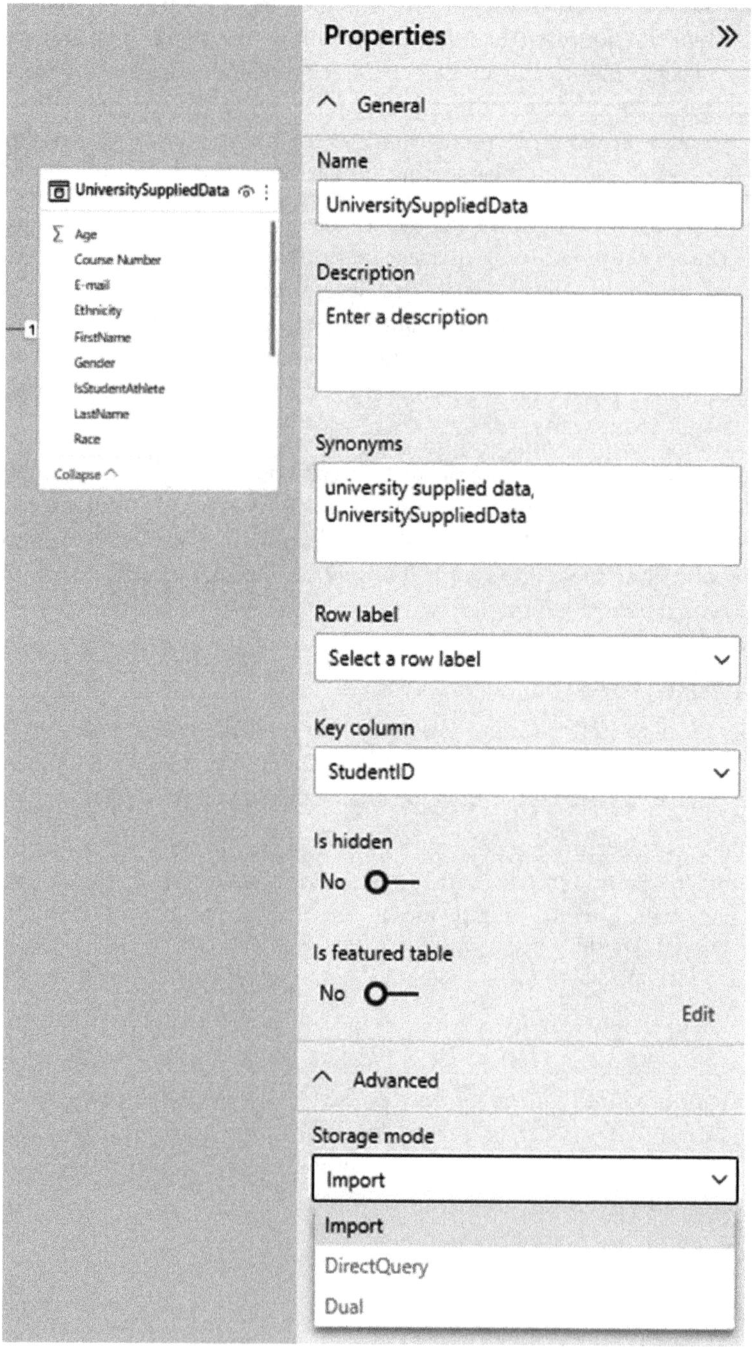

Figure 3-19. The Properties pane has information that's useful for organization, linguistics, keys, and a table's storage mode

The Key column allows you to identify a column that contains only unique values. I like to highlight the column that serves as the basis for that table's relationships with other tables. Also, when a column is identified as the key column, it will get a special icon next to it in the Fields pane.

If "Is hidden" is set to Yes, the table will be hidden from the Report view so that you can't add items from that table to report items. Note that if you already had objects created using that table, those objects will stay visible, but you won't be able to add data elements from that table to new visualizations. Finally, if a table is a featured table, people in an organization with featured tables enabled can search for this table from the Power BI service.

When an individual column is selected, you can see the Name, Description, Synonyms, Display folder, and Is hidden flags. In the Formatting section of the pane, you can see the column's data type and the data's format. Finally, in the Advanced section, you can select another column to sort by, identify a data category if relevant (think of these as identifications for very specific types of data that Power BI might need to use in very specific situations), and set a default summarization. You can also identify whether a column should be able to have null values in this section of the pane. All the guidance from our preceding table section applies, but I want to talk about display folders a little bit.

Display folders can be a great way to keep a data model clean by grouping data elements into a subfolder inside a table. No actual data is modified or manipulated here; this is strictly for visual cleanliness. You can also place measures into display folders, and I find this to be particularly helpful when I want to group specific items together that may not be convenient in the larger alphabetical sorting that Power BI does in the Fields pane.

Conclusion

So, to wrap up this chapter, we got a ton done. We took our first steps into Power Query, loaded our data into our model, have relationships to support our analysis, and now we can start creating our dashboard that will help us learn more about our students' performance over the course of the semester in our class.

To facilitate that, in the next chapter I'll be going into depth on the visualization options in Power BI and discussing use cases for each type of visual. We'll also practice drawing inferences from our data from these visualizations to learn a little bit more about the students. Great job following me so far. You are definitely on your way to earning a Cool School University sweatshirt.

CHAPTER 4

Let's Make Some Pictures (Visualizing Data 101)

Previously we discussed the basics of the Power BI user interface, touching on the Report, Data, and Model views, as well as Power Query. In the preceding chapter, we imported our first set of data from our Cool School University dataset.

In this chapter, we're ready to go over some basic ideas about why we visualize data. Then, using our data from the preceding chapter, we'll do a walk-through of the multiple visuals available by default in Power BI.

Why Visualize Data?

Imagine this. The year is 1950, and you're an accountant at a small manufacturing firm in the Midwest. You served in World War II as an accountant at the Department of War, ensuring those war bond funds were spent efficiently to help the Allied war effort.

To do all your work, you had a ledger book. That was it. So, every day you'd log your transactions from one account to another, making sure all the money was where it was supposed to be.

One day, the floor manager of the plant comes to the accounting office to ask you a few simple questions. "Hey, I'm curious. Which of our products actually makes us the most money? What about on a per unit basis? And are they the same product?"

Now, as a 1950s accountant, would you willingly just hand over your ledger book? Absolutely not. Never. The ledger book was an accountant's lifeblood, and back then someone would have had to pry it from your cold, dead hands before you'd part with it.

What you would do is, using the data compiled, put together a table that would show the list of products, the total profits by product, and the profit per unit for each product. One might call that table a very simple data visualization.

Now, for sake of argument, let's say that a different accountant (not you, you're too smart) would consider just handing over their ledger book, saying, "Sure. You can figure it out. Here's the record."

Would that make sense? No. It doesn't make sense for two reasons. First, the floor manager and their team aren't going to be as familiar with the data. They didn't compile it. They didn't do all the math, and they're likely not accountants. So, even if an accountant did hand over the ledger book, the floor manager and their team might have a hard time following the logic. Second, the accountant had already done all this work, so why would they ask someone to do it again? That's just not efficient.

Let's get back to our example and the data. We discover that widget A has the highest total profitability and widget B has the highest profitability per unit. The follow-up question becomes, "Is that true just for this year or is it true historically?"

I could create an even more complicated table. I could have columns for each year and do the calculation by product and put together a nice matrix. While some people can look at the matrix and follow along, some of our audience now isn't getting the impact of the data.

I want to make the data as comprehensible as possible, so I create a simple graph with an x-axis for year and a y-axis for profitability. I plot the points and draw a very simple line that shows the trend for those products, separating them into their own graph for clarity.

Which do you think will better stick in people's minds? The matrix or the graphs?

Answer this question for yourself. You've likely been in a meeting or presentation where someone showed data in the form of a long, drawn-out table, and maybe that's when you felt yourself start to drift off a bit. Another presenter showed data using graphs and images. Which one did you find more engaging?

I'm willing to bet that the overwhelming majority of people find the graph approach much more engaging. I feel confident of that because we are inherently drawn to stories. We're drawn to stories because we're more naturally able to take a story and learn lessons from it than we can from a list of facts.

The fact that we find it easier to identify with these anecdotes over hard data is taken advantage of. For example, it is possible you've had a bad experience with an undocumented immigrant. That anecdote left an impression and when a new organization pushes individual stories of misdeeds, it becomes easier to latch onto that qualitative story over the reams of data that shows that undocumented workers commit crimes at a far lower rate than native born citizens.

We have all sorts of biases that we must contend with, and we have to be able to view and understand the facts to overcome them. But if the choice is between data that tells no story and a story that serves our bias, the story that serves our bias will win.

Data visualization fundamentally uses that phenomenon of storytelling as teaching to our advantage. Data visualization uniquely triggers all three parts of the ancient Greek modes of persuasion: ethos, pathos, and logos. The art of doing the work to create the visualization demonstrates your mastery of the data, giving you an ethos credibility. Showing the data in the form of images that are easily understood and enable you to tell a story is the core of the pathos, or emotional appeal. Finally, the data itself, assuming it's been collected and managed properly, should only tell you the truth. At its core, the data elements are the facts, and the facts make the argument's logos appeal.

We visualize data because we are storytellers. We don't tell our stories from the whimsy of our imagination. We tell our stories from the facts, establishing our credibility and understanding of those facts. From there, we make that story as digestible as possible. And, again, the story is based on thousands or millions or billions of data points, not just a few anecdotes, which lends to credibility.

Remembering the adage that a picture is worth a thousand words, a good graph can be worth millions or billions of rows of data. You are a storyteller, and you're the best kind of storyteller, one who makes sense of what's really happening. Whether finding the answer or finding the truly important question that needs to be answered, storytelling with data visualization can help you get there.

So, let's talk about the visualization tools Power BI gives us to tell that story with our data. Think of these tools as the alphabet. Once you get familiar with them, you'll learn how to make words from them, then get to the point where you are telling stories with them, and, with time and practice, you'll figure out how to use each visualization to maximum effect. With that in mind, let's talk about where that all begins, the Visualizations pane.

The Visualizations Pane

The *Visualizations pane* is your go-to spot for adding visualizations, modifying them by adding the requisite data points, formatting your visualizations, or adding additional analytics capabilities that Power BI supports in some of these visuals. The Visualizations pane consists of three major parts: Fields, Format, and Analytics. See the recently updated Visualizations pane in Figure 4-1.

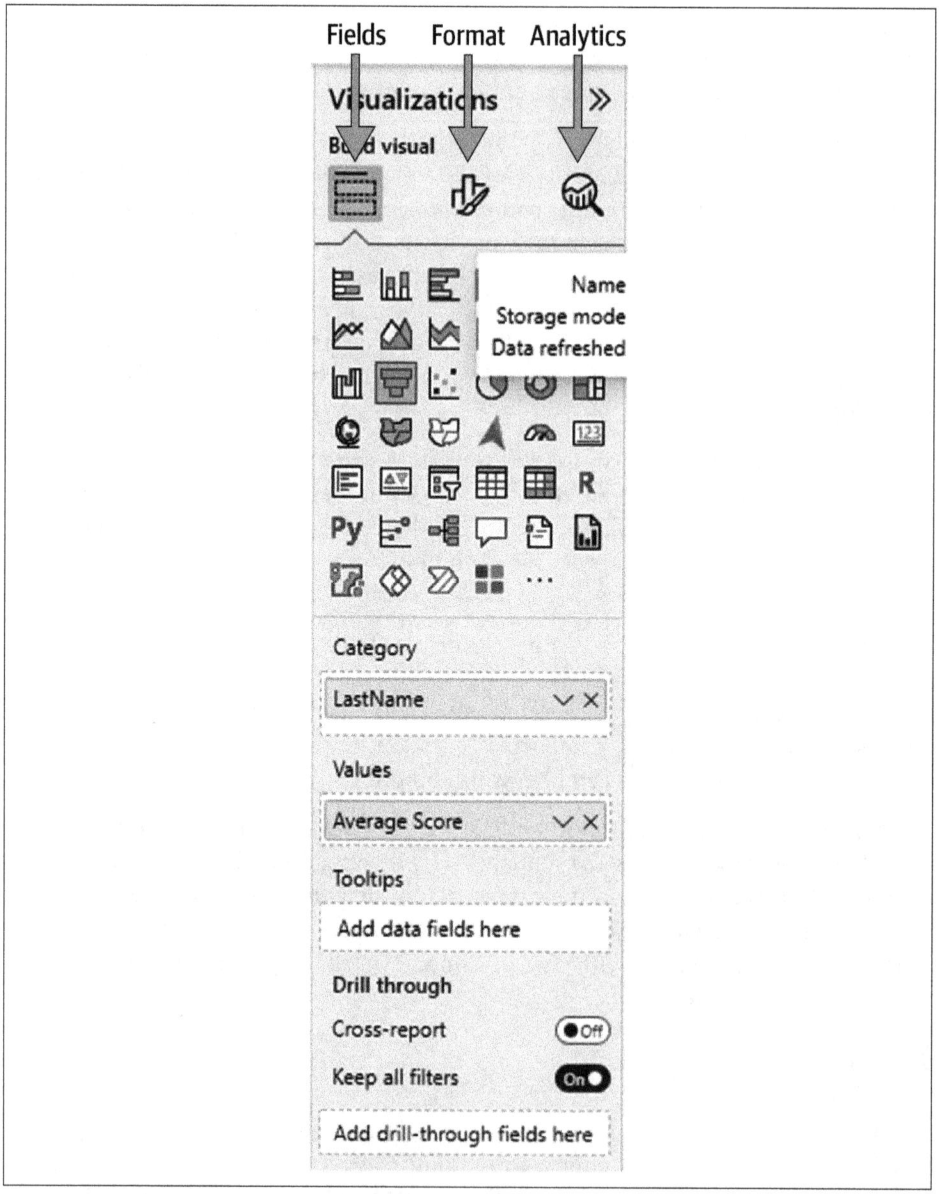

Figure 4-1. *The Visualizations pane is our visualization toolbox. Don't leave home without your toolbox!*

Fields

It's important to note that each visualization will look different from other visualizations in the Fields area because they all accept different inputs. A map visual isn't going to be the same as a bar chart, which isn't going to be the same as a matrix. If you have fields in a visual already and choose to change the type of that visual into something else, Power BI will try its best to reallocate the selected fields and measures to the new visual; but it's not guaranteed to work as you intended. You can change the type of a visual already on the canvas by selecting that visual and clicking a different visualization in the Visualizations pane. That's it.

Common elements that will show up in many visuals in the Fields pane include Axis, Legend, and Values. An *axis* defines how you are categorizing your data. A *legend* splits the data into subsections and highlights those distinctions. *Values* are the actual values you want to aggregate across those groupings.

In Fields, there will always be a section at the bottom for "Drill through" options. This cool feature allows you to take a visual and apply the filters currently on that visual to another visual on another page, taking you directly to that report page and its set of visuals. "Drill through" is a really great way to take insights from one portion of your report to another and to keep that context in sync.

Format

In previous versions, the Format pane was depicted by a paint-roller icon. Now, when a visual is not selected, it appears as a paintbrush over a page. But when a visual on the canvas is selected, it looks like a paintbrush over a bar graph. Format allows you to customize the look and feel of a given visualization to meet your specific needs.

Much like with Fields, the eligible options under Format are contextual to the visualization being modified. Many options are available, and if you've ever used PowerPoint, many should feel familiar to you. Each section in Format has an arrow next to it that allows it to be open or collapsed. This can be helpful for navigation purposes. Some features under Format have distinct functionality, but for the purpose of this exercise, focus on the thought that Format is where you go to make your visualizations really pop.

Analytics

The Analytics functions, accessed by clicking the icon of a magnifying glass looking at a graph, don't work on all visualizations, and it's important to note that no custom visuals can leverage the Analytics area. However, for visuals where Analytics does work, you can use this functionality to add in constant lines for comparison, minimum value lines to identify when something is below a given threshold, a maximum line for the obverse purpose, an average line, a median line, a percentile line, or a trend line, or even do anomaly detection.

There's so much functionality under Analytics, but using it effectively is context dependent, so don't be afraid to try things to see what works or doesn't for you and your project.

Visual Interactivity

Before we get into details of actual visuals, we should discuss one of the most powerful features on a Power BI report page: visual interactivity. By default, any visualization you put onto a report page can filter any other visual on the page. This enables a user to quickly get to specific combinations of data they could be looking for.

In Figure 4-2, you see a simple report page with two visuals. One is a map visual showing the number of students I have in my class from each state, and the second is a simple bar showing the average score across all assignments.

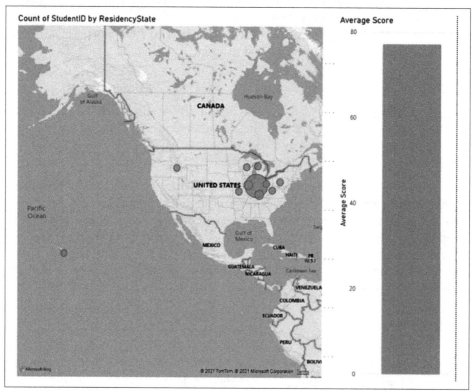

Figure 4-2. This shows a combination of data detailing where our students came from. I think our student from Hawaii is lost.

When I click any of those bubbles in the map, the average score visual will change to reflect the specific subgroup I've selected from the map visual. Looking at the map visual, I can see many of my students are from Indiana. But I want to see how my students from other states might compare to the average, for instance. When I choose the bubble in Michigan, I get the result shown in Figure 4-3. For demonstration purposes, I've captured the image while I was hovering over the result for the column graph to make it clearer to you.

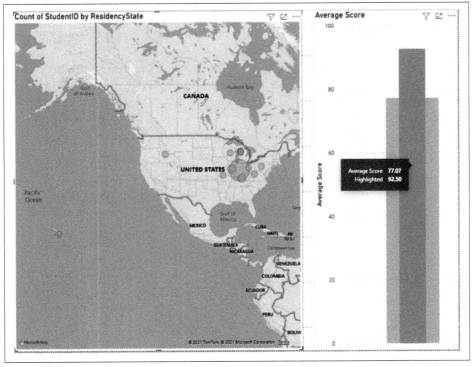

Figure 4-3. Here we demonstrate cross-filtering across visuals. We can see our students from Michigan perform above the average of the rest of the class.

You can see in the map visual, all the other bubbles are transparent now, indicating I've selected one. Now, on the right, you'll see that the column graph shows a new result. It shows a highlighted column, and behind that highlighted column, you can see the original result. From this, I can quickly see that the average score for my Michigan students is higher than my average for the entire group of students. You'll note, though, that it doesn't immediately give me the original average without the Michigan students. This type of cross-filtering, which highlights a value, doesn't remove the selection from the original value.

So, this compares the Michigan student average to the entire student average, which still includes the Michigan students. If we wanted to do something a little different, we could do so with some custom measures, and we'll discuss that more in our chapter on DAX fundamentals.

Now, at times you might not want a certain visual to cross-filter or be cross-filtered, and not all visuals have the same types of cross-filtering display options. When you have a visual selected, in the ribbon under the Format tab, you'll see a button called "Edit interactions." Unlike other buttons we've discussed, this is either on or off. When it's on, you will see in the corner of each visual on your report page some different icons; again, not every icon will be on every visual.

Let's take, for example, the column graph from our preceding figures; with "Edit interactions" on and the map visual selected, we would see three icons, as shown Figure 4-4. The icons are very small. I wish Microsoft would make these interaction icons a little bit more obvious, but they're not. When I talk about an icon being selected, it will show as being "filled in," as compared to being see-through. In the example, you can see the middle button is filled in, so that's the type of cross-filtering that is done by the map visual against the column visual.

On the left is the Filter option. This would strictly filter the result to show only the filtered result; so, in this case, we would see only the Michiganders' result, instead of the result against the entire average. The second option is the Highlight option, which does what you saw in Figure 4-3. The final option is None, which means that the selected visual will not cross-filter that visual at all.

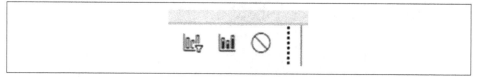

Figure 4-4. From left to right: Filter, Highlight, and None

Column and Bar Charts

Column and bar charts typically have a very simple x-/y-axis design. Take the values and compare them across two dimensions, and garner some insight from that. Some charts allow us to add in a second y-axis to use when we want to overlay one value against another. In the column and bar chart category, Power BI has the following visuals by default (in their order in the Visualizations pane, left to right, top to bottom, skipping over visuals that aren't relevant to this portion of the text):

- Stacked bar chart
- Stacked column chart
- Clustered bar chart
- Clustered column chart
- 100% stacked bar chart
- 100% stacked column chart
- Waterfall chart

Stacked Bar and Column Charts

The *stacked bar* and *column charts* accomplish the same goal with different verticality. Which one is your x-axis, and which one is your y-axis? As a good rule of thumb, use bar charts when comparing against discrete values and use columns when you're measuring against continuous values like time, for instance. This isn't a hard-and-fast rule, though.

For this chart, I'm going to look at the difference between students for whom this is their first class in the department and those for whom it is not. I'd like to know their average score, and I'd like to see how many office hours were attended by each group.

We can see both the bar and column examples in Figure 4-5. Note that for these two charts, the values you lay on top of each other form a summation of whatever values make up the visualization—in this case, the average assignment score and the sum of each group's office hours. This gives us a combined value that allows us to quickly compare multiple columns and find results that may not be intuitive on the surface.

Looking at both charts, they share the same inputs from the Visualizations pane. You define an axis. You can add a legend as a category to further subdivide the bar or column, the values you want to review, small multiples, and tooltips.

The *tooltip* is what you see when you hover over a certain part of the visual with your mouse cursor. When the tooltip is empty, Power BI will put together a list of values into the tooltip based on what's in the visual. Think of it as a quick table you can make appear for a given set of data to help you read the visual. You can also put things into the tooltip that aren't necessarily in the visual.

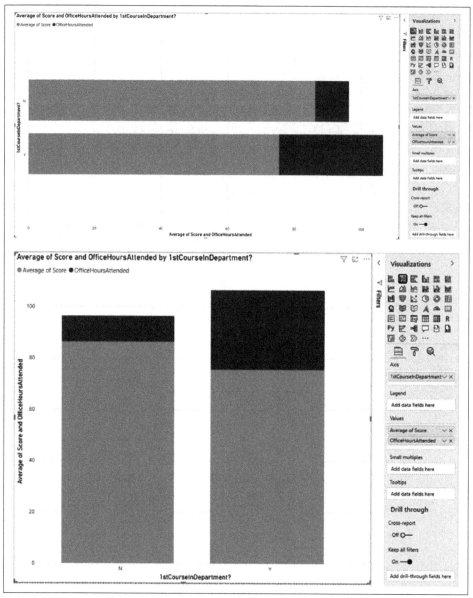

Figure 4-5. Bars versus columns

Clustered Bar and Column Charts

A *clustered bar* or *column chart* takes the values and separates them into discrete items against an axis, as opposed to aggregating them together. In the stacked charts, we basically got one bar or column combining all the values together. In the clustered chart, we get a separate bar or column for each value across our x-axis.

In the example in Figure 4-6, I want to see if there is any real discrepancy between the average scores by ethnicity and by age. I want to see each ethnicity highlighted separately, but I want to see how the ages compare against each other and how the average score compares on a more apples-to-apples basis. I can do this by separating out the values for the average age and average score. Figure 4-6 shows us what this looks like in both bar and column form.

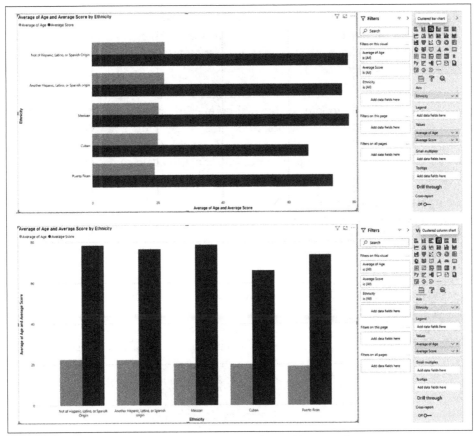

Figure 4-6. Clustered charts split out, as opposed to pulling together

This set of charts does a nice job of showing that the way you present data matters. If we look at the top portion of Figure 4-6, it's easier to see the difference in the average age that exists in each ethnic grouping. I think this is a little harder to see in the column example. Both the column and bar charts here do a good job of showing the difference in the average score, though.

Sometimes changing a value from an x- to a y-axis can make a big difference, and remember that by default axes are dynamic. That's something for you to consider when choosing bar versus column charts or if you feel the need to manually set axis values (which you could do in the fields area for this group of visualizations under the relevant axis category).

100% Stacked Bar and Column Charts

The 100% stacked bar and column charts take a given set of values across dimensions and figure out, for that total, what percent of the total belongs to each specific section of the grouping. This normalizes the result across categories because it's based on percentages instead of absolute values.

For example, in our class we have way fewer student athletes than students who are not athletes. If we were to look at the total number of office hours attended by each group, the nonathletes would just look like a much larger group. However, what if I'm trying to figure out if a particular assignment got more office hours in one group than another? That's an example where normalizing the data can come in handy, as we see in Figure 4-7.

Here we have 13 assignments with office hours attended. We can see that our student athletes attended office hours for only assignments 5, 6, 7, and 12. Assignment 12 noticeably had 20% more office hours than the other assignments. We see that, for the nonathletes, the distribution is fairly uniform across assignments. Not perfectly uniform, but close.

If we were teaching this class, this could lead us to ask some additional questions. Was there an issue in sporting schedules that made getting to office hours more difficult? Was the extra interest at the end of the semester because the student athletes weren't performing well, or was it just coincidence? Some of these questions I can answer from the data, and some of them I probably can't, but hopefully you can see some example questions I might want to ask as I develop my report or my research into the topic.

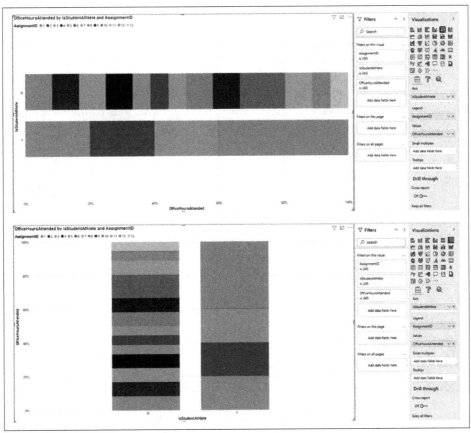

Figure 4-7. Percentage-based comparisons can be useful; however, with many categories it can become unreadable

Small Multiples

Small multiples is a feature that lets you split the visual into slices while maintaining common axes. Say I wanted to divide this into four quadrants using the student athlete identifier and the gender flag. I could see this broken out for all four combinations—not an athlete and female, not an athlete and male, is an athlete and female, is an athlete and male—while keeping my core axis value. That gets us the view represented in Figure 4-8, which also contains an example of a tooltip value that isn't elsewhere in the visual (in this case, the average age for that grouping of data).

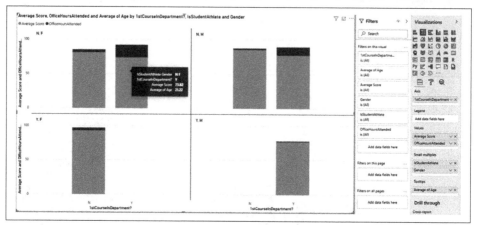

Figure 4-8. Small multiples are a great example of what puts the Power in Power BI

Let's take a second and talk about the inferences we can draw. We know that there are no male athletes for whom this is not their first course. We know the inverse is true of female athletes. We can see the average score is higher across all groups for those people for whom it is not their first class. And, generally, we know that those who were taking their first class in the department attended more office hours, but those office hours didn't quite get the first-timers up to the level of the more experienced students in the department.

Waterfall Chart

A *waterfall chart* compiles by a given category how a value changed over that category until it shows you the final total value. This can be useful when you have a combination of positive and negative features that contribute to a total, so that you can break them out and compare them to each other. We don't have negative grades for anyone, so Figure 4-9 demonstrates a single-directional waterfall chart showing the calculation of office hours attended by AssignmentID before showing the total number of office hours attended for the semester.

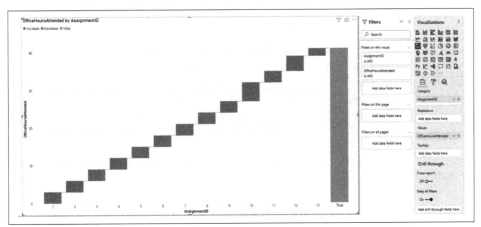

Figure 4-9. Sometimes it's OK to chase those waterfalls!

Line and Area Charts

Line and area charts, like column and bar charts, have a very x- and y-axis focused theme. The difference is often that it can be easier to see trends or do comparisons with lines or areas, seeing where data in a time series might overlap or observing where certain categories might intersect.

Also, Power BI has a set of charts that combine column charts with line charts that we will discuss in this section. Again, the list of visualizations in this category is read from left to right, top to bottom, skipping visualizations that aren't in this section:

- Line chart
- Area chart
- Stacked area chart

- Line and stacked column chart
- Line and clustered column chart
- Ribbon chart

Line Chart

A *line chart* isn't really that different from a column chart, except that it's easier to see trends with lines than it is to see them with columns. Line charts also work best with a continuous axis because when there's a gap, the line chart will break the line and pick it back up for the next value in the axis series. If you look at the options in the Visualizations pane for column and line charts, you'll see that they look incredibly similar, except that the line chart has one additional option for Secondary values. That section is there in case we want to do two y-axes against each other, which is the unique feature about line-type charts. This can be useful when you want to compare trends of two values, but they might have very different orders of magnitude.

A good business example of this is comparing my average product price to my total profit. Average price for my products is going to be lower than my total profit (or at least it should be, or you have much bigger problems than this book can really solve.) If I were to put those values on the same axis—say, profit in millions and average price in the hundreds—the average price line would look virtually flat and near zero compared to millions in profits. However, if I put them on different axes, with each y-axis measuring its own order of magnitude, we can solve that problem and better see the trends together.

In Figure 4-10, I've put a line chart together showing average score by assignment ID alongside the student ID count for each assignment. Even in the example provided, the number of students doesn't reach the level of the average score on any assignment, even the lowest-scoring one.

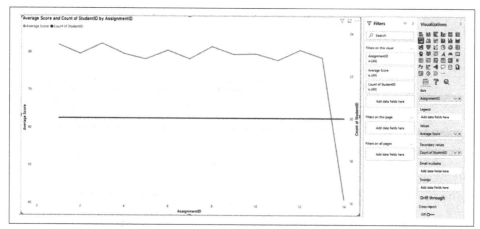

Figure 4-10. What happened on assignment 14? Stay tuned to find out!

Area Chart

An *area chart* has all the same category options as a line chart. Think of an area chart as a line chart with the values below the line filled in. Voila, area chart! The area chart does two things in my mind that provide good use cases. The first use case is when you have data that changes over time, and you want to give the reader a sense of the proportion of that change. A good example of this is looking at the change in population over time.

You can also use an area chart to see more easily where two or more values overlap, or —usually the more interesting case to me—where they don't. Figure 4-11 is the same as Figure 4-10, except it's an area chart. At the very end of the chart, for assignment 14, you'll see that the area that's filled in under the student count line isn't also filled in by the average score because the average score dropped. That filled-in area serves as a great visual indicator that something there is abnormal or may be worth further investigation.

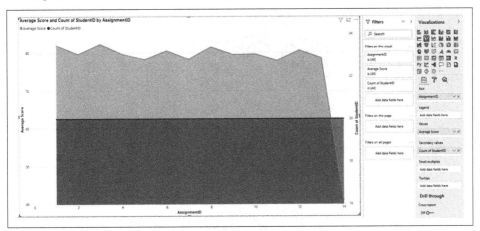

Figure 4-11. That little triangle at the end begs so many questions!

Stacked Area Chart

A *stacked area chart* is a bit different from an area chart in that it not only shows you the individual values in the area, but also creates an aggregate of the values of the area, allowing you to see both the individual parts of a total and the total at the same time.

Imagine you are in a business that has multiple subscription models: silver, gold, and platinum. The stacked area chart can be great in an example like this because it will show you the silver, gold, and platinum areas on top of one another, allowing you to see the combined subscriptions as well as their component parts.

Figure 4-12 demonstrates a stacked area chart so that we can see our average assignment scores per assignment by the number of years a student has been in school. Looking at AssignmentID 3, we can see that, for some reason, students with one year in school really struggled with this assignment. Maybe they've gotten used to sleeping in already?

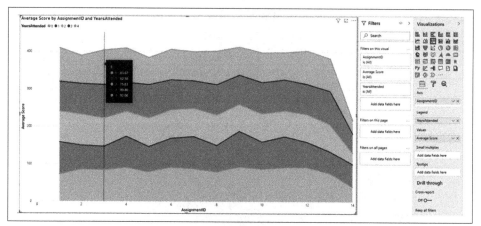

Figure 4-12. Students with one or two years of attendance seem to struggle on this one

Line and Stacked Column Chart/Clustered Column Chart

We discussed stacked and clustered column charts earlier in this chapter. What does adding a line do for these charts? Quite a bit, as it turns out! The ability to take a column chart and then overlay a line value on a different axis can really expand analysis.

For example, in Figure 4-13, I break down my average score by race for the line, but use a clustered column on the total sum of all the scores. This view tells me very quickly that White people are the majority in my class, but the Black or African American students have the highest average score. However, the inclusion of the second y-axis also tells me that the difference in the average score between my racial groups isn't that large, ranging from about 76 to a high of 80. If I were a teacher who was concerned about my course being pedagogically attuned to the needs of all my students, I would take this result in a very positive light!

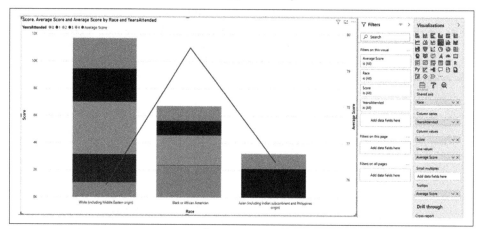

Figure 4-13. Sometimes just an extra line and axis can tell us so much

Ribbon Chart

A *ribbon chart* is somewhat like an area chart, but what it really excels at is showing how things rank against each other. You can see how the ribbon flows across the category. The tooltips for ribbon charts are also exceptionally detailed when hovering over the "transition" part of the ribbon. That's what I call the portion of the charts that aren't the columns being compared.

You can get a good idea of a simple ribbon chart in Figure 4-14, where we're looking at the rank of the average score for those who attended office hours versus those who didn't. We can see at the beginning of the semester that those who didn't attend office hours were doing better, but then that changes in Week 5, so that those who were attending office hours were doing better. What are some of the questions this raises in your mind?

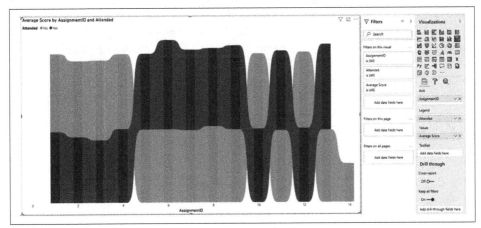

Figure 4-14. I want to know when office hours make the most impact

Donuts, Dots, and Maps, Oh My!

This next section of charts covers a bit of a broader spectrum than the previous two categories. I like to group these things together because they don't necessarily fit as neatly into other categories for me. They tend to be about demonstrating the effect of categories rather than summarizing a value across a category. Put another way, what does a given category contribute to something? That brings us to the following list of charts, again listed in their order in the Visualizations pane, reading from right to left, top to bottom:

- Funnel chart
- Scatter chart
- Pie chart
- Donut chart
- Treemap

Funnel Chart

A *funnel chart* is a flexible visualization. At its core, a funnel chart is about comparing a collection of data to another collection of data to see how close or far away it is.

One of my favorite examples of a funnel chart was from when I worked in operations analytics in a call center. That call center did telephonic coaching, and it was important to know how many times we would successfully connect or engage. I would use a funnel chart to show off our total eligible population, and then the number of people we engaged with once, then twice, then three times, etc. Each successive reach was harder to get, and you couldn't reach someone for a third time unless you'd reached them a second time. This allowed us to quickly understand our conversion rate at each level of customer engagement.

In our example in Figure 4-15, we're looking at a different use case for the funnel: a presorted list of average scores by student. Pay special attention to the tooltip, the information in the black box in Figure 4-15. It shows the percentage of the highlighted value in comparison to the top value. Mr. Schmitz, with an average score of 85.36, has an average that is 92.28% of the top score (Montegalegre's) and an average score that is 97.47% of Boomhower's.

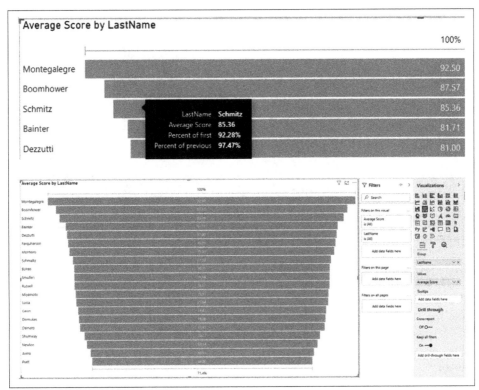

Figure 4-15. Visualizing rank

Scatter Chart

The *scatter chart* is one of the most useful and most maddening visuals in Power BI. I'll be blunt: it's fickle. There are way too many ways to get an error out of this visual when you are constructing it. If you have data that you can represent nicely in X and Y pairs, the scatter chart is fantastic. One of its other uses is to display how values change over time. Just as an additional note, your y-axis must always be numeric; it cannot be categorical. Your x-axis can be either numeric or categorical.

In the example in Figure 4-16, we are looking at our average score by assignment between student athletes and nonathletes. What we have added that is unique to the scatter chart is the Play axis, which allows us to cycle through some categorical filtering in sequence to see how these values change over time. This can work really well with continuous data that uses dates or, as in this case, I'm using the assignment IDs, which are numerical, to play through the change in assignment order.

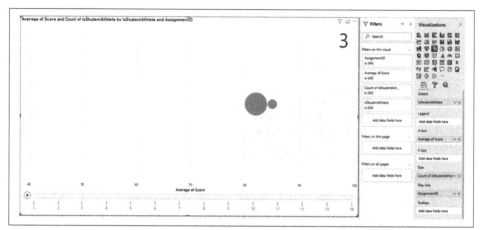

Figure 4-16. Moving pictures. They're weird, but I bet they'll be big someday.

Pie and Donut Chart

Oh, I can hear the screaming of finance professionals everywhere, "Jeremey! Why are these together? They're *totally* not the same thing!" I want everyone to be clear on this. A *donut chart* is a pie chart with a hole in the middle. They do the exact same thing, which is demonstrate the percent of a total value that represents a certain category.

Now look at me, and by look at me, I mean stop reading, lift your eyes to the sky and hear my disembodied voice in your head. Pie and donut charts are overrated and overused. Does this mean they are bad? No, of course not. However, naturally it is easier to compare lines and bars against each other than it is to compare "areas" of values.

Does your pie chart have 74 values that it is comparing? That's bad. Is it a real sugar crème pie from Zionsville, Indiana? Then it's good. Is your donut made of some vegan, gluten-free flour substitute from a back alley in Portland, Oregon? Probably not good. Seriously, go to Coco's. Voodoo is overrated. Figures 4-17 and 4-18 show good pies and donuts versus bad ones.

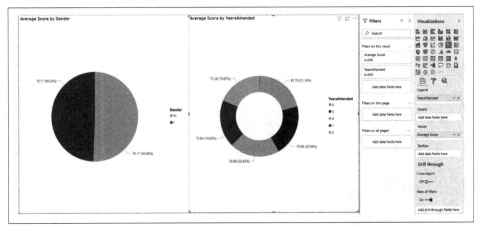

Figure 4-17. Good pie, good donut. Why? Because they're both readable.

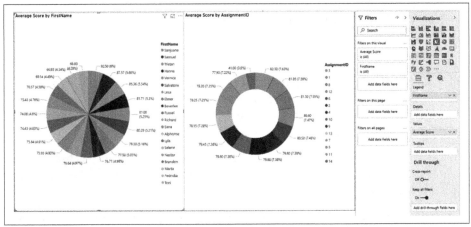

Figure 4-18. Don't do this! Here's an example of pie and donut charts that are not readable. As the kids say, "Y u do dis?"

Treemap

The *treemap* is the donut chart for the 21st century, which is to say, it can be used well and can be destroyed by too many categories filling it up. However, one advantage the treemap has over its pie and donut counterparts is that it is easier to tell the difference between big squares and little squares. I like to use treemaps as a cross-filter on many report pages where categories and subcategories exist naturally to highlight specific subsections of data for more analysis.

A larger treemap like the one in Figure 4-19 is helpful for identifying large groups at a glance. In this case, we are looking at combinations of gender and ethnicity to see which groupings attended the highest number of office hours. We can easily see females attended more hours than males, and we can see which ethnic groups attended those hours.

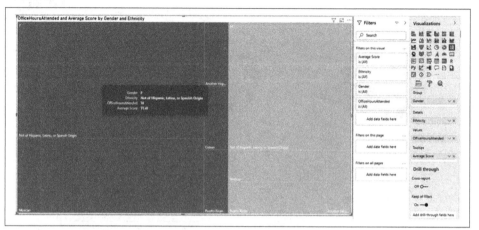

Figure 4-19. Group and Detail divisions make treemaps shine

Map Visuals

Map visuals do exactly what you think they do: they align data with geographic categories to show you details about data across those categories. Pretty straightforward. Power BI has several map visuals that can help you get to where you want to go.

The basic map visual offers the ability to define a location or to offer data points for latitude and longitude to define your map parameters. The filled map is basically the same as the map, except it fills in the relevant geographic categories, as opposed to putting in size-based dots.

By the time you get this book, the shape map visual might finally be out of beta (where it has been for years). The shape map does not use Bing or Azure to power it, but it uses custom TopoJSONs to define the map's shape and structure. A *TopoJSON* is a special file format that contains semistructured geographic data. If you are in a place where you need a custom map, check to see if you have a TopoJSON built inhouse or find one of the many great resources online to get a TopoJSON of the map you need.

The Azure map allows you to define latitude and longitudinal boundaries that can be passed to TomTom to generate a map much like the shape map visual. With map visuals, my suggestion is to try each map visual and see which one works best for you and your needs.

The "Flat" Visuals

Flat visuals exist to display simple, straightforward information that you want your reader to see. These visuals generally do not cross-filter others, but are cross-filtered themselves, with one obvious exception: the slicer visual. These visuals may seem simple, but they often add that magical, extra little bit of context to a report that turns the data into a story that makes sense. They do so by highlighting those specific things that you really want your audience to understand. In this category, we have the following visuals:

- Gauge
- Card
- Multi-row card
- KPI

- Slicer
- Table
- Matrix

Gauge

Gauges are one of the oldest forms of data visualization we have. They've been used in machines and engineering for most of the 20th century. A *gauge* fundamentally tells you how a value is doing compared to its minimum and maximum values alongside a target. The gauge is helpful for setting targets and seeing quickly if you are above or below that target value. It can also be useful when you want to keep a value in a specific range, not too hot or not too cold.

In the example in Figure 4-20, we compare the average score with our goal average score measure.

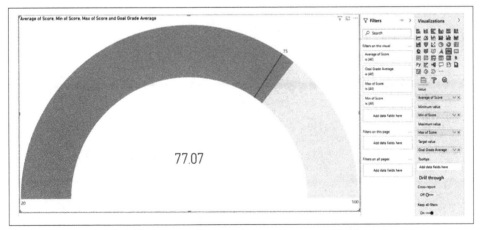

Figure 4-20. Gauge has been around; gauge has seen some stuff. That's because gauges are among some of the earliest data visualizations.

Card/Multi-Row Card

The *card visual* is one of the simplest visuals in Power BI. It's also one of the most self-explanatory from its name. When given a value, it takes that value and puts it into a square card with a brief note on what it is that's being viewed.

For me, the card does two things well. First, in its simplicity, it's easy to understand what you're reading. Combine this with cross-filtering, and the card visual can quickly highlight a specific value for any combination of data easily. Second, it helps the storytelling process by drawing readers to specific values you think they should care about, either because they're important on their own or because they provide necessary context that makes the other visuals on your report page more meaningful.

The *multi-row card visual* is like the card visual's cousin whom your aunt and uncle dote on constantly at Thanksgiving, but you're not actually sure they're all that great. The multi-row card puts, unaspiringly, multiple values into a single card-like space. If all the values are aggregations, it will look fairly clean. However, if you have aggregations and then some dimension that categorizes those aggregations, the multi-row card will create multiple rows on the card, detailing the aggregated values for each categorical value.

In Figure 4-21, we have a simple card on the left and two multi-row cards on the right: one with only aggregations at the top, and sliced by StudentID on the bottom to tell the difference more easily. Note how the second multi-row visual also has a scroll bar to help navigate the visual because it's now longer than the assigned space.

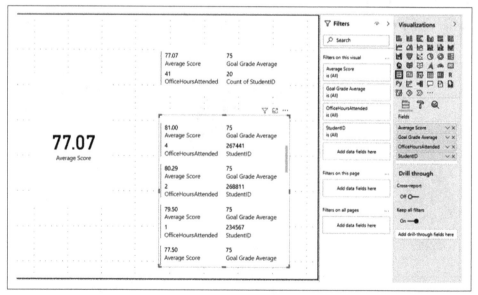

Figure 4-21. You get a card, you get a card, everyone gets a card! This shows the difference between a card and a multi-row card.

KPI

The *key performance indicator (KPI)* visual is one of those things that on the surface sounds great, but inevitably leads to a place of frustration. It's not as bad as the scatter chart, but the KPI visual is not intuitive at first.

There is an indicator field, and this is what you are actually measuring. There's a trend axis, which is how the visual will display the results on an x-axis that isn't displayed. Then there's the target goal, which we should be either higher or lower than.

A classic example of a KPI use case is something like current year revenue versus previous year revenue by fiscal month. In our example, we are looking at our average score compared to our goal grade average of 75. The visual then shows how we did compared to that goal.

The infuriating thing about the KPI is that it always displays the value for the last value in the axis, regardless of what happened before it, even though it will visualize those values in the chart portion. You'll notice in Figure 4-22 that I've left the Filters pane open so you can see what the visual looks like in two scenarios: one where I ignore Assignment 14, which is special, and one where I do not, so you can see the difference in the way the KPI visualizes those results.

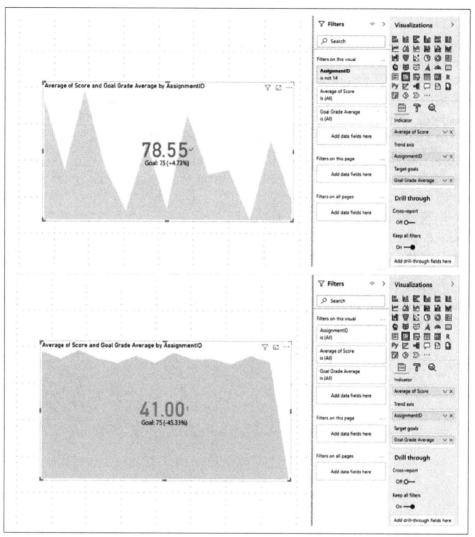

Figure 4-22. Sometimes I wish I could give the KPI visual a red card

Table/Matrix

So, I'm going to apologize, because this is one time I'm going to deviate from the order and skip over Slicer. I'll come back to it after the table and matrix visuals. These are easy to understand if you've used Excel or Google Sheets or looked at a database table.

The *table* is exactly what it sounds like. No bells and whistles here. The table visual, in the Visualizations pane, has only one insert, and that is into a values field. Everything is a field (column), and all the values are assigned to that column. It might seem counterintuitive to have a table visual in a data visualization tool, but the table visual can provide some more specific detail that can offer extra context.

In many scenarios, I might prefer a table to a multi-row card for highlighting specific data points. The other cool thing I've done with table visuals is put them at the end of reports to make for easy data extraction for analysts who might want to use the data of that table for other analysis.

The *matrix* is more akin to a pivot table in Excel, with the ability to have multiple levels of row features to drill into. Matrices can also be overused, but when used to highlight specific sets or combinations of data, they can help illuminate specific items for readers or provide extra context to analysts who can figure out what questions they need to go answer quickly.

For many years, exporting data from a matrix visual would lose its matrix formatting, as Power BI would put it into a table first and then export it. However, that's not true anymore, so if you have a need to export data in a matrix format, maybe for a presentation or something, you can do that as well. Figure 4-23 shows a table on the left and a matrix on the right.

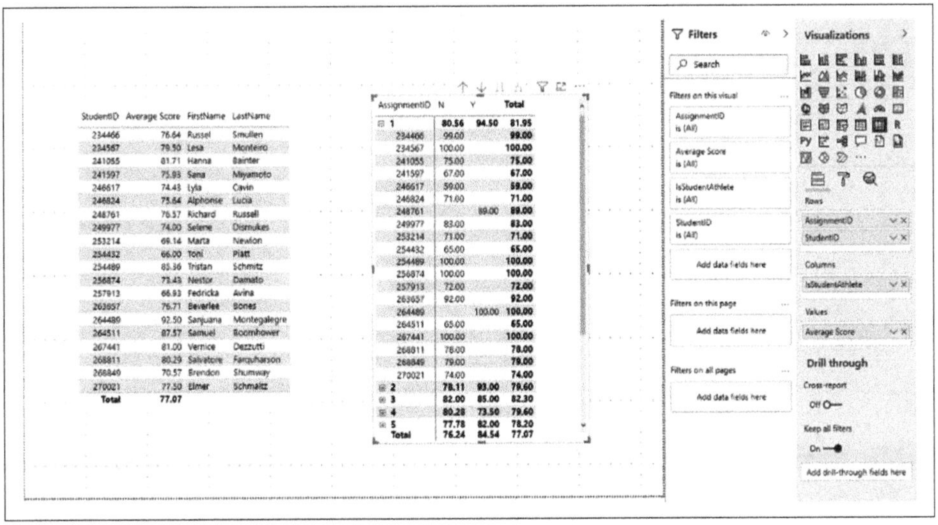

Figure 4-23. Fine, you want tables? Have some tables.

Slicer

I saved the slicer for last because its functionality is fundamentally different from every other visual we have reviewed, but that doesn't mean it's less important. A *slicer* takes the visuals on a page and filters them in alignment with the selected value(s) on the slicer.

A slicer isn't too different from having a column selected via the "Filters on this page" button in the Filters pane. What is different, though, is that as a visual on a report page, you can edit how it interacts with every other visual on the report page by using the "Edit interactions" function on the Format tab of the ribbon; and slicers can be synced across pages of your choosing using the "Sync slicers" pane. This can make slicers much more flexible and more intuitive for your report readers. This also gives you, as the author, another chance to identify which dimensions you feel are important for helping your readers understand how they should be thinking about the data.

In Figure 4-24, you can see the slicer visual selected in the bottom-left corner, using the assignment ID. Note how the values change when I select different combinations of the assignment ID I want to look at.

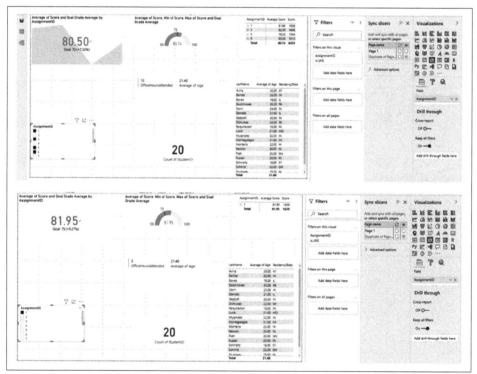

Figure 4-24. Slice, slice, baby!

Conclusion

Yes, the Visualizations pane has a few other visuals, but those aren't really visuals for the 101 section. If you're able to do R or Python scripting, you already know how to use the R and Python visuals, and we'll discuss the AI-powered visuals a bit more in Chapter 7. Power Apps, Power Automate, and Paginated Reports are a bit beyond the scope of this book, but plenty of resources are available if you have an interest in those topics.

In this chapter, we've gone through the basics of visualization in Power BI and walked through many of the visuals that are available right out of the box in Power BI Desktop. And we've discussed some of their use cases. In many of the visual examples, we used a simple measure, the average score, to use as a point of reference, but how did we make that measure? That's where DAX comes into play, and that's what we'll be moving to next. Excited? You should be.

CHAPTER 5

Aggregations, Measures, and DAX

In Chapter 1, we had a long conversation about the storage engine and the formula engine of Power BI. In Chapter 3, we were really talking about how the storage engine works and what it means to store data in your own personal Analysis Services instance. Now we'll dive into the other half of what makes Power BI special: the formula engine.

Taking stock of our progress so far, we've put our data in Power BI and reviewed most of the visuals available in Power BI out of the box. We dragged and dropped values into visualizations to get results, but how did Power BI know what to display?

This chapter details the roles of aggregations, measures, and DAX as they relate to visualizations. What is an aggregation? What is a measure? What exactly is DAX? We'll answer all these questions and explain what you need to know.

A Primer on the DAX Language

Data Analysis Expressions (DAX) is the language of the formula engine of Analysis Services Tabular and Power BI. It is a multifunctional query language that can be used to obtain specific results or create calculated tables or columns. Anytime you create a visual in Power BI, it generates DAX behind the scenes to get the data from the Power BI storage engine.

DAX is incredibly powerful, but like everything else in Power BI, it is really defined at the columnar or table level. That's different from software like Excel, where things are defined at the individual cell level. DAX cannot modify individual points in space or cells like Excel. It has to modify a table or column of data. Remember, our underlying database is columnar, so we need a language that can modify and query columns, not individual cells of data. Being able to modify and query columns is much more powerful because it's faster, and you don't have all the overhead of needing to be able to write formulas against specific cells.

Measures

A *measure* is the result of a DAX formula that leads to a single-value result. This result can be modified by either row or filter context. You will discover that row and filter context are two of the most important concepts in DAX, so we'll discuss them in more detail later in the chapter. The short version for now is that row context occurs when you are dealing with records in a table; filter context happens when things try to cross-apply to one another, like, for instance, using a slicer visual.

In Power BI, this context can be passed implicitly through other factors in a visual. For example, when we discussed the "average score" previously, that was a measure. It's a DAX statement that will return the average score based on whatever context exists, either explicitly in the DAX statement itself or implicitly through visual implicit context.

Think about it with a simple table visual. With no context and just the measure, I will get the average score across all assignments for all students. When we add assignments to the table, we then get the average score for all students for each specific assignment. If I add student last name to that table, I'll get the average score for an individual student for an individual assignment. These examples show how a measure can be contextual.

Calculated Columns

A *calculated column* is the result of a DAX statement that will return a result for each individual row in a given table. A simple example of this is to concatenate the last name and first name into a single column. We would write a DAX statement that would return a value for each record.

In Power BI Desktop, when you right-click the Fields pane, you'll see the options to create new measures or calculated columns. These options help Power BI identify how it should treat the DAX statement. If it knows the goal is to create a calculated column, it will evaluate the DAX in that context, and the same for a measure.

A common example is the desire to concatenate last name and first name. DAX has a concatenate statement, but if I try to do this with a measure, the IntelliSense in Power BI won't allow me to choose the columns. However, it will allow me to do that as a calculated column. I recommend that you create columns in Power Query and use DAX-calculated columns as a last resort. My general rule is that we always want to modify our data as close to the source system as possible. A DAX-calculated column is really the furthest point away from that data source.

Calculated Tables

A *calculated table* returns a table of values, rows, and columns, based on a DAX statement that references other tables in the same data model. You can think of a calculated table almost as a SQL query result. You query a database in SQL, and you get a set of results in the form of a table based on which columns you selected.

A calculated table is the same idea, except it exists in memory and can be referenced in the data model as its own unique object. It can also be used in relationships. If you find yourself querying a Power BI dataset or Analysis Services instance, thinking about DAX in this context will be helpful.

The other common use of calculated tables in Power BI development is in the process of "role-playing" dimensions. In the most common example, you have a fact table with multiple dates and need to be able to interact with different dates based on the reporting requirement. Your date table can have only one active relationship. So you can use a calculated table to create another set of dates to build another relationship to that fact table. Then you have two different date tables that you can use, depending on which date you might need to use from a given fact table.

Types of Functions

DAX functions are grouped into families, or *types*, that identify the goal that they should accomplish. A DAX formula is a construction of one or more DAX functions.

I certainly don't use every DAX function available within the examples in this book, simply because there are hundreds. For that reason, it can be helpful if you know how DAX functions are grouped in case you need to quickly look up the details on how a specific function works or you're trying to find a function that fits the type of analysis or data manipulation you are trying to perform. Here's a list of how DAX functions are grouped:

- Aggregation functions
- Date and time functions
- Filter functions
- Financial functions
- Information functions
- Logical functions
- Math and trigonometric functions
- Other functions
- Parent and child functions
- Relationship functions
- Statistical functions
- Table manipulation functions
- Text functions
- Time intelligence functions

To see sample syntax of some commonly used functions, please refer to Appendix A.

Aggregations, More Than Some Sums

The mysteries of the complexities of database storage aren't really that important to an end user, but figuring out how to make that stored data say something meaningful is. This is what DAX lets us do. It takes the data and allows us to aggregate it into insights that enable us to tell a story about what is happening.

I don't know about you, but I can't read 5,000 records, much less 5 million. I can, however, figure out an average value across a certain column of that data, tell you the earliest or most recent date of activity, tell you the first or last relevant value to a given combination of data, or give you a count of records that match a certain data collection. These are all *aggregations*, and Power BI allows us to use each of them with specific types of data.

Aggregations are more than just sums. Table 5-1 helps demonstrate the types of aggregations, the types of data that can have that aggregation applied, and then, finally, whether it can be set as a default aggregation. I'll discuss default aggregations a little later in the chapter, but for now, let's go through the aggregation types at a high level and talk about possible use cases for some of them. If you see an X in the table, that's because that aggregation type doesn't make sense for that data type.

Table 5-1. The selectable aggregations by data type in Power BI

Aggregation type	Numeric	Text	Date	Default eligible?
Sum	Y	X	X	Y
Average	Y	X	X	Y
Minimum	Y	X	X	Y
Maximum	Y	X	X	Y
Count (distinct)	Y	Y	Y	Y (only for numeric)
Count	Y	Y	Y	Y (only for numeric)
Standard deviation	Y	X	X	X
Variance	Y	X	X	X
Median	Y	X	X	X
Earliest	X	X	Y	X
Latest	X	X	Y	X
First	X	Y	N	X
Last	X	Y	N	X
Don't summarize	Y	On by default	On by default	Y (only for numeric)

Sum

The old reliable. We all know what a *sum* is. It's addition. You've known how to add numbers forever. If you're reading this book, I'm going to go out on a limb and say you've probably already used sum functions in Excel or similar products. The good news is that Sum functions in the same way in Power BI. For a given column of numbers, we will get a sum, or addition, of those numerical values for each given combination of data that is represented in a visual.

This, like so many data concepts, is easier to understand visually. Since that is why we are here, to visualize data, it seems fair to show you rather than tell you what I mean. In Figure 5-1, we see two tables. Both have a sum of office hours attended. They both get the same total, but they have different values for each combination of data.

Course Number	Term Start Date	StudentPreferredPronouns	UsedPowerBI?	OfficeHoursAttended
ISOM 210	Monday, January 04, 2021	He / Him	N	8
ISOM 210	Monday, January 04, 2021	He / Him	Y	6
ISOM 210	Monday, January 04, 2021	She / Her	N	22
ISOM 210	Monday, January 04, 2021	She / Her	Y	4
ISOM 210	Monday, January 04, 2021	They / Them	N	1
Total				**41**

LastName	AssignmentID	OfficeHoursAttended
Avina	12	1
Bainter	8	1
Bainter	9	1
Bainter	10	1
Bones	2	1
Bones	6	1
Bones	7	1
Bones	11	1
Boomhower	4	1
Boomhower	8	1
Cavin	1	1
Cavin	5	1
Cavin	13	1
Damato	10	1
Dezzutti	3	1
Dezzutti	7	1
Dezzutti	11	1
Dezzutti	12	1
Dismukes	8	1
Farquharson	9	1
Farquharson	13	1
Lucia	4	1
Lucia	10	1
Miyamoto	1	1
Miyamoto	2	1
Miyamoto	11	1
Montegalegre	5	1
Montegalegre	6	1
Montegalegre	7	1
Montegalegre	12	1
Monteiro	3	1
Newlon	3	1
Piatt	4	1
Total		**41**

Figure 5-1. Yeah, you get sum!

The table at the top shows the sum of office hours attended by several categorical groupings. So, in this case, the people who attended the ISOM 210 course that started on January 4, 2021, who have the preferred pronouns of she/her, and never used Power BI before the course started, totaled 22 of the 41 total office hours. Here, the total represents the sum of the values in the OfficeHoursAttended column.

The table at the bottom is much different. It shows the breakdown by a student's last name and, for a given assignment ID, the number of office hours they attended. We can see we get the same total hours, but the distribution is different.

If you were to look at the Grades table, you'd note that no student attended more than one office hour for any given assignment ID. In this case, the sum is still calculating a summation; it just happens to be a summation that gets down to one cell's worth of data.

The reason I wanted to show this example is to demonstrate that, by default, Power BI will not show data collections that don't return a value for a given summation. So, we know Ms. Avina attended only one office hour, and that was for Assignment ID 12. We can tell that much more quickly by seeing only data where an actual value is returned, as opposed to viewing results that don't return any data.

Average

There are lots of types of averages. To describe the default aggregation as shown in the options under the Visualizations pane, Power BI is creating a simple average. That simple *average* can be defined as the sum of a given set of values, filtered by all the relevant categories on a visual, then divided by the count of records that are also filtered by all relevant categories on a visual. So, if we had, for a given combination of data, a sum score of 240, and three records made up those 240 points, we would have an average of 80.

Just like the sum, if we end up getting to a combination of categories that returns only one record's worth of data, a value divided by one is itself; that's still technically an average. In Figure 5-2, I've created two new tables with average scores, but I've also included on the left the sum of office hours attended, which we saw in Figure 5-1, and the average of the office hours attended on the right.

Course Number	Term Start Date	StudentPreferredPronouns	UsedPowerBI?	OfficeHoursAttended
ISOM 210	Monday, January 04, 2021	He / Him	N	8
ISOM 210	Monday, January 04, 2021	He / Him	Y	6
ISOM 210	Monday, January 04, 2021	She / Her	N	22
ISOM 210	Monday, January 04, 2021	She / Her	Y	4
ISOM 210	Monday, January 04, 2021	They / Them	N	1
Total				41

LastName	AssignmentID	OfficeHoursAttended
Avina	12	1
Bainter	8	1
Bainter	9	1
Bainter	10	1
Bones	2	1
Bones	6	1
Bones	7	1
Bones	11	1
Boomhower	4	1
Boomhower	8	1
Cavin	1	1
Cavin	5	1
Cavin	13	1
Damato	10	1
Dezzutti	3	1
Dezzutti	7	1
Dezzutti	11	1
Dezzutti	12	1
Dismukes	8	1
Farquharson	9	1
Farquharson	13	1
Lucia	4	1
Lucia	10	1
Total		41

Figure 5-2. Always be careful with averages, and avoid averages of averages at all costs

Two things about Figure 5-2 might pop out at you. First, just like the sum in Figure 5-1, the total Average of Score across both tables is the same. Second, doesn't the Average of OfficeHoursAttended on the right look strange? It's an average of 1, but there are blank values. What does that mean? Why are there blank values? Didn't I just say the default behavior was not to show values where there is no data? The table at the bottom of Figure 5-1 showed us that, indeed, for any given assignment, no one attended more or less than one office hour. However, blanks are not zeros. True blanks, or *nulls* in database parlance, are not uncommon in many datasets.

The important takeaway is that Power BI does not treat nulls as zeros and ignores them when generating a count of values. If nulls are ignored in generating a count, our calculation description for the average in Power BI still holds true, and that total average in Figure 5-2's right table still makes sense.

Now, the big question is how to calculate an average for Ms. Avina. Should it be 1 hour divided by 1 instance of attending office hours, or should it be 1 hour divided by 14 opportunities to attend office hours, with 13 zeros? It's a question we can only answer for ourselves, as the analyst or report author, and that really depends on what we want our average to mean.

The second question is why are there blank values being returned for the Average of OfficeHoursAttended on the right table in Figure 5-2? I did say that the default behavior was not to return values when there would be no data to display. However, on a visual where there is a second aggregation that does return a value for a given combination of data, all other aggregations will still display, even if they return a blank value.

Figure 5-3 is a simple rendition, taking Figure 5-2's right table and making a second copy of it without the average score. You can see the two tables together and find that, indeed, it is the inclusion of that second aggregation that causes the blank values to appear in the visual. It also helps demonstrate the previous point about average calculation ignoring blank values.

LastName	AssignmentID	Average of Office Hours Attended		LastName	AssignmentID	Average of Score	Average of Office Hours Attended
Avina	12	1.00		Avina	1	72.00	
Bainter	8	1.00		Avina	2	76.00	
Bainter	9	1.00		Avina	3	72.00	
Bainter	10	1.00		Avina	4	71.00	
Bones	2	1.00		Avina	5	90.00	
Bones	6	1.00		Avina	6	94.00	
Bones	7	1.00		Avina	7	61.00	
Bones	11	1.00		Avina	8	74.00	
Boomhower	4	1.00		Avina	9	54.00	
Boomhower	8	1.00		Avina	10	66.00	
Cavin	1	1.00		Avina	11	66.00	
Cavin	5	1.00		Avina	12	55.00	1.00
Cavin	13	1.00		Avina	13	66.00	
Damato	10	1.00		Avina	14	20.00	
Dezzutti	3	1.00		Bainter	1	75.00	
Dezzutti	7	1.00		Bainter	2	74.00	
Dezzutti	11	1.00		Bainter	3	99.00	
Dezzutti	12	1.00		Bainter	4	100.00	
Dismukes	8	1.00		Bainter	5	93.00	
Farquharson	9	1.00		Bainter	6	100.00	
Farquharson	13	1.00		Bainter	7	64.00	
Lucia	4	1.00		Bainter	8	89.00	1.00
Lucia	10	1.00		Bainter	9	77.00	1.00
Miyamoto	1	1.00		Bainter	10	88.00	1.00
Miyamoto	2	1.00		Bainter	11	68.00	
Miyamoto	11	1.00		Bainter	12	100.00	
Total		1.00		Total		77.07	1.00

Figure 5-3. Blanks? We don't need no stinkin' blanks! Yet including a second aggregation will cause blank values to appear in a visual.

Minimum and Maximum

Minimum and Maximum can be tricky because they don't always lead to the results you're looking for. These are two separate summarizations, but they are inverses of each other.

We've all been in a scenario where we needed to know the highest and lowest values for a given category. Imagine being an engineer reviewing data for how a new machine is performing. You know what the tolerances are, let's say, for the internal temperature of the machine. There's a sensor that's giving you readings of the internal temperature and sending that data to your data warehouse, where you are looking at it in Power BI. You need to know if the machine is ever getting too hot or too cold. A quick check of the minimum and maximum temperatures might help you do that.

In our school scenario, we want to know the highest and lowest score for each given assignment. While we are not grading this class on a curve, it's helpful to know how big the gap was between our top performer(s) and our bottom performer(s). You can imagine a teacher wanting to know if the gap is consistent. Was there a specific assignment that was possibly too hard or too easy? Understanding the local minimum and local maximum can help answer those questions.

Remember that, as with all aggregations, the minimum and maximum are context dependent. If I add last name or first name to the minimum value, I'm going to see that individual's minimum value. Don't confuse the minimum and maximum with global minimum or maximum! When you add extra columns or use a slicer, remember that your new min or max is the min or max in the context you have provided. We can see an example of this in Figure 5-4. I show the min and max scores by AssignmentID on the left. On the right I do the same, except I add LastName. But it doesn't give me the result I'm looking for. Instead, it adds LastName as a category to the visual.

Now, for the example, I must create a way to take the value result and link it back to whatever criteria I want to discover about the minimum or maximum. I created a DAX measure that gives me the score holder's name, if one person matches, and tells me its multiple if multiple people have that minimum score and assignment combination.

Left table:

AssignmentID	Min of Score	MIN SCORE HOLDER	Max of Score
1	59	Cavin	100
2	53	Bones	100
3	50	Multiple	100
4	54	Multiple	100
5	50	Multiple	100
6	55	Multiple	100
7	57	Multiple	100
8	55	Multiple	100
9	54	Multiple	100
10	56	Multiple	100
11	51	Piatt	100
12	55	Multiple	100
13	56	Multiple	100
14	20	Multiple	80
Total	20	Multiple	100

Right table:

AssignmentID	Min of Score	Max of Score	LastName
1	72	72	Avina
1	75	75	Bainter
1	92	92	Bones
1	65	65	Boomhower
1	59	59	Cavin
1	100	100	Damato
1	100	100	Dezzutti
1	83	83	Dismukes
1	78	78	Farquharson
1	71	71	Lucia
1	67	67	Miyamoto
1	100	100	Montegalegre
1	100	100	Monteiro
1	71	71	Newlon
1	65	65	Piatt
1	89	89	Russell
1	74	74	Schmaltz
1	100	100	Schmitz
1	79	79	Shumway
1	99	99	Smullen
2	76	76	Avina
2	74	74	Bainter
2	53	53	Bones
2	98	98	Boomhower
Total	20	100	

Figure 5-4. Getting the answer on the left is harder than it should be

For this type of example, we might be better off trying to shape our data a little bit to help us target the type of result we're looking for. We could go back to the source data (an Excel spreadsheet) and do some calculations there that would add that data preingestion, maybe do a Power Query transformation to get the student's name into the Grades table. Or we could write a DAX measure that would return a specific value. Remember, our general rule for data transformation is to do transformation as close to the data source as possible.

We can't do complex data shaping in Excel, but we could probably add some columns to our Grades worksheet with some MINIFS and MAXIFS functions, and then do some VLOOKUP magic on those values. But in Excel, that would return only the first value where those conditions were true, not all of them, and it wouldn't identify if there were multiple. Could we continue down this Excel rabbit hole until we got to a point where it was working? Sure. Am I going to tell you that you're wrong if you were to do that? Absolutely not.

If this were in a SQL Server database and you wanted to write a query against the table that got the min and max values grouped by AssignmentID, then wrote some sort of subquery to join on those results, and then got the name or names of the people who had those scores, would I tell you that you're wrong? Again, no. In my case, because this is the Aggregations, Measures, and DAX chapter, I chose to do an example with a DAX measure. What I would say is that if you feel like you need to modify the shape or form of data to get a result that you're looking for, make sure you document your work and changes for later!

Standard Deviation, Variance, and Median

If you look at Table 5-1, Standard Deviation, Variance, and Median are the last of the numeric-only aggregations, and these are not selectable as default aggregations. These aggregations are more statistical in nature and tend to have more specific use cases, which is why they're not available to be default summarizations. Microsoft even helps us a little by putting them at the bottom of the list, so as to not draw attention to them to prevent confusion, as we can see in Figure 5-5.

Out of these three, the median is the most familiar. For a given array of N numbers in numerical order, the *median* is the number that leaves an equal amount of values on either side of the array from that value. If N is even, then the median is the average of the two values in the middle of the array that leave an equal number of values on either side of the array. In shorthand, it would be okay to call the median the middle number of an array.

Variance and standard deviation go hand in hand. Variance measures how spread out a set of numbers is from that set's average value. To calculate variance, you get the average value for a set of numbers and then, for each and every value in that dataset, you take the square of that value minus the average and sum all of those variances to get the total variance. The standard deviation is the square root of the variance. The *standard deviation* is often used to describe how close values tend to be to the average for that set.

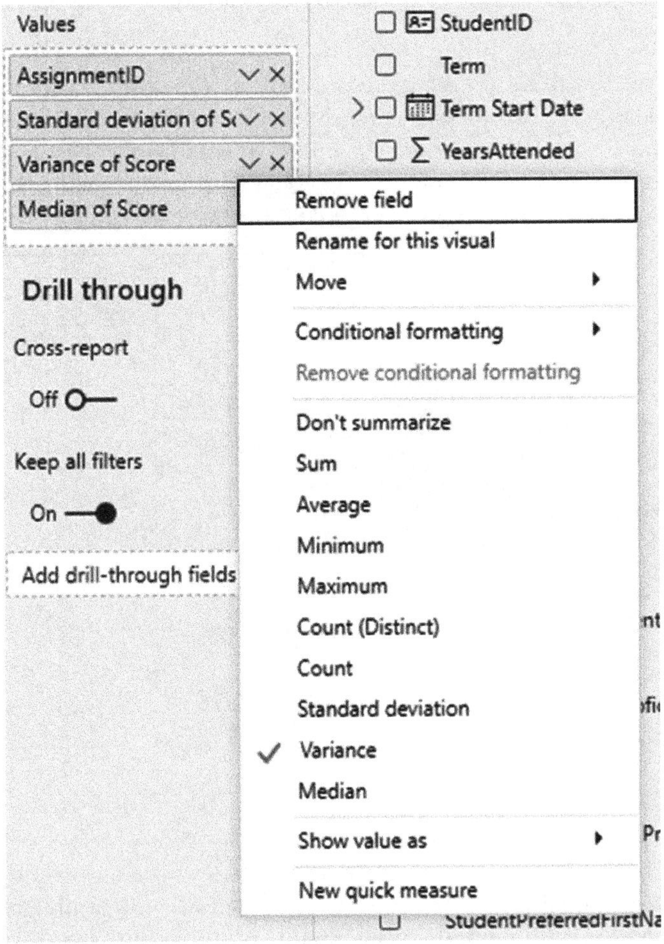

Figure 5-5. Selecting an aggregation is as easy as pie, not pi, 3.1415. Note that Standard deviation, Variance, and Median cannot be defaults.

Count and Count (Distinct)

Count and Count (Distinct) are two very useful aggregations that can be used by any data type. You can use these to count occurrences of text, dates, or numerical instances of data. The difference between the selections Count and Count (Distinct) are that Count will count duplicate instances of that data, whereas Distinct won't. This count is performed against the column of data that is being referenced.

Figure 5-6 has four demonstrations of Count and Count (Distinct). First, on the top left is a list of scores across all assignments. For that table, I am not aggregating the score, so I'm getting the raw values and then performing a Count of score and a

Count (Distinct) of score to see the number of times that score appeared for that assignment.

One thing to note, with most aggregations, Power BI will create an alias to help readers identify the aggregation if it isn't sum. However, Power BI aliases Count (Distinct) in the same way it aliases Count, so I've manually aliased Count (Distinct) in the visuals for clarity. You can alias any object in a visual by double-clicking the item in the Values section of the Visualizations pane and typing in a new name.

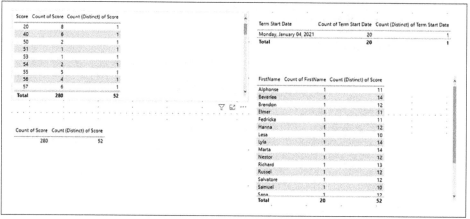

Figure 5-6. Count and Count (Distinct) are amazing, as long as you know which one you're looking at

Note in the top-left example, we have the raw score, the number of times that score appears in the dataset, and then the distinct count, which is one for every value. The total shows 52 unique values. But in the visual where each value is listed, the distinct count of that individual value will always be 1. When we look at the bottom left, it's the same visual, just with the score value removed, and we can see the total number of scores, 280, and the number of distinct score values, which is 52.

The top-right example shows us a count for the occurrences of a specific date, in this case, the term start date. At this time, we have only one semester's worth of data in the dataset, so we have one unique term start date. That value appears 20 times in the table from which it originates. Remember, the way this table is constructed, the distinct count would be 1 no matter what because the table specifies a value, and a distinct count of that value will always be 1.

The bottom-right example shows the scenarios we've looked at in a bit of a different light. We have a list of students' first names and the count of those names, which are all 1. This is not a distinct count; we just happen to have no names that appear twice. But then we can take the Count (Distinct) of scores and can see how many unique scores each individual obtained. With 14 assignments, we would expect the distinct count of scores by person to be high, but notice it's not uniformly 14 either. Some people had the same score more than once over the course of the semester.

First, Last, Earliest, and Latest

I've grouped these together because they're not really aggregations in the classic sense. These do not group together; in fact, they really do the opposite. They also don't do what you think they would, which would be to serve as a filter (or at least they don't do that without additional context or having a bidirectional relationship). As we note in Table 5-1, First and Last are unique to text fields, while Earliest and Latest are unique to date and time fields.

First will provide the first value, alphabetically, that matches a given set of data criteria as listed in the visual. If it's used by itself, First will provide the first alphanumeric value in the column.

Last does the inverse of this. It will provide the last value, alphabetically, that matches the given criteria. A quick example can be seen in Figure 5-7, where we see on the left a list of students by their last names and their average scores for their assignments. But notice that Ms. Avina's average score in the table on the right doesn't match what it is on the left. In fact, the average score on the right is just the average score of the class. This is happening because our relationship between the Survey Data table and the Grades table is unidirectional. The same thing happens if we were to use the last LastName. Note, though, that when we give just a little extra context, as we do on the far right side of Figure 5-7, we get the expected result.

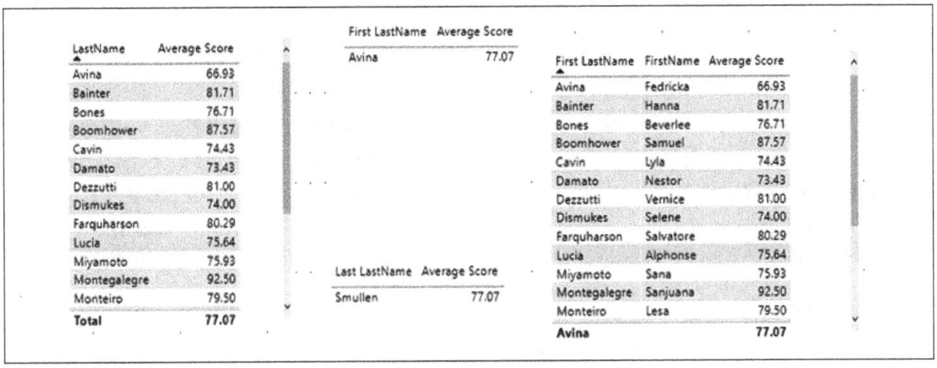

LastName	Average Score
Avina	66.93
Bainter	81.71
Bones	76.71
Boomhower	87.57
Cavin	74.43
Damato	73.43
Dezzutti	81.00
Dismukes	74.00
Farquharson	80.29
Lucia	75.64
Miyamoto	75.93
Montegalegre	92.50
Monteiro	79.50
Total	**77.07**

First LastName	Average Score
Avina	77.07

Last LastName	Average Score
Smullen	77.07

First LastName	FirstName	Average Score
Avina	Fedricka	66.93
Bainter	Hanna	81.71
Bones	Beverlee	76.71
Boomhower	Samuel	87.57
Cavin	Lyla	74.43
Damato	Nestor	73.43
Dezzutti	Vernice	81.00
Dismukes	Selene	74.00
Farquharson	Salvatore	80.29
Lucia	Alphonse	75.64
Miyamoto	Sana	75.93
Montegalegre	Sanjuana	92.50
Monteiro	Lesa	79.50
Avina		**77.07**

Figure 5-7. First and Last aren't as intuitive as they should be

In the figure, we can see the average scores for the students, then see the weirdness that happens with First and Last when left alone. Then, on the far right, we see what happens when First and/or Last is given additional context. My general rule of thumb when using First or Last is to not use them as filter conditions, but treat them more like values you are seeking to find. What is the first value where conditions A, B, and C are true? What is the last value where those conditions are true?

Earliest and *Latest* function the exact same way, but they do it with dates instead of text and order the items chronologically. It is important to note that there is also an EARLIEST DAX function that is not quite identical to the aggregation happening here, so if someone does mention Earliest, you can ask if they're talking about the default aggregation options for dates or the DAX function.

Measures and DAX Fundamentals

We aggregate data so we can understand the data points underneath. Sometimes we want to make sure that the calculation is performed in a specific way, or that future users can see an explicit calculation in our data model. Sometimes our column name is sufficient for understanding what an aggregation is doing. What is often not understood, though, is that whether you are dragging a column into the Values section to get a sum or average or creating a DAX measure to perform a calculation, a measure is being used to create that aggregation in both scenarios.

Implicit and Explicit Measures

Since Power BI writes DAX behind the scenes to power every visual, and we aren't required to write out every measure, we see that there are both implicit measures and explicit measures.

An *implicit measure* is not strictly defined before being brought into a visual. This happens when you drag a column in, and it sums, or you tell it to average or perform some other aggregation.

An *explicit measure*, on the other hand, is a specific DAX measure that you create in your data model with a predefined calculation that you then add to a visual. Implicit measures are convenient but are limited to the aggregations we talked about previously. Explicit measures allow for more complicated calculations or specific groupings that might be hard to achieve without additional fields or columnar context.

It is also entirely possible to see the DAX that is generated when you use an implicit measure. You can, in fact, see the DAX that generates an entire visual in Power BI! As in Chapter 3 when we discussed using the Advanced Editor to see M that is generated in Power Query, you can use the "Performance analyzer" pane to see DAX that is generated when a visual is refreshed.

I've created a simple table that shows the Average Score by AssignmentID (Figure 5-8). We've seen this before. What I'm doing differently here is using the measure for Average Score and the implicit measure by using the Score column and setting the aggregation to average. You'll note that they get the same results. That's a good sign!

LastName	Average Score
Avina	66.93
Bainter	81.71
Bones	76.71
Boomhower	87.57
Cavin	74.43
Damato	73.43
Dezzutti	81.00
Dismukes	74.00
Farquharson	80.29
Lucia	75.64
Miyamoto	75.93
Montegalegre	92.50
Total	**77.07**

First LastName	Average Score
Avina	77.07

Last LastName	Average Score
Smullen	77.07

First LastName	FirstName	Average Score
Lucia	Alphonse	75.64
Bones	Beverlee	76.71
Shumway	Brendon	70.57
Schmaltz	Elmer	77.50
Avina	Fedricka	66.93
Bainter	Hanna	81.71
Monteiro	Lesa	79.50
Cavin	Lyla	74.43
Newlon	Marta	69.14
Damato	Nestor	73.43
Russell	Richard	76.57
Smullen	Russel	76.64
Avina		**77.07**

Figure 5-8. If it gets aggregated, it's a measure at some point

Now if we click the "Copy query" link in the "Performance analyzer," we can see the DAX that is generated. In Figure 5-9, I've copied the DAX and put it into my favorite DAX writing tool, DAX Studio.

I want you to focus on lines 6 and 7. The other lines aren't important right now. Line 6 is calling our explicit measure, the Average Score measure. Line 7 is calling an implicit measure, our chosen aggregation of Average of Score.

```
 1 // DAX Query
 2 DEFINE
 3    VAR __DS0Core =
 4       SUMMARIZECOLUMNS(
 5          ROLLUPADDISSUBTOTAL('Grades'[AssignmentID], "IsGrandTotalRowTotal"),
 6          "Average_Score", 'Grades'[Average Score],
 7          "AverageScore", CALCULATE(AVERAGE('Grades'[Score]))
 8       )
 9
10    VAR __DS0PrimaryWindowed =
11       TOPN(502, __DS0Core, [IsGrandTotalRowTotal], 0, 'Grades'[AssignmentID], 1)
12
13 EVALUATE
14    __DS0PrimaryWindowed
15
16 ORDER BY
17    [IsGrandTotalRowTotal] DESC, 'Grades'[AssignmentID]
18
```

Figure 5-9. Power BI's DAX generator knows the power of CALCULATE, and soon you will too

When Power BI needs to create a measure to satisfy the implicit need, we can see it creates an explicit piece of code to generate that measure for the internal calculation engine. In this case, that looks like this:

```
CALCULATE(AVERAGE('Grades'[Score]))
```

If you go into the PBIX file for Cool School University ISOM 210 and look at the measure for Average Score that already exists, you'll notice it's the exact same syntax. `Average_Score` and `AverageScore` from lines 6 and 7 are actually the same, except in line 6 it's calling the explicit measure I've created, and in line 7 it's creating an implicit measure to accomplish the same task. And Power BI also happened to generate the same code I used to create my measure.

A lot is going on in Figure 5-9, and not all of it is super relevant to measure creation in DAX, but what we can do is evaluate code that is generated and try to learn from it to see how DAX syntax works.

DAX Syntax Fundamentals

To learn the basics of DAX syntax, we're going to start with a simple calculation using an AVERAGE function against a single column. We will then add to our simple example a use of the CALCULATE function and that will look like line 7 from Figure 5-9. Let's look at Figure 5-10 to get a look at our simplified DAX average.

```
X  ✓  | 1 Simple DAX Average Score = average('Grades'[Score])
```

Figure 5-10. DAX syntax sounds scary, but I promise it's not

Here, from left to right, we first have the title of our measure, in this case "Simple DAX Average Score." The equals sign sets the title apart from the actual calculation that is to follow. Average is our function. The function then accepts certain criteria, in our case, a column reference.

The first parenthesis sets the function apart from the arguments or criteria it's looking for. Next, we have the table name enclosed in single quotes and column name enclosed in brackets that we are looking to pass to the function.

The second parenthesis identifies that all the arguments for the preceding function are present. Let's put that all together and make it sound a little more like English.

I have a DAX measure called Simple DAX Average Score. That DAX measure is defined as the Average function using the Score column from the Grades table as its parameter to calculate against. In our case, this will return the average score from the Grades table and is open to be modified by any applicable context. For your reference, all table names that have a space are always enclosed in single quotes, and all column names are always enclosed in brackets. As far as best practices when writing your own DAX, I always recommend putting your table names in single quotes regardless of whether they contain spaces.

Looking at this in a more technical way, all the simple aggregations we looked at earlier have the same basic DAX syntax for their function. Sum, Average, Count, DistinctCount, Min, and Max are all the same. First, Last, Earliest, and Latest are just calculations of the Min or Max. That syntax is as follows.

```
FUNCTION('TABLE'[COLUMN])
```

That's it. That will get you a simple explicit measure that will be filtered by all other context in the visual and any applicable slicers on your worksheet. With this basic context understood, let's go one step up from here, get back to the full version of line 7 from Figure 5-9, and talk about CALCULATE.

CALCULATE

The CALCULATE function is, in many ways, the Swiss army knife of DAX functions. Like many things in life, 80% of DAX problems can be solved with 20% mastery. If you can master CALCULATE, you will be well on your way to that early level of mastery.

The CALCULATE function is very simple. It is a wrapper that evaluates an expression in a modified filter context. What does that mean? You can evaluate functions and then preset filter contexts.

Think about being able to use a WHERE clause in SQL. You want to limit results to where X = Y or Z > 100, for instance. CALCULATE allows you to pass these WHERE clause–type parameters into your DAX formula in an explicit way, which means that they will always apply, regardless of any other context. You can probably think of tons of use cases where this would be helpful.

Want to compare this year's sales to date to the sales year-to-date of the previous year? CALCULATE can help you do that. Maybe you need to see how another product's sales count compares to a different set of products? You can do that. Do you want to provide a dynamic calculation that passes filter context based on the results of another calculation, like yesterday's date? You can do that.

So, let's review line 7 of Figure 5-9 and discuss the DAX that Power BI put together when it created our implicit measure:

```
"AverageScore" = CALCULATE(AVERAGE('Grades'[Score]))
```

AverageScore is the name of the implicit measure. We know how to read the Average function from the previous section. CALCULATE wraps that function into a larger function. That's what the parenthesis in front of AVERAGE and on the other side of the first right parenthesis are doing.

Let's say we want to compare our students' average scores, but want to compare them to another group result quickly. A great example of this is to take a category and then see how people did against others in that category. Let's look at the average score of students who have a self-described intermediate level of proficiency in Excel, and see how each of those students performed against their cohort's average.

As we have seen, getting everyone's individual average in a visual isn't hard, but let's say we want to compare that value to the average of a specific category. For instance, is the average score higher or lower than the average score of those people with intermediate Excel proficiency? The CALCULATE function helps us with this by allowing us to define the filter context. Let's look at the code for our new example in Figure 5-11 and break it down.

```
1  Intermediate Excel Average Score =
2  CALCULATE (
3      AVERAGE ( 'Grades'[Score] ),
4      'Survey Data'[ExcelSelfDescribedProficiency] = "Intermediate"
5  )
```

Figure 5-11. Ah, the beauty of properly formatted DAX

As we are going to break down a more complicated DAX statement, I wanted to make sure that the code was formatted to be easier to read. Several DAX formatting options are available online and through the previously mentioned DAX Studio. Let's go through this line by line.

In line 1, we have the name of our measure, in this case Intermediate Excel Average Score.

In line 2, we have established our CALCULATE wrapper and put down the first parenthesis of the CALCULATE function to identify that what comes next is the function that will be called.

In line 3, we call the AVERAGE function, as we did previously in our simple example. Again, note inside the parenthesis of the AVERAGE function, we identify the table name with the single quotes and the column name in regular brackets. Then, at the end of line 3, we have our first new wrinkle, and that's the comma after the right parenthesis.

Now we can look at the syntax for the CALCULATE function to understand what is about to happen. CALCULATE's syntax always follows the following format:

```
CALCULATE (Function(), Filter Statement 1, Filter Statement 2, ...,
    Filter Statement N)
```

Notice that the first comma separates the function from the first filter statement, and then commas are used to separate each filter statement that comes after the first from the last. Yes, that's right, CALCULATE can pass multiple filter conditions. But now that we understand what that comma is doing in line 3, separating the wrapped function from the filter condition that is about to come after, we can move to line 4.

In line 4, we have a very simple true/false, or Boolean, statement. In the Survey Data table, we have a column called ExcelSelfDescribedProficiency. We want to calculate the average score for only the people who have a self-described intermediate level of proficiency, so after the comma in line 3, we identify a table name and a column name and set it to be equal to a value. Notice that `Intermediate` is wrapped in double quotes. Text must always be wrapped in those double quotes, and if it is wrapped in those double quotes, Power BI will treat the value as though it were text. We will come back to this issue in a little bit.

Finally, in line 5 we have the last right parenthesis, which identifies to the `CALCULATE` function that everything is now wrapped and ready to go. Now let's look at Figure 5-12 to see what that looks like in a table with our students, their level of proficiency, and the average score.

LastName	ExcelSelfDescribedProficiency	Average Score	Intermediate Excel Average Score
Avina	None	66.93	
Bainter	Intermediate	81.71	81.71
Bones	None	76.71	
Boomhower	Intermediate	87.57	87.57
Cavin	Intermediate	74.43	74.43
Damato	Beginner	73.43	
Dezzutti	Beginner	81.00	
Dismukes	Advanced	74.00	
Farquharson	Beginner	80.29	
Lucia	Beginner	75.64	
Miyamoto	Beginner	75.93	
Montegalegre	Intermediate	92.50	92.50
Monteiro	Advanced	79.50	
Newlon	None	69.14	
Piatt	None	66.00	
Russell	Beginner	76.57	
Schmaltz	None	77.50	
Schmitz	Advanced	85.36	
Shumway	None	70.57	
Smullen	Beginner	76.64	
Total		**77.07**	**84.05**

Figure 5-12. CALCULATE can enforce its own filter context

When we look at this simple table, we can see the average score we've seen multiple times before, but notice that our new Intermediate Excel Average Score measure shows values for only the people who have intermediate self-described proficiency! This is a great example of basic DAX wrapping in `CALCULATE` to show you how that works.

However, what if we wanted to show in this table the total Intermediate Excel Average Score for everyone, so we could quickly see how each person did compared to that 84.05 number, regardless of their proficiency?

We Heard You Like DAX, So We Put Some DAX in Your DAX

As mentioned before, the CALCULATE function can take multiple filter context conditions. However, those filter conditions can themselves also be DAX functions. In Figure 5-12, we saw that we could use CALCULATE to get the specific average for our intermediate Excel users, but we didn't quite get all the way there to make it nice and easy to compare those users.

What I really want to do is compare everyone to the 84.05 value, which is the average score of everyone who had intermediate Excel proficiency. What we need is a calculation that takes the average score of those intermediate Excel users and ignores all the other context or filters. We can do this with the ALL statement.

ALL is an operator that returns all the records, ignoring any filters that might have been applied. ALL comes in a couple of flavors. We will use the simplest one for our example, but the ALL statement can accept a table value or column value to target a specific context to remove filters from. You can also pass no value in the ALL statement to remove all of the filter context. As we did in Figure 5-11, let's take a look at Figure 5-13 to see how we can modify CALCULATE with a second filter function using another DAX statement as the filter condition.

```
1   Intermediate Excel Average Score with ALL =
2   CALCULATE (
3       AVERAGE ( 'Grades'[Score] ),
4       ALL (),
5       'Survey Data'[ExcelSelfDescribedProficiency] = "Intermediate"
6   )
```

Figure 5-13. Just one step down the DAX rabbit hole

You may notice Figure 5-13 doesn't look that different from Figure 5-11. We really added only one line, but remember to put it into the context of how CALCULATE works: CALCULATE(Function (), Filter 1, Filter 2, ..., Filter N).

What we are doing now is adding a filter, in this case, replacing filter 1 and making what was formerly filter 1, now filter 2. For the example provided in Figure 5-13, the order of the filters doesn't matter, but, as a warning, it might in more complicated examples. The ALL function now serves as filter 1, and when the ALL function is followed by nothing within parentheses, it means to remove all filter context for the result.

Think of the DAX statement in normal terms like this. I am going to calculate the average score of intermediate Excel users. When I display that value, I want it to display the average of all intermediate Excel users, regardless of any other context that exists in the visual or any other slicers or filters that might normally apply. To see how this result is different, look at Figure 5-14.

LastName	ExcelSelfDescribedProficiency	Average Score	Intermediate Excel Average Score	Intermediate Excel Average Score with ALL
Avina	None	66.93		84.05
Bainter	Intermediate	81.71	81.71	84.05
Bones	None	76.71		84.05
Boomhower	Intermediate	87.57	87.57	84.05
Cavin	Intermediate	74.43	74.43	84.05
Damato	Beginner	73.43		84.05
Dezzutti	Beginner	81.00		84.05
Dismukes	Advanced	74.00		84.05
Farquharson	Beginner	80.29		84.05
Lucia	Beginner	75.64		84.05
Miyamoto	Beginner	75.93		84.05
Montegalegre	Intermediate	92.50	92.50	84.05
Monteiro	Advanced	79.50		84.05
Newlon	None	69.14		84.05
Piatt	None	66.00		84.05
Russell	Beginner	76.57		84.05
Schmaltz	None	77.50		84.05
Schmitz	Advanced	85.36		84.05
Shumway	None	70.57		84.05
Smullen	Beginner	76.64		84.05
Total		**77.07**	**84.05**	**84.05**

Figure 5-14. Take a look at ALL the 84.05s

What is our new measure doing? It's calculating the average score of everyone with an intermediate Excel proficiency and then applying that value to every data combination in the visual, regardless of its filter context. When we look at the Intermediate Excel Average Score that we put together for Figure 5-12, we can see it did not return results for users who were not of intermediate proficiency. That would make sense. The calculation is filtered by the visual's context.

Likewise, while we see the total Average Score in Figure 5-12, everyone who is an intermediate user returned their individual average, and we can see their individual average was the same as their average. That doesn't help us compare the result, though.

However, with this consistent value in place, I could do something very simple like turn this into a line and clustered column chart to quickly see which of my students are above or below this new average line. We can see an example of this in Figure 5-15, along with a slicer that would allow us to look at different groupings to see how they might compare.

In this case, we will look at the students who claimed advanced Excel proficiency and see how they compare to the intermediate average. Notice in Figure 5-15 that our 84.05 line is not affected by the slicer being set to Advanced because, with the ALL statement inside our CALCULATE filter, it's ignoring that filter context.

LastName	ExcelSelfDescribedProficiency	Average Score	Intermediate Excel Average Score	Intermediate Excel Average Score with ALL
Avina	None	66.93		84.05
Bainter	Intermediate	81.71	81.71	84.05
Bones	None	76.71		84.05
Boomhower	Intermediate	87.57	87.57	84.05
Cavin	Intermediate	74.43	74.43	84.05
Damato	Beginner	73.43		84.05
Dezzutti	Beginner	81.00		84.05
Dismukes	Advanced	74.00		84.05
Farquharson	Beginner	80.29		84.05
Lucia	Beginner	75.64		84.05
Miyamoto	Beginner	75.93		84.05
Montegalegre	Intermediate	92.50	92.50	84.05
Monteiro	Advanced	79.50		84.05
Newlon	None	69.14		84.05
Piatt	None	66.00		84.05
Russell	Beginner	76.57		84.05
Schmaltz	None	77.50		84.05
Schmitz	Advanced	85.36		84.05
Shumway	None	70.57		84.05
Smullen	Beginner	76.64		84.05
Total		**77.07**	**84.05**	**84.05**

Figure 5-15. It's ALL about the filter context

Row and Filter Context

The most important lesson that you will learn about DAX as you develop your skills will be to understand row context and filter context. In many ways, this is the least intuitive but most important lesson about DAX you can learn, which will take your mastery of DAX to the next level.

DAX is a language that queries columns. Analysis Services Tabular and Power BI store their data in columnar data store databases. DAX statements query columns to get results for measures or reference other columns when building calculated columns.

When we look at our data in the Data view, we see that the data is still a collection of rows and columns, and when we look at the table visuals we've built to showcase our DAX examples, they're tables with rows and columns. Those row values impact our measure results.

Going back to Figure 5-12, our intermediate Excel average score showed results only where the row contained a record indicating a user's intermediate level of Excel proficiency. This would still be true even if we removed the specific field regarding proficiency from the visual; it's because the LastName field comes from the same table and implicitly identifies their Excel proficiency status, being just a different field in the same table.

This brings us to row context. *Row context* occurs anytime a table is iterated on, or said another way, anytime a formula calls for going over a table row by row. This can happen both explicitly, as seen in Figure 5-12, or implicitly, as we described in the previous scenario. Row context always applies when we create calculated columns using DAX because the results of a given record for a calculated column are always calculated at the row level.

Certain DAX functions always iterate over a table. These functions can, therefore, be useful when you want to do more than get a simple aggregation for a column because what you really want is an aggregation based on some combination of data for each row of data. You want to return a value that is an expression for each row in a table. I like to call these functions the *X functions* SUMX, AVERAGEX, COUNTX, MINX, MAXX, and PRODUCTX.

You can imagine these X functions as making implicit calculated columns and then taking the desired aggregation of those calculated columns. A classic example of when you might use a function like this is for a sales table with price and quantity sold. If you try to take the sum of the quantity times the sum of the prices, you're going to get a result that doesn't make a ton of sense.

What you really want is something more like the sum of each record's price multiplied by quantity. That's what SUMX does, and it does this with row context. Row context is often seen at the visual level, but always happens at the data storage level. Just because Power BI stores its data as columns and computes its data as columns doesn't mean that rows and row context don't matter!

With row context out of the way, we can talk about *filter context*. The first thing to note is that while we discuss filter context second, computationally, it happens first. Filters are applied to the data before any DAX gets computed. This has the benefit of getting to run a calculation against a smaller amount of data instead of over the entirety of the column each time. It's easier to filter out 50 of 100 records and then add the 50 records than it is to add the 100 records, then pick out each record that isn't relevant, and then subtract those records from the total.

Filters on tables apply to all rows of the table that meet the filter condition. From our instance in Figure 5-12, the calculation says to calculate the average score for people with intermediate proficiency. It first filters the table to only those people who have intermediate proficiency and then runs the result. If there were no other columns but LastName and that measure, we would see only the last names that would return values because the table gets filtered first and then passes that filter along its relationship to the other table.

If more than one filter is in place, only the records that meet all the filter criteria are shown. If you want to think of it as a Venn diagram with filter A and filter B, if both filters were on, you would get only the result that would meet both, or the overlapping part of that diagram. In SQL terms, you could think of it as an INNER JOIN, in which only the records where both conditions were true would be shown. Remember, filters always get applied first and do not interact with row context.

One Final DAX Example

With these things in mind, let's try our hand at creating one more DAX measure to go a couple of levels up in difficulty from what we've done previously. We are going to start with the measure we made for Figure 5-13 and build on it from there. This example uses some unique DAX functions, and I don't want you to worry about those specifically, but see how the context comes together with the syntax to make a readable DAX statement.

In this example, we want to expand our analysis. We don't want to compare everyone to the intermediate cohort. We want to compare everyone to their own cohort. However, to do that, we need to find a way to pass a specific value—in our case, someone's level of Excel proficiency—through the CALCULATE function.

The next problem is, there are four possible values, and we want to make sure that each is called correctly, but we also want the function to work if no value is selected. There are certainly a couple of ways to tackle this problem. However, I intentionally tried to find the most obnoxious one so I could demonstrate how context and syntax come together to make the DAX statement understandable. Let's look at that example in Figure 5-16.

```
1   Filtered Excel Proficiency Average Score =
2   IF (
3       HASONEVALUE ( 'Survey Data'[ExcelSelfDescribedProficiency] ) = TRUE (),
4       CALCULATE (
5           AVERAGE ( 'Grades'[Score] ),
6           ALL (),
7           'Survey Data'[ExcelSelfDescribedProficiency]
8               = SELECTEDVALUE ( 'Survey Data'[ExcelSelfDescribedProficiency] )
9       ),
10      CALCULATE ( AVERAGE ( 'Grades'[Score] ), ALL () )
11  )
```

Figure 5-16. It's not as bad as it looks, I promise!

So, the first thing we have here is going to be familiar to our Excel users. In line 2, we have an IF statement. IF statements in DAX are similar to the way they function in Excel:

```
IF (Conditional Statement, Conditional Statement is True result,
Conditional Statement is False result).
```

Immediately, I know I'm looking to see what the conditional statement is and what the results are based on whether the conditional statement is true or false. Let's go to line 3.

Our conditional statement here is to say that if the column of ExcelSelfDescribedProficiency is returning one result, for whatever reason, then do the first thing; otherwise, do the second thing. A conditional statement must have a condition to be met. So, in this case, the HASONEVALUE statement is testing whether the column has more than one value and then returning a TRUE or FALSE statement.

Lines 4 through 9 detail what should happen if the statement is true. In this case, we have the first couple of lines we've seen before until we get to line 7. Here we are adding another filter condition to the CALCULATE wrapper and saying that the function should also have a filter for the column that is the actual selected value from that column. Why does this work? Remember, filter context is figured out first, before row context!

If I'm using a slicer to determine which value to choose or my visual has that field in its results, it must pass that filter condition to the function and, at that point for that specific version of the calculation, we are returning one specific value.

If for some reason we are in a situation where we are not looking at the average score by Excel proficiency or by a field in the same table as Excel proficiency from which filter context could be derived (say, for the total row), we then go to the conditional formula for when it's not true. To do that, you use a simple CALCULATE function of the average, removing all filter conditions with the ALL function.

If you were to look at this DAX statement in Power BI or another DAX editing tool, there is a feature called intellisense that we could use to identify what each parenthesis groups together for a given DAX statement. But this statement isn't too far removed from what we have discussed so far. If you can do that, you can figure out how to solve most other DAX problems. With the preceding DAX statement, we can get to a result like we see on the far right column of the table in Figure 5-17.

LastName	ExcelSelfDescribedProficiency	Average Score	Complex Filtered Excel Proficiency Average Score
Dismukes	Advanced	74.00	79.62
Monteiro	Advanced	79.50	79.62
Schmitz	Advanced	85.36	79.62
Damato	Beginner	73.43	77.07
Dezzutti	Beginner	81.00	77.07
Farquharson	Beginner	80.29	77.07
Lucia	Beginner	75.64	77.07
Miyamoto	Beginner	75.93	77.07
Russell	Beginner	76.57	77.07
Smullen	Beginner	76.64	77.07
Bainter	Intermediate	81.71	84.34
Boomhower	Intermediate	87.57	84.34
Cavin	Intermediate	75.57	84.34
Montegalegre	Intermediate	92.50	84.34
Avina	None	66.93	71.14
Bones	None	76.71	71.14
Newlon	None	69.14	71.14
Piatt	None	66.00	71.14
Schmaltz	None	77.50	71.14
Shumway	None	70.57	71.14
Total		**77.13**	**77.13**

Figure 5-17. See!? We figured it out.

With what you've learned here, you can create a measure or calculated column that gets you what you need for your analysis. Just remember, any DAX used to create a calculated column will always be row-context dependent because you're adding data to your data model. Now we're ready for some real data analysis.

Conclusion

At this point, we've got the data into the data model, we've built the relationships, we have the visuals we need, and finally we have enough DAX to create the explicit measures we want when an implicit measure won't do the job.

In the next chapter, we are going to put everything we've discussed together into a real-world workflow using our dataset. We will append data for an extra course into the data model using Power Query, do some cleanup transformations, build some measures, and learn a little bit more about Cool School University.

CHAPTER 6

Putting the Puzzle Pieces Together: From Raw Data to Report

In the first five chapters of this book, we laid a foundation for the use of Power BI. In this chapter, you'll learn how to go from raw data in Excel to a Power BI report.

To facilitate that, we'll bring in the Cool School University data that we've already worked with so far and add data from a second class's grades using Power Query to wrangle our data into the desired form. Then we'll build out the relationships we need so that we can get the data to fit together. After that, we'll build some measures to help us get deeper insights.

Finally, we'll build our first report page with some easy, out-of-the-box visuals that will help us learn a little more about our students' performance. This first, simple report should allow our users to gain valuable insights about our classes that they didn't have before, and that will help us tell a story that will inform our future decision making.

Your First Data Import

Let's begin by importing the data you need. First locate the six Excel files within the ZIP file associated with this text (*https://oreil.ly/MS-power-BI-files*). We'll initially focus on three files, ignoring the other three whose names have "Chapter6Addition" at the end. Don't worry, we'll get to them in the next section.

Before we start, if you want to take time to familiarize yourself with all of the data, feel free to open the files and look around. I recommend saving copies of the files so that you can try different things with the data in Excel and, on your own, try to get those same answers out of Power BI. I also highly encourage you to change some of the data in those files to see how that might impact some of the results after you feel comfortable with the process that will be laid out through this chapter. Taking that step will help you get more familiar with the functionality and might just make you a Cool School star.

So, ignoring the Chapter 6–specific additions, we're left with three files:

- *CoolSchoolUniversityGradesPowerBIVersion.xlsx*
- *CoolSchoolUniversityInstructorGatheredInformation.xlsx*
- *CoolSchoolUniveristySchoolSuppliedDataClassStart.xlsx*

Choose and Transform the Data When You Import

Let's bring these into Power BI. We'll go through the files one at a time, but remember to not just choose to import the data, but to transform it too, even if we don't necessarily have transformations to make immediately. This is the same process that was discussed in Chapter 3: Get data → Excel workbook → Navigate to the file we want to import → select file → choose "Transform data" in the Navigator window.

To do this, click the "Excel workbook" button on the Home ribbon to first take a look at our school-supplied data. It's the beginning of the semester, and the university provides us a specific set of data about our students for the course.

In the Explorer window that appears (Figure 6-1) you'll see the Navigator menu, discussed previously. For an Excel workbook, each worksheet appears as its own item, as do any named tables.

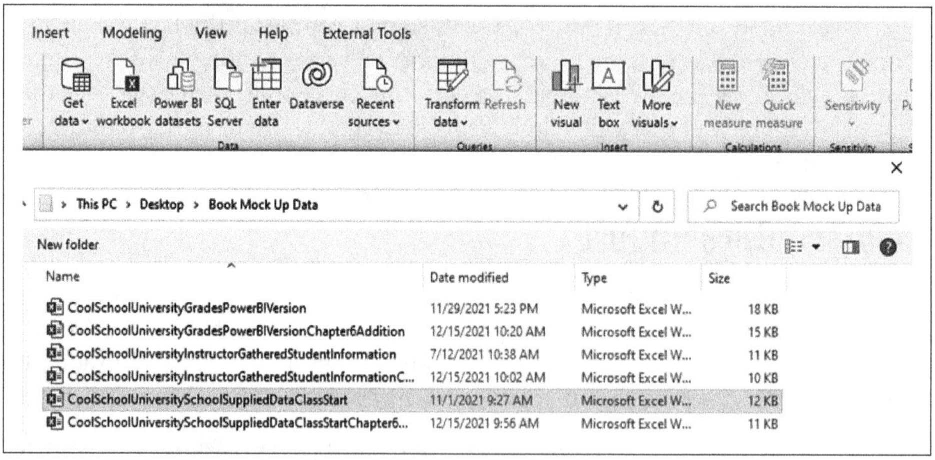

Figure 6-1. Ahh, let's open up our first data, chronologically

Now select the file called *CoolSchoolUniversitySchoolSuppliedDataClassStart*, which has only one Excel worksheet named Sheet1. Then choose "Transform data" and take a look at Figure 6-2, which shows what you should now see—a preview of the data in the file.

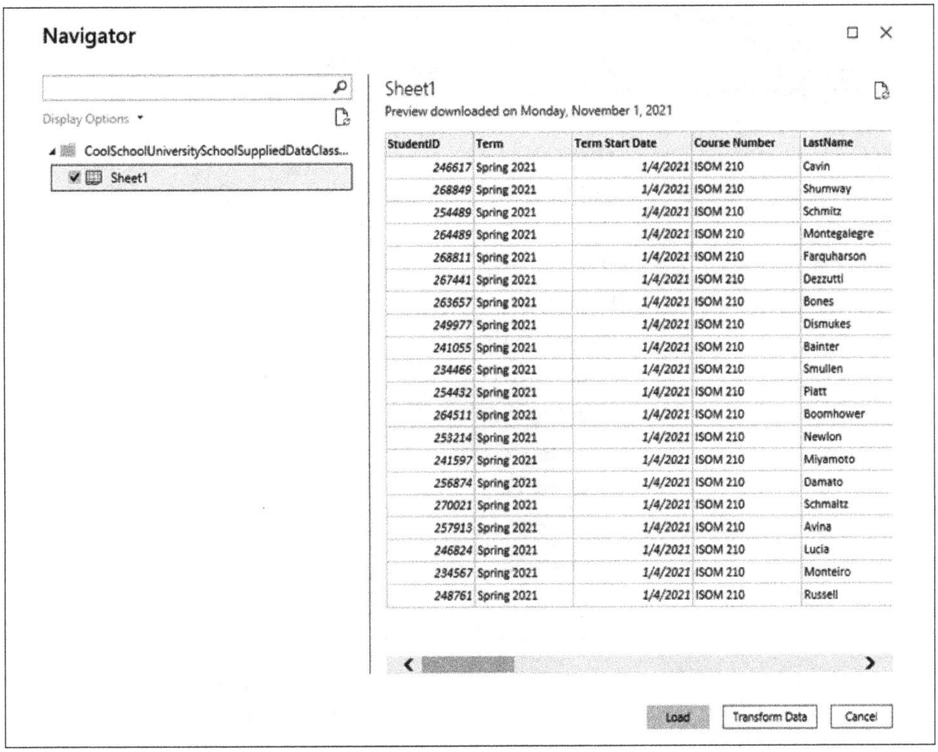

Figure 6-2. The Navigator window is great for a quick preview of data

Transformations in Power Query

After selecting "Transform data," we are brought into Power Query. We can see in Figure 6-3 that Power Query has taken the liberty of applying some basic transformations to help accelerate our development—in this case, the steps of Source, Navigation, Promoted Headers, and Changed Type. You'll notice that Power Query by default will show you the view of the data as of the final transformation, and you'll see that Changed Type is now highlighted in the Applied Steps window on the right.

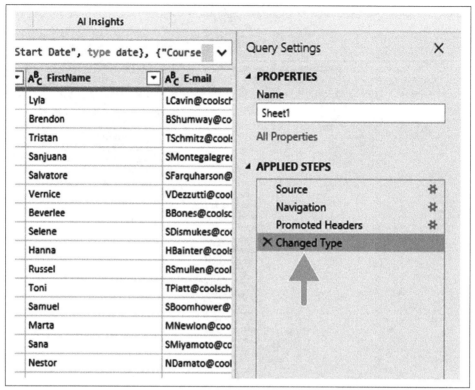

Figure 6-3. Power Query helps us get a head start by applying some basic transformations for us to see

Under Applied Steps on the right, the Source is almost universal for any type of data. This is what Power BI uses to identify the data source so that it knows how to access the data. For an Excel workbook, this will look like a list of worksheet names and table names from the workbook we are looking at. In a database source, it will look like a list of tables and views you have access to.

When using the Navigator window, what we are doing is walking through the first step of Source and the second step of Navigation. This is how Power Query builds a type of map that will allow it to remember what data to get and where in that dataset the specific information we are looking for is located. In a database, the source would be a given database, but the navigation would lead us to a specific table of data. From Excel, the source identifies which Excel file it is, but navigation identifies what worksheet or named table range the data we are looking for is in.

Speaking of Navigation, this is the first view of the data that Power Query gets. If you look at the Power Query window with Navigation selected, you'll notice that the data doesn't look very clean at all. You can see in Figure 6-4 that the column names aren't there, and the data itself isn't well defined, as each column has a data type of Any.

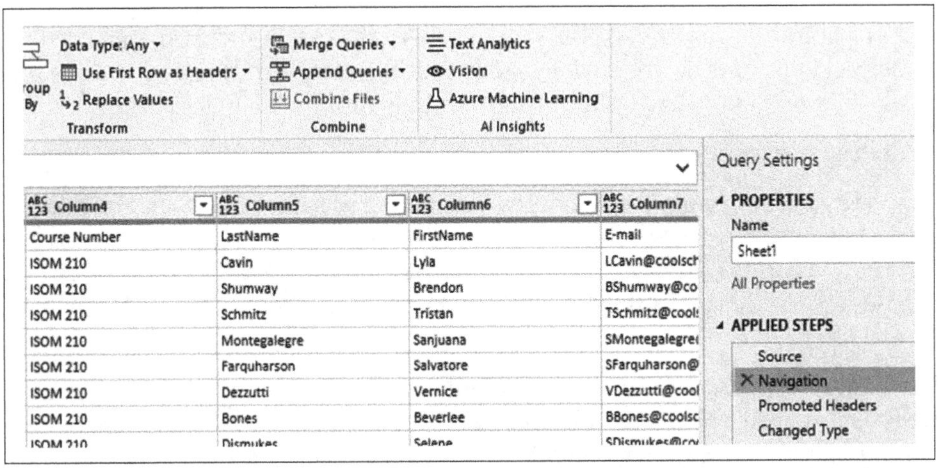

Figure 6-4. The Navigation step is only the beginning, as it's your first view of the data in an unclean format

However, Power Query is helpful here and intuits that the first row should, in fact, be column headers. Power Query automatically changes the data types to fit based on a review of the data in the columns themselves. That's why Promoted Headers and Changed Type appear under Applied Steps in Figure 6-4.

While Power Query's accuracy with these steps is incredibly high, that doesn't mean it's perfect. Therefore, I always like to take a cursory glance at these steps when they're applied to confirm that's indeed the behavior I want.

Also, sometimes if Power Query can't intuit these steps for whatever reason, these steps might not appear. If that happens, you can apply these steps manually from Power Query as discussed in Chapter 3.

There will also be data for which the Promoted Headers applied step won't be necessary because the data source provides that metadata detail in advance. This is true most often with database data sources, but it can also be true of other data sources, such as named Excel tables.

If you'd like, you could certainly review the Advanced Editor to look at the M that is generated by Power Query, but I think the last thing to do here is to change the name of the table to something more meaningful. Sheet1 just doesn't have a great ring to it. You can name the table whatever you like, but I'll keep things simple and call it "UniversitySuppliedData." Note that if your naming conventions are not the same as mine, you'll need to adjust whatever DAX is used in this chapter accordingly.

You could insert spaces in that name, as well, but I'm not a fan of putting spaces into table names. From a metadata perspective, it's generally not a database best practice. Also in my experience, DAX IntelliSense tends to get weird when dealing with table names that include spaces. So that's why I removed the spaces and used capital letters at the beginning of each word to help readers identify how to read the table name. It's a stylistic choice more than technical impact, but in my opinion it does help.

With that, we have our first piece of data in Power BI! Congratulations!

Now let's go get the other two files and look at some specific cases where the process might differ from what we did. In fact, we can add more data from within Power Query by using the New Source button, so let's use that. Remember, the button's drop-down arrow makes a shorter list of most used data sources, and Excel is the first on that list.

Next, chronologically, would be our student survey data from the beginning of the term. This is the file within our file list called *CoolSchoolUniversityInstructorGatheredStudentInformation.xlsx*. This is another single-sheet Excel workbook, so the Applied Steps are going to look identical to the first worksheet we imported. Let's rename this table "StudentSurveyData" and move on to our last initial data import.

Finally, we get our grades sheet at the end of the term that we've theoretically been updating throughout the year. You'll notice that *CoolSchoolUniversityGradesPowerBIVersion.xlsx* has two worksheets: AssignmentDIM and GradeScores. We want both of them, so in the Navigator window select Both.

If you're doing this from outside Power Query, remember to choose "Transform data" and remember that is the default behavior inside Power Query. Thankfully, as these sheets are named inside Excel, Power Query makes those sheet names the default table names, which in our case is perfect. First data import complete! So now we have four tables. Next, we need to bring in our second semester's worth of data.

Second Data Import and Wrangling

Our second set of data importing starts very much like the first. We have three files that we are going to bring in for this portion, and the first part of it is the same as what we just did—except we're importing the files with the Chapter6Addition filenames.

When you import those four sources exactly as we did before, your query list should look like Figure 6-5. You'll notice I didn't make any modifications or any other edits to these tables yet. I just imported them. When something is imported that would have the same name as a query that already exists, it will have a number (N) automatically added to it, where N is the number of items with the same name.

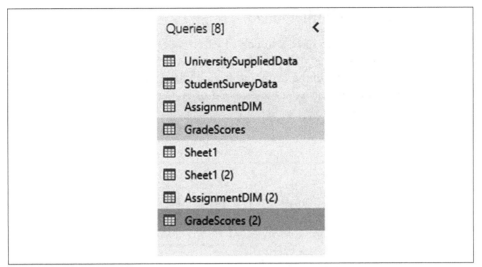

Figure 6-5. Your query list after importing your second set of data

Looking through these tables at a glance, it looks like AssignmentDIM is the same. There's no new data there, so let's remove that second AssignmentDIM from our queries list. How? You can either select it and press the Delete key or you can right-click it and select Delete.

Next let's rename those remaining sheets with more meaningful names. I did the university-provided data first and the survey data second, so my query list looks like Figure 6-6. Note that for my own clarity I added the (2) to the names in the list.

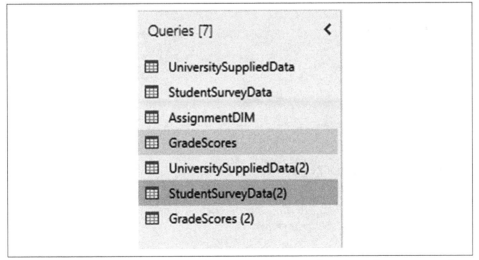

Figure 6-6. We've removed our second AssignmentDIM and can now focus on wrangling our three new queries

Consolidating Tables with Append

Inevitably, we don't want to have a bunch of extra tables in our final model, so we would like to consolidate these tables where we can. We can do that with the Append Queries function, as shown in the Combine section of the Home ribbon. If we choose the drop-down menu, we can select to Append or Append as New. In this case, we will just Append. Select the first table and click Append Queries. Select University-SuppliedData(2) from the "Table to append" list, and when we do that, we'll see what's shown in Figure 6-7.

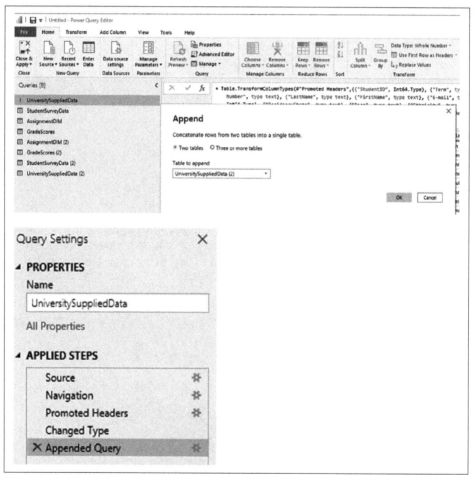

Figure 6-7. Consolidate tables with the Append Queries function. Appending proves that sometimes things are really better together.

Notice in the Applied Steps list that there is a new step called Appended Query, and we can see this single table now contains all the values from both UniversitySupplied-Data and UniversitySuppliedData(2). That's exactly what we want.

Now we cannot delete UniversitySuppliedData(2). That query is now referenced in the M script that allows the append to happen. When we finalize the load with the Close & Apply button, this table will also load. For demonstration purposes, I'm leaving them alone so that I can talk about hiding tables from the Report view later, but another option would be to right-click UniversitySuppliedData(2) and click "Enable load" so that the option is unchecked. This makes that query like a staging query that isn't loaded into the final dataset.

Now when we repeat the Append step for StudentSurveyData, we get a problem. Notice, I didn't say an error. There's nothing technically wrong. However, our data now has a problem. Look at the ClassID column in this appended StudentSurvey-Data. It's not unique. It has duplicated values, as we can see in Figure 6-8.

IDs should be unique. It's clear that the professor when considering these class IDs didn't think ahead to future courses and the impact of using the same IDs. However, we can create a unique ID for each record with something called an Index Column.

In the Add Column portion of the ribbon in the General section, you can see the Index Column with a drop-down. The default behavior for any Index Column is to start from 0, which really annoys me. So I will use the drop-down menu and select to start from 1. When we do that, we get a column named Index that appears at the far right side of the table.

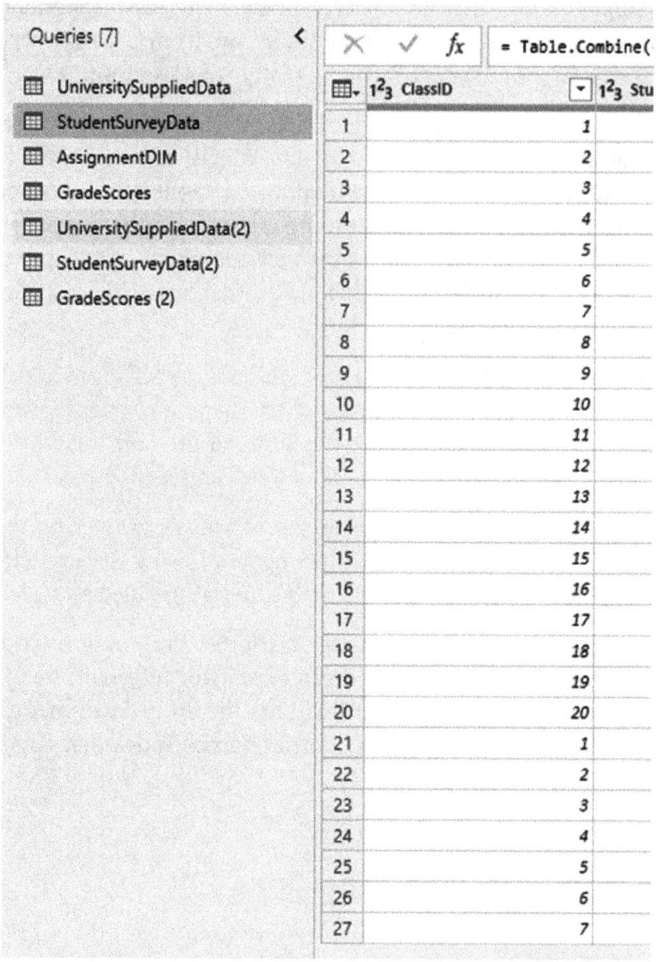

Figure 6-8. Danger four-letter name, son-of-a-robin person! We can't have duplicate values in a column that is supposed to be unique.

I personally like to see my primary ID on the left side, so I will right-click the column name and select Move → To Beginning to get it on the far left of the table. You could alternately click the Column Name, hold, and drag it all the way to the left. You can see the menu options when right-clicking a column in Figure 6-9.

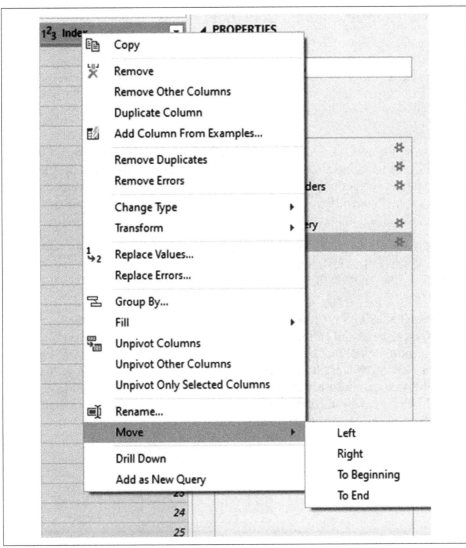

Figure 6-9. Here are your options when you right-click a column. Learn to love this menu, because you'll use it often.

We can also rename the Index Column, as we see the Rename option just above the Move option in Figure 6-9. In this case, I'm going to rename the Index to "TrueClassID" so that I know that's the unique value.

Using Merge to Get Columns from Other Tables

This gets our student survey data into a good spot, but our grades are going to be even more weird because of the issue with the ClassIDs. Notice that GradeScores and GradeScores (2) don't have any other way to identify students. If we were just to append them now, we really wouldn't have a good way to identify which person with ClassID 1 we're talking about. For instance, would it be the fall or summer student with that ID?

In this case, we need to find a unique value that we can match to each class ID. Thankfully, we have those in the student survey data tables in the StudentID. So we're going to do two merges here. We're going to merge GradeScores with StudentSurvey-Data to get the StudentID into that table, and then we will do the same thing with GradeScores (2) and StudentSurveyData(2).

Merging is a little more complicated than appending. Appending is, at its core, about making a table longer. Merging is about making a table wider. Another way to think about it is that appending is about adding rows, and merging is about adding columns.

Let's select GradeScores (2) and go back to the Home portion of the ribbon so we can select Merge Queries and perform the merge this time with StudentSurveyData(2). As with Append Queries, the drop-down menu will allow you to choose to Merge or Merge as New. We will again just merge. When you select Merge, you'll see an interface that is very reminiscent of the relationship creation interface. It autoselects the currently selected query and puts it on top, and then you can choose the second table, StudentSurveyData(2). Select ClassID in both tables. When we do that, we get what you see in Figure 6-10.

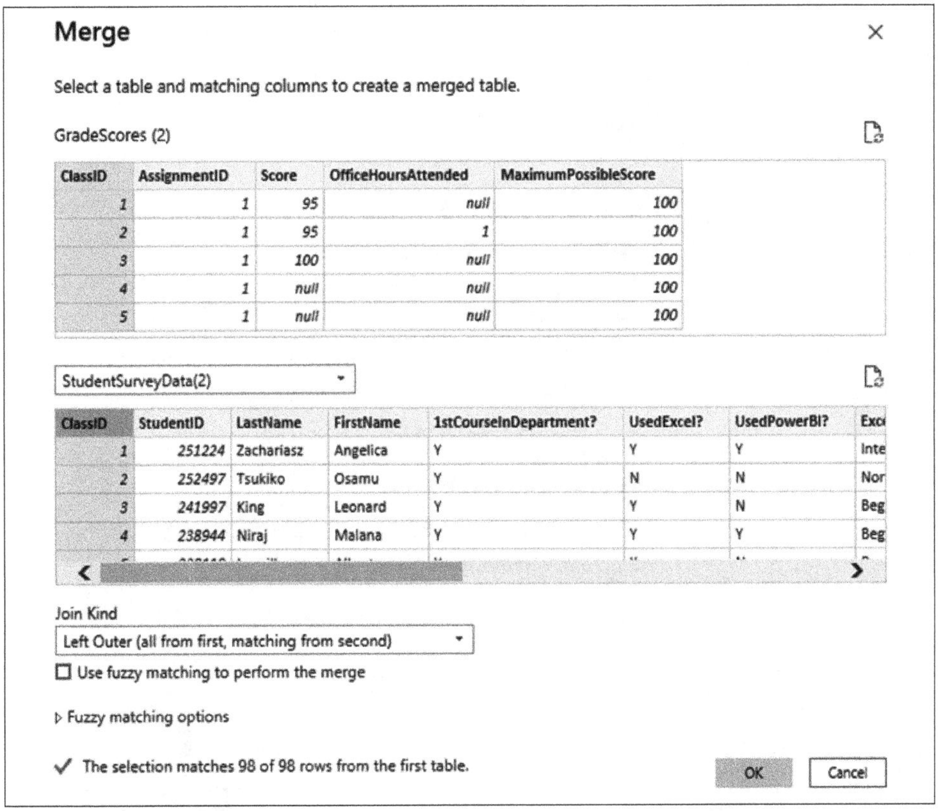

Merge   ✕

Select a table and matching columns to create a merged table.

GradeScores (2)

ClassID	AssignmentID	Score	OfficeHoursAttended	MaximumPossibleScore
1	1	95	null	100
2	1	95	1	100
3	1	100	null	100
4	1	null	null	100
5	1	null	null	100

StudentSurveyData(2)   ▼

ClassID	StudentID	LastName	FirstName	1stCourseInDepartment?	UsedExcel?	UsedPowerBI?	Exc
1	251224	Zachariasz	Angelica	Y	Y	Y	Inte
2	252497	Tsukiko	Osamu	Y	N	N	Nor
3	241997	King	Leonard	Y	Y	N	Beg
4	238944	Niraj	Malana	Y	Y	Y	Beg

Join Kind

| Left Outer (all from first, matching from second)   ▼ |

☐ Use fuzzy matching to perform the merge

▷ Fuzzy matching options

✓ The selection matches 98 of 98 rows from the first table.   [OK] [Cancel]

Figure 6-10. Merging is like a SQL join: bring two tables together and get the fields you need from each of them

Once the Merge is confirmed and you click OK, you'll notice that a column appears on the far right that has "Table" for every single record. This column also has a different symbol next to the column name, compared to the typical filter button on the other columns. That button next to the column name enables you to choose which columns you want to merge into the table. Figure 6-11 shows what that menu should look like. In this case, the only column I'm selecting is StudentID.

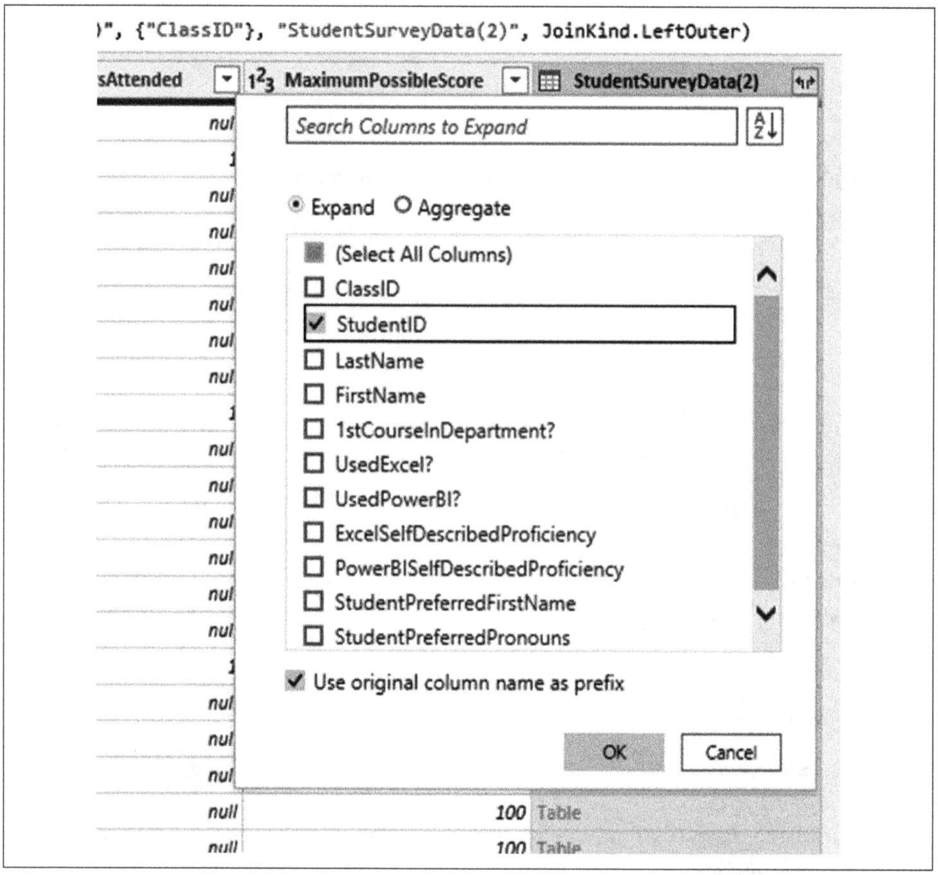

```
)", {"ClassID"}, "StudentSurveyData(2)", JoinKind.LeftOuter)
```

Figure 6-11. You don't need everything. Be judicious. Take only the extra fields you need.

Now that I have the StudentID column in this table, I can create a new column that will create a unique combination of ClassID and StudentID. We can do this by using the Column From Examples feature in the General section of the Add Column ribbon. To do this, hold down the Ctrl key and select the ClassID and StudentID columns so that we can choose From Selection from the button's drop-down list. Figure 6-12 shows the result.

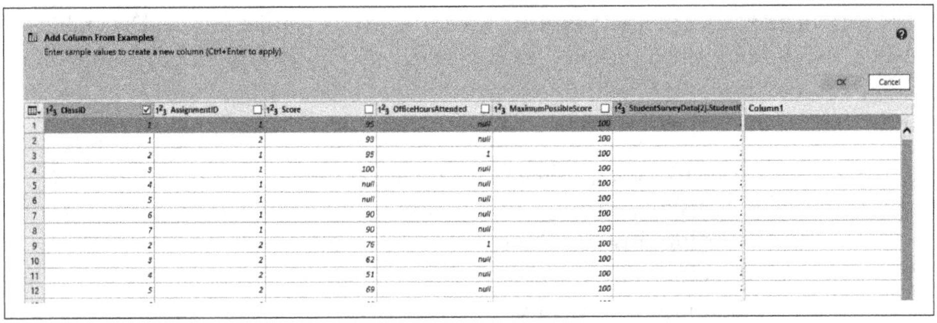

	ClassID	AssignmentID	Score	OfficeHoursAttended	MaximumPossibleScore	StudentSurveyData(2).StudentI[	Column1
1	1	1	95	null	100		
2	1	2	93	null	100		
3	2	1	95	1	100		
4	3	1	100	null	100		
5	4	1	null	null	100		
6	5	1	null	null	100		
7	6	1	90	null	100		
8	7	1	90	null	100		
9	2	2	76	1	100		
10	3	2	62	null	100		
11	4	2	51	null	100		
12	5	2	69	null	100		

Figure 6-12. Column From Examples is an example of actual magic. Power Query's ability to intuit here is impressive.

Using this process, I'm going to create what I call a *composite key*. This will be a concatenated value or values that together form a unique combination for each record. In this case, I'll use ClassID and StudentID with a hyphen to separate them for readability, but this isn't required.

See Column 1 in Figure 6-12. In that first blank record, I put 1 for the listed ClassID, then a hyphen, and then the StudentID number, 251224. I get 1-251224. We can see that Column 1 will populate the appropriate values for all the other records, like an autofill process. You'll notice it's not perfect, and when I did this, it didn't quite get me the result I wanted.

I then went down the first record where the ClassID was 2 and put in 2-252497, and the rest of the records then filled the way I wanted. You can see that result in Figure 6-13. You'll notice in the gray area above the columns, it will also show you what M script is generated to populate the column. Click OK and then rename the column TrueClassStudentID.

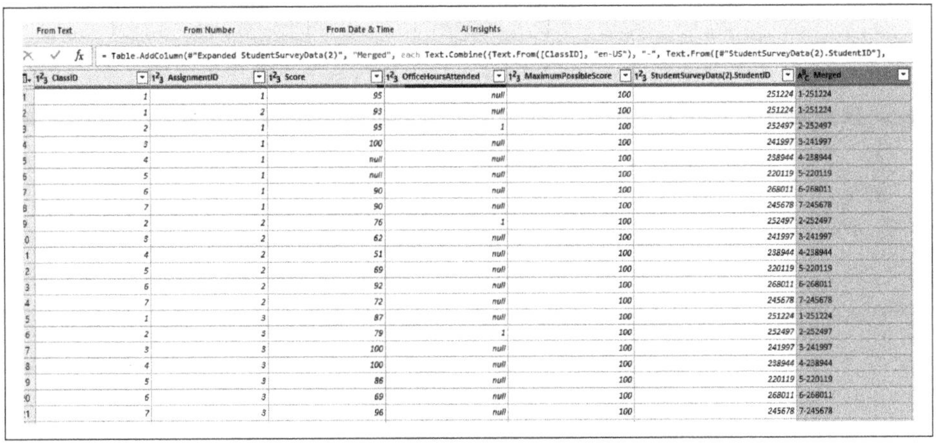

	ClassID	AssignmentID	Score	OfficeHoursAttended	MaximumPossibleScore	StudentSurveyData(2).StudentID	Merged
1	1	1	95	null	100	251224	1-251224
2	1	2	93	null	100	251224	1-251224
3	2	1	95	1	100	252497	2-252497
4	3	1	100	null	100	241997	3-241997
5	4	1	null	null	100	238944	4-238944
6	5	1	null	null	100	220119	5-220119
7	6	1	90	null	100	268011	6-268011
8	7	1	90	null	100	245678	7-245678
9	2	2	76	1	100	252497	2-252497
0	3	2	62	null	100	241997	3-241997
1	4	2	51	null	100	238944	4-238944
2	5	2	69	null	100	220119	5-220119
3	6	2	92	null	100	268011	6-268011
4	7	2	72	null	100	245678	7-245678
5	1	3	87	null	100	251224	1-251224
6	2	3	79	1	100	252497	2-252497
7	3	3	100	null	100	241997	3-241997
8	4	3	100	null	100	238944	4-238944
9	5	3	86	null	100	220119	5-220119
0	6	3	69	null	100	268011	6-268011
1	7	3	96	null	100	245678	7-245678

Figure 6-13. First composite key complete

Next, we will add this TrueClassStudentID column to the StudentSurveyData table by creating a Column From Examples using ClassID and StudentID. It's the same thing we did with GradeScores (2) earlier. Remember that the StudentSurveyData table has already been appended at this point.

Now that we have our two composite keys, we can get the Student IDs to the original GradeScores table by using a merge on ClassID and TrueClassID. However, we're also going to use an inner join instead of a left outer join to keep the table clean. We will expand two columns into GradeScores: StudentID and TrueClassStudentID. When we have done these things, GradeScores should look like Figure 6-14.

With these steps done, we're just about ready to append GradeScores (2) to GradeScores. However, if we do it without making sure the column names are the same, we won't get the results we want, so make sure you rename the StudentID and TrueClassStudentID columns in both tables to ensure they're the same. Then you can append them together, as we did the tables before.

The last thing we could do now is to bring back in the TrueClassID from the StudentSurveyData into our GradeScores table via Merge. We do this so we'll have a nice, clean ID from 1 to 27 to work with merging on the TrueClassStudentID as an inner join condition. I'm going to go ahead and do that in my example.

Admittedly, I didn't do this in the most efficient way because I wanted to work through using Append and Merge, but a good exercise would be to take the steps we've talked about here and to optimize this transformation process to get all the data together.

At this point, our data has been transformed, and we're ready to load the data, build our relationships, and clean up our model. Click Close & Apply in the upper-left corner, and we'll move on to the next step of our work.

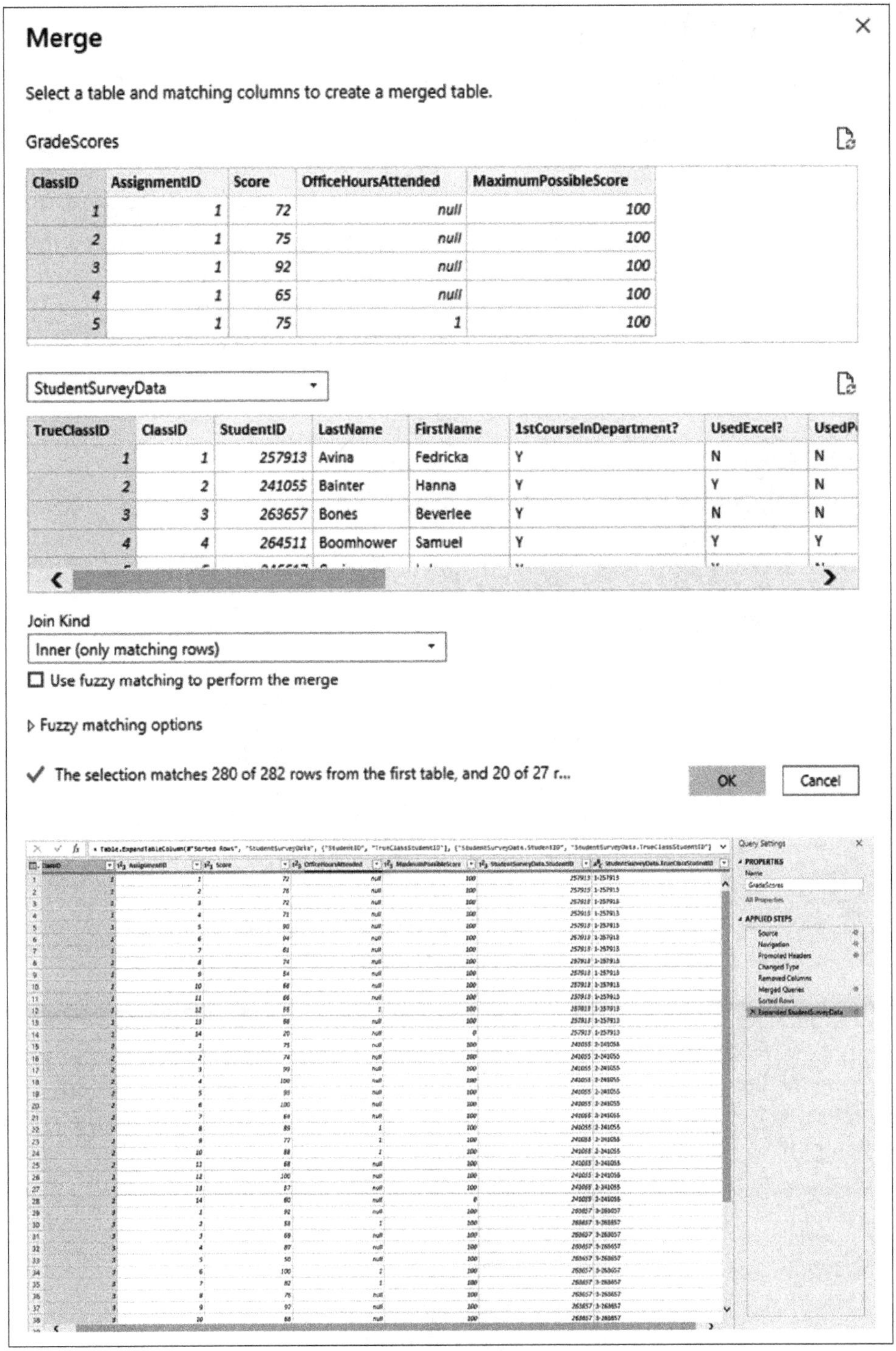

Merge

×

Select a table and matching columns to create a merged table.

GradeScores

ClassID	AssignmentID	Score	OfficeHoursAttended	MaximumPossibleScore
1	1	72	null	100
2	1	75	null	100
3	1	92	null	100
4	1	65	null	100
5	1	75	1	100

StudentSurveyData ▾

TrueClassID	ClassID	StudentID	LastName	FirstName	1stCourseInDepartment?	UsedExcel?	UsedP‹
1	1	257913	Avina	Fedricka	Y	N	N
2	2	241055	Bainter	Hanna	Y	Y	N
3	3	263657	Bones	Beverlee	Y	N	N
4	4	264511	Boomhower	Samuel	Y	Y	Y

Join Kind

Inner (only matching rows) ▾

☐ Use fuzzy matching to perform the merge

▷ Fuzzy matching options

✓ The selection matches 280 of 282 rows from the first table, and 20 of 27 r...

OK   Cancel

Figure 6-14. Grades are ready to be appended...after one more thing

Building Relationships

You might remember in Chapter 3 that my personal preference is to have Power BI *not* try to find default relationships. You can adjust this behavior from Power BI Desktop by choosing File → Options and Settings → Options → Current File → Data Load and unchecking the boxes for Relationships. If you do have that enabled, though, and you load your data, your Model view is going to look something like Figure 6-15. It's not super easy to read. It has a ton of inactive relationships, and we're going to hide more than half of these tables anyway.

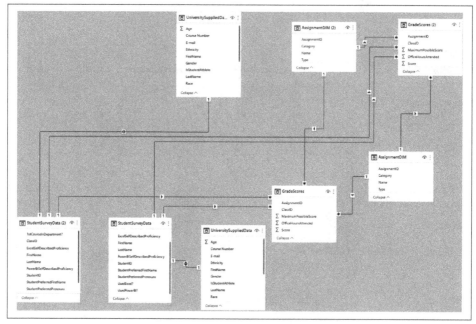

Figure 6-15. Yes, "Autodetect relationships" can be helpful, but you see an example here of when it isn't. I prefer not to enable "Autodetect relationships."

If you did have" Autodetect relationships" enabled, let's go ahead and remove all of them so we're starting from a fresh canvas together. You can delete relationships by clicking the line that shows the relationship and pressing the Delete key. Or you can go into the Manage Relationships section through the ribbon and remove the relationships from there.

Hiding Tables

As we just mentioned, we went through a lot of trouble to consolidate our data into the GradeScores, StudentSurveyData, and UniversitySuppliedData tables. The (2) tables are important in that they're called by Power Query and must exist, but that doesn't mean we need them for our analysis. For tables like this, which are functionally staging tables that we use to get the data into a certain shape so that we can work with it more easily, I like to go to the Properties window for these staging tables and move them to hidden status, as shown in Figure 6-16.

Now, it's important to note that "hidden" doesn't mean hidden from every view. It means it's hidden from the Report view. Therefore, you can still have tables that have relationships and serve important functions but not be available to report on.

However, what I want to do for now is, in the Model view, move all the (2) tables away from the core data model and make sure they're all hidden. You can see that when a table is hidden, it has a crossed-out eye next to the table name in the Model view. I'm going to collapse them to prevent looking at items I don't really care about, and I'll do that by clicking the Collapse button at the bottom of the table.

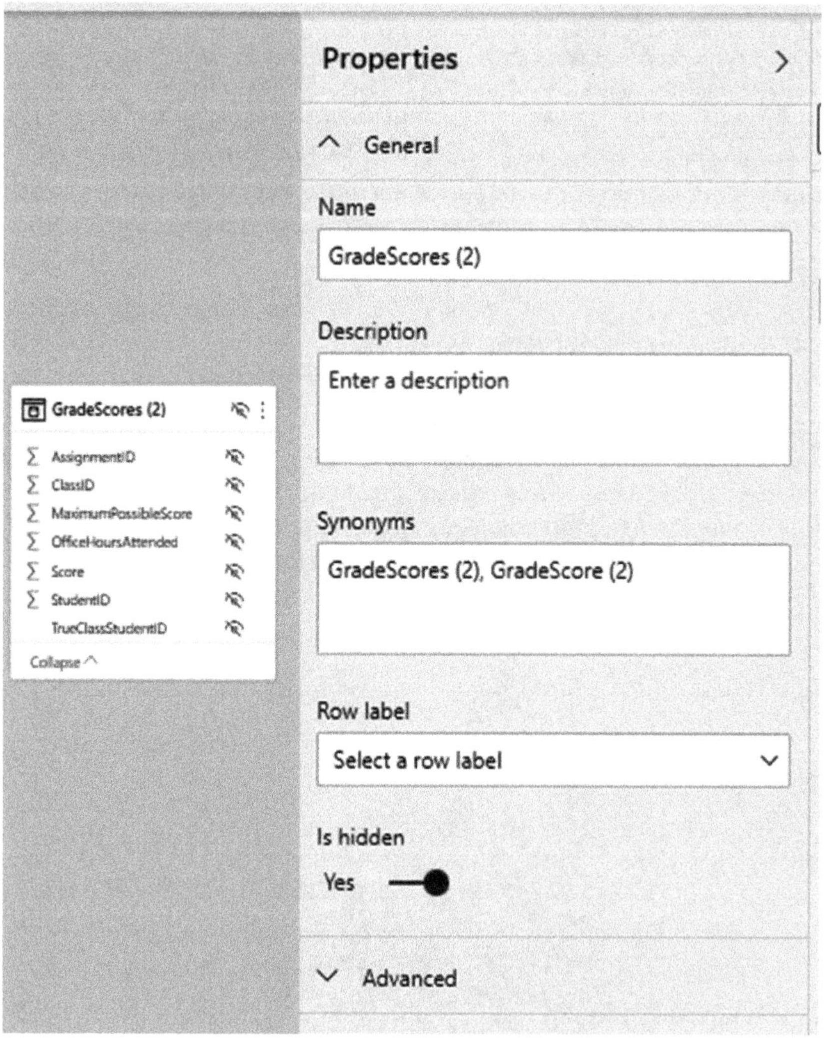

Figure 6-16. You've served your purpose, GradeScores (2), so now you can rest. That is done by hiding the data in the table.

Identifying Our Relationship Columns

Now we can start working with our four core tables to build out a simple data model that we can use for reporting. We achieve that by creating relationships between tables.

Remember, these relationships serve as the pipes that allow data to flow from one table to another, connecting all the pieces together so that the internal query engine

---

can get all the data it needs to process a report request. Also remember that, as much as we can, we want a data model that uses as many single-directional relationships as possible while avoiding many-to-many relationships whenever possible.

To do that, we want to find columns that have only unique values, and we want to find that same column in our primary fact table—in this case, GradeScores. This would be our one-to-many relationship. In the Data view, as noted in Chapter 2, we can look at the table's data and observe different elements of the data, one of which is the ability to see how many distinct values and total values exist in a table for a given column. Let's take a look at AssignmentDIM this way in Figure 6-17.

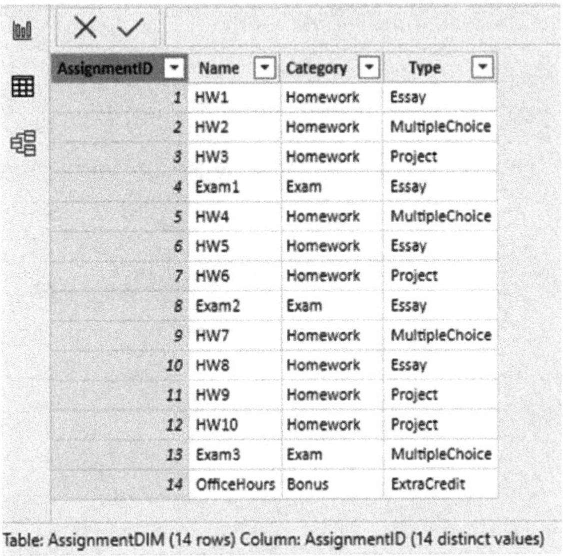

AssignmentID	Name	Category	Type
1	HW1	Homework	Essay
2	HW2	Homework	MultipleChoice
3	HW3	Homework	Project
4	Exam1	Exam	Essay
5	HW4	Homework	MultipleChoice
6	HW5	Homework	Essay
7	HW6	Homework	Project
8	Exam2	Exam	Essay
9	HW7	Homework	MultipleChoice
10	HW8	Homework	Essay
11	HW9	Homework	Project
12	HW10	Homework	Project
13	Exam3	Exam	MultipleChoice
14	OfficeHours	Bonus	ExtraCredit

Table: AssignmentDIM (14 rows) Column: AssignmentID (14 distinct values)

Figure 6-17. You have to get down with the uniqueness. The building block of a table relationship is having a column of unique values that relates to another column in another table.

As we see, when we select the AssignmentID column, in the bottom-left corner we see 14 rows and 14 distinct values. That's the column we are looking for. When we check GradeScores, we see that it also has an AssignmentID column, and those values line up with one another, with every value of AssignmentID in the GradeScores table being between 1 and 14.

Time to Get Building

We can create the relationship between AssignmentDIM and GradeScores in two ways. The first option is to use the Manage Relationships Wizard from the ribbon in the Model view. After we bring up the wizard and click New, we select our two tables and identify the columns that will be the basis of the relationship by clicking the column names in each table (Figure 6-18). We click OK, and that relationship is built.

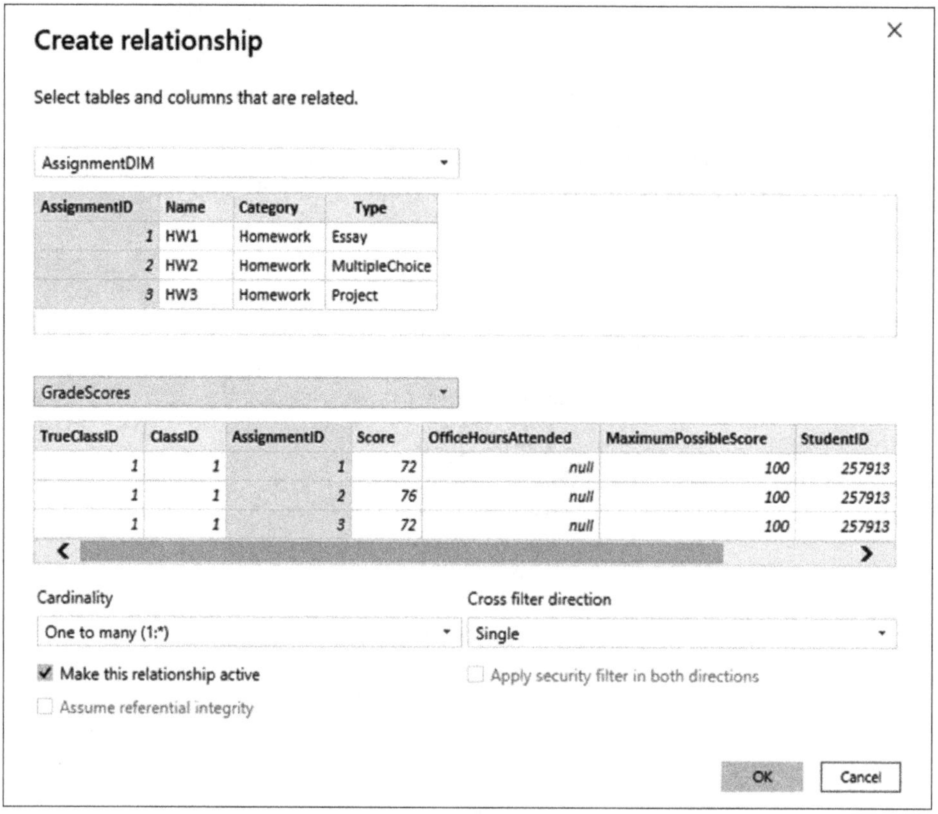

Create relationship   ×

Select tables and columns that are related.

AssignmentDIM   ▾

AssignmentID	Name	Category	Type
1	HW1	Homework	Essay
2	HW2	Homework	MultipleChoice
3	HW3	Homework	Project

GradeScores   ▾

TrueClassID	ClassID	AssignmentID	Score	OfficeHoursAttended	MaximumPossibleScore	StudentID
1	1	1	72	null	100	257913
1	1	2	76	null	100	257913
1	1	3	72	null	100	257913

⟨   ⟩

Cardinality   Cross filter direction

One to many (1:*)   ▾   Single   ▾

☑ Make this relationship active   ☐ Apply security filter in both directions

☐ Assume referential integrity

                                               OK   Cancel

Figure 6-18. Here we're making a one-to-many relationship between AssignmentDIM and GradeScores on AssignmentID to AssignmentID

The second option to build relationships is, frankly, much faster. In the Model view, you click any column in a table, hold down your mouse button, and drag it to the column you want to build that relationship to in another table. Then you release your mouse button and, voila, relationship!

The downside to this approach is that it is easier to make mistakes by dragging from or to the wrong column. It's also more prone to error when you have tables with many columns and you must drag onto parts of a table that have to be scrolled through to find the right column; that can quickly get tedious, and that's when mistakes happen.

With AssignmentDIM connected to GradeScores, we need to connect StudentSurveyData to GradeScores, and UniversitySuppliedData to GradeScores as well. Thankfully, in our Power Query transformations, we got StudentID into GradeScores where it wasn't there before. We can also see StudentID is unique in both of the two tables mentioned, so creating relationships on StudentID from UniversitySuppliedData and StudentSurveyData to GradeScores is simple enough.

After those relationships are built, we should have a core data model that looks like Figure 6-19. This gets us to a star schema of many dimension tables interacting with our fact table, surrounding it like a star. This has optimization benefits, but more importantly, makes the model incredibly easy to read and understand. You instantly know which tables can filter the fact table(s) you care about and how that filter behaves, either in a single direction or bidirectionally.

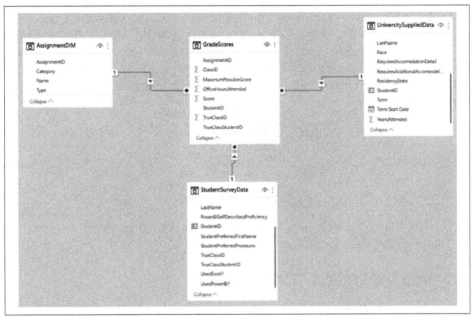

Figure 6-19. "When the line hits your eye like a star in the sky, that's amore." Our core data model is set up in a star schema, where many dimension tables surround a fact table.

Let's Get Reporting!

We've got our data in, we've got it transformed, and we've got it modeled. Now we can start getting those insights we're so interested in. There are tons of questions we could ask. From here, I'm going to focus on creating a first-level report page and some measures that will support our analysis. After you've gone through this chapter, think of some questions you might have from the data and try to find some answers! Now let's start with building that report page.

We Need a Name...

Here's some advice: I often find in reports that a simple thing like a title that reminds users what they're looking at can pay big dividends. This title could be something we reuse on multiple pages, identifying it as the title of the report, or in theory we could use different titles for each page. We could also have an entire report page that would serve strictly as some sort of title introduction.

Each approach has advantages and disadvantages, but, in this example, I'm just going to provide a simple title for the report at the top of the page. I'm going to do this with the classic text box. Just as we talked about in Chapter 2, the "Text box" option is under the Insert section of the ribbon in the Report view. I know that a text box is not terribly exciting, but it's helpful. As shown in Figure 6-20, I've put the text box at the top of my reporting area, center-justified it, and put some nice italics on it because I'm personally a sucker for italics. I like the Segoe font, as well as the default Power BI font, and I want it to be nice and legible, so I made it quite large.

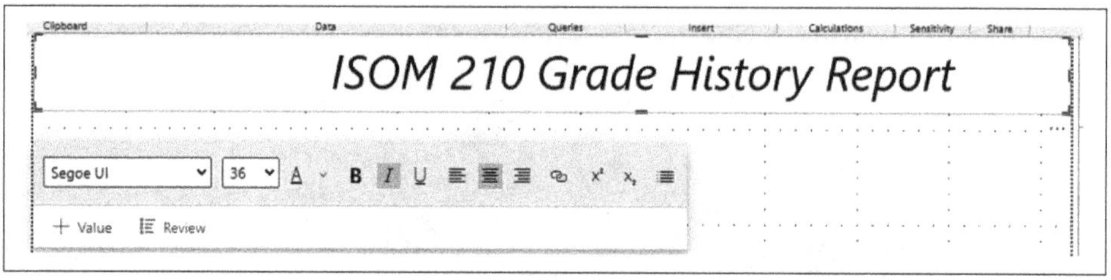

Figure 6-20. I like to make my titles large and in charge. Including a title in a report is a small touch that makes a big difference.

Cards Help Identify Important Data Points

Next, I want to highlight specific values that I think are valuable for understanding how our cohort of students performed and items that identify something unique about those students. I also like "lines" of information. I love blocks; I can't help it.

Our first card is a count of those students for whom ISOM 210 was their first class in the department. This uses the 1stCourseInDepartment? column in the StudentSurveyData table. However, if you make a card visual and drop that column into it, you'll probably see something like Figure 6-21.

Figure 6-21. A single data point for a text-based column might not get you the intended result. N is not what we're looking for....

Let's note a couple things that are happening here. First, it's not a numeric column, so it does not have a default summarization. However, card visuals always display some summarization of data, and in this case, it is displaying the first result from the table that matches our filter context, which in this case is no filter context. So, we need to change the summarization from first to count. We do that by clicking the down arrow next to the column name in the Fields list in the Visualizations pane and then select the summarization we want—in this case, Count. Looking at Figure 6-22, we can see we're getting much closer now, but we're still not quite there.

27

Count of 1stCourseInDepartment?

Figure 6-22. That's just a count of students! It's still not quite right.

So, we've got the card now displaying count instead of first, which is good. However, looking at the data in the table, we know there are 27 records in that table, so this is just a count of the nonblank records for this column.

We need to provide filter context. We want Power BI to give us a count, but we want a count of only the "Y" values. Currently in the Filter pane for this visual, we can see there's no real filter context.

Let's add some context by dragging the 1stCourseInDepartment column to the Filters on this visual area of the Filter pane and use Basic filtering to select only "Y" values. It is worth noting that the Count version of this field exists already since it's what we are displaying. We need to add the column to the Filter pane again to get its base values to filter as demonstrated next. When we do that, we get the 24 number we're looking for. Let's alias the column name by double-clicking the column name in the Fields section of the Visualization pane and renaming it to whatever you like. In this case, I chose 1st Course in Department Count. I now have the card I want and show the filter condition and aliasing, as you see in Figure 6-23.

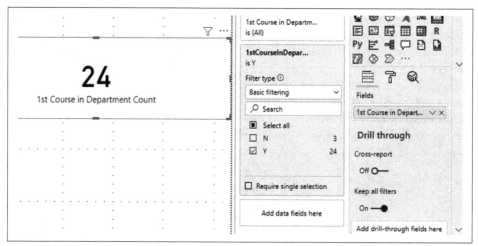

Figure 6-23. One card down, three to go!

The second card is very straightforward. Using the OfficeHoursAttended column in the GradeScores table, we can see that column is numeric and has a default summarization of sum. We make a card visual, drag that column into the Fields list, and that's about it. I did go ahead and alias the column name again so that would reflect in the card visual, so I had Office Hours Attended.

The third card is the Total Grade card. This should be able to calculate an individual's total grade for a given combination of assignments, as well as the entire class's total grade for a given combination of assignments. It's also important to note that assignment 14, which is extra credit, should be added to the numerator of someone's grade, but not the denominator.

We're going to need a measure here. The good news is that we did note a maximum possible score in the GradeScores table, and for assignment 14 that value is zero. Looking at the data in the table then, we should be able to sum up the Score and divide it by the maximum possible score to get the percent grade.

The one issue we have is that if someone were to choose only assignment 14, they would get a divide-by-zero error (#DIV/0!) because Assignment 14's maximum possible score is zero, and zero plus zero is zero. No problem. A DAX function that will be helpful in this case is called the *divide function*. Power BI does support the "/" operator in DAX to represent a divide function. However, if the result of that division would return an error, you're a bit out of luck. The divide function allows us to pass an alternate value at the end of the function that functions like an IFERROR clause. We can see the example DAX in Figure 6-24.

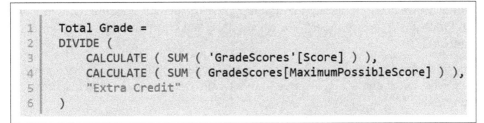

```
1   Total Grade =
2   DIVIDE (
3       CALCULATE ( SUM ( 'GradeScores'[Score] ) ),
4       CALCULATE ( SUM ( GradeScores[MaximumPossibleScore] ) ),
5       "Extra Credit"
6   )
```

Figure 6-24. The DIVIDE DAX function allows us to automatically define a replacement value for a division error

Breaking down this DAX function, we start with a DIVIDE function that has a syntax of (Numerator, Denominator, Alternate Value). Our numerator is a CALCULATE(SUM) of Score. The denominator is a CALCULATE(SUM) of the MaximumPossibleScore. Finally, the alternate value is Extra Credit because I know the only time this would come back with a divide-by-zero error would be on Assignment 14, which is the extra-credit assignment based on office hours attended.

This gets us the result, but if we try to use it now, we're going to get a decimal result to two decimal places. That isn't necessarily bad, but typically we show grades as a percentage (at least we do in the United States; if it's different where you're from, do what would make the most sense to you).

I want this to be a percentage with zero decimal places, so I'm going to select the measure from the Fields pane that will show the Measure tools portion of the ribbon in the Report or Data view. I want the formatting section for this measure to look like Figure 6-25.

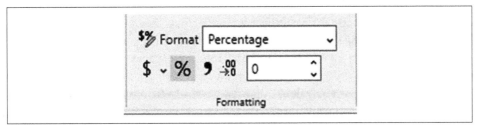

Figure 6-25. A little sprinkle of formatting dust

Now when we make our card visual and bring the Total Grade measure onto the Field list for that visual, we should see a card that looks just like that third card in Figure 6-27.

Our final card is the letter grade of that Total Grade. If your grade list was different from what I'm about to use, feel free to modify the DAX we're about to discuss to fit your needs.

To accomplish this, we need a DAX statement that will take the result of our Total Grade measure and provide a conditional result based on the result of that first value. In SQL, we could use something like a case when statement. In Excel, we could do a nested IF statement, and we could do that in Power BI too, but nested IF statements can get difficult to read very quickly, and in Excel and Power BI, nested IF statements aren't very performant.

To get the Total Letter Grade, I'm going to use a combination of the SWITCH function and the TRUE function. Often in Power BI or DAX, you'll see these two statements together and often referenced together as a SWITCH/TRUE statement.

SWITCH is a function that returns a value based on a condition. The example used in Microsoft's own documentation is a statement that takes the number of a month and offers the month's name as the switch value. So, 1 would be January, and 2 would be February, and so on. SWITCH calls first an expression, a value result of that expression, and then what to display instead if that value exists:

```
SWITCH(<expression>, <value>, <result>[, <value>, <result>]...[, <else>])
```

TRUE is a simple function that returns the logical value TRUE. However, a conditional statement can also be reviewed to see if the result of that value is true.

So, a SWITCH/TRUE function is basically saying that, for a list of conditions, when you get to the condition that is TRUE, switch to that value. In this case, my grade range needs to be between a given maximum and minimum value for a particular letter grade, so I will use the && operator to function as an AND operator. This can be useful alongside its OR operator equivalent of ||. The benefit these operators have over their explicit DAX AND/OR statement counterparts is that they're not limited to two passed functions, and I find them easier to read in statements like the one in Figure 6-26.

```
1    Total Letter Grade =
2    SWITCH (
3        TRUE (),
4        [Total Grade] >= 1.00, "A+",
5        [Total Grade] < 1.00
6            && [Total Grade] >= .925, "A",
7        [Total Grade] < .925
8            && [Total Grade] >= .895, "A-",
9        [Total Grade] < .895
10           && [Total Grade] >= .875, "B+",
11       [Total Grade] < .875
12           && [Total Grade] >= .825, "B",
13       [Total Grade] < .825
14           && [Total Grade] >= .795, "B-",
15       [Total Grade] < .795
16           && [Total Grade] >= .775, "C+",
17       [Total Grade] < .775
18           && [Total Grade] >= .725, "C",
19       [Total Grade] < .725
20           && [Total Grade] >= .695, "C-",
21       [Total Grade] < .695
22           && [Total Grade] >= .675, "D+",
23       [Total Grade] < .675
24           && [Total Grade] >= .625, "D",
25       [Total Grade] < .625
26           && [Total Grade] >= .600, "D-",
27       "F"
28   )
```

Figure 6-26. Really not that bad! Here we're just providing what to display for a given result. Check result, display result.

We read the preceding statement as saying the following:

- Find the result of Total Grade.
- If that Total Grade is greater than or equal to 1, it's an A+.
- If that Total Grade is less than 1 but greater than 0.925, it's an A.
- Etc. etc.
- Sorry, you failed.

For each time Total Grade is calculated and this measure is on the canvas, it will figure out for that result which condition in the SWITCH statement is TRUE and then switch the TRUE statement for the Grade Score we've acquired.

Notice that for the calculation, I still used the decimal values for the conditional statements and not percentages. Even though we display the result of Total Grade in a percentage form, it's still calculated as a decimal value.

With that measure put together, we can simply drag the measure to the Field list of that last card visual, and our cards are complete! We can see our four cards together in Figure 6-27.

Figure 6-27. Our bottom row of cards gives readers quick, high-level information they might be looking for

Bars, Columns, and Lines

Let's put some pictures on this darn canvas already, right? I've got three visuals here, two bar charts and one line and column chart, and we will walk through those as shown in Figure 6-28.

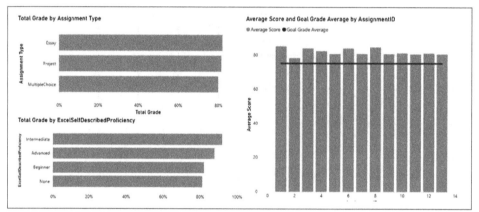

Figure 6-28. This page is starting to come together!

The first graph I'll deal with is the bar graph in the upper-left corner, Total Grade by Assignment Type. To add the visual to the canvas, I simply selected the clustered bar chart from the Visualizations pane and moved it over to the upper-left corner by clicking and dragging the outline of the visual to where I wanted it to be. The goal of this visual is simple: for each assignment type, I want to know the total grade. I put Assignment Type from AssignmentDIM into the Axis list (Y-axis area in more recent versions) and Total Grades into the Values list (X-axis area in more recent versions) in the Visualizations pane by dragging those columns from the Fields pane into the relevant sections on the Visualizations pane with the visual selected. That was it, right?

The eagle-eyed among you who are trying this will probably see something quite strange! At first, this graph will show ExtraCredit, and it will be a blank bar! That's not very helpful at all. In fact, we know that Total Grade for ExtraCredit is going to be blank because ExtraCredit Assignments have a maximum score of zero, and as we discussed in the creation of our Total Grades measure, in a divide-by-zero situation, the measure should return "Extra Credit," which isn't a value we can display on a bar chart. So in the Filter pane, with that visual selected, you'll see that I've filtered out ExtraCredit, and that's how I get the result in Figure 6-28 for that bar chart, as shown in detail in Figure 6-29.

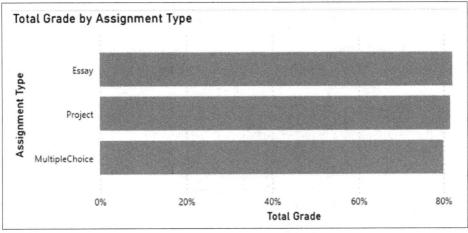

Figure 6-29. This is a great example of why mastery of the data matters!

That's straightforward. Let's go down to the second bar chart, Total Grade by Excel-SelfDescribedProficiency. This looks exactly like the first chart with a different axis, in this case the ExcelSelfDescribedProficiency column from the StudentSurveyData table.

I have done something different with this visual, though. I've added a second axis to make it drillable. I have two self-described proficiency columns in StudentSurvey-Data, one for Excel and one for Power BI. I put the PowerBISelfDescribedProficiency column under the Excel column in the Axis list. When I do that, I get the result shown in Figure 6-30. I could now use the drill options to drill into a specific combination of data between these two categories or show the results for every combination of these two columns that exist in the dataset.

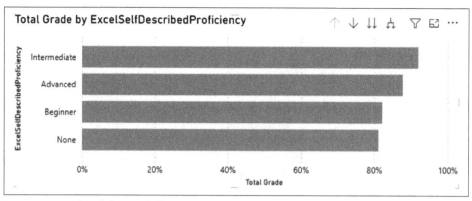

Figure 6-30. The ability to drill into a visual allows you to quickly change the dimension you're reviewing or combine dimensions for more categories to analyze

Finally, we have the line and column chart on the right side showing the Average Score and the Goal Grade Average with Assignment ID on the x-axis. In this example, I made a measure called Grade Goal Average, and it's literally equal to 75:

```
Goal Grade Average = 75
```

That's it. Nothing fancy, the measure equals a number that gets me this very convenient line.

Now, another way I could accomplish this same task would be to use a simple clustered column chart and use the Analytics section of the Visualizations pane to add a constant line of 75. I prefer the flexibility of the line and column chart, but it's important to note that there are multiple ways to accomplish something like this.

I want to fix one thing, though. We can see that Power BI is making a default axis, highlighting values at every even numbered interval. So, it shows 2, 4, 6, 8, etc., including Assignment 14, and it is showing this even though I currently have Assignment 14 filtered out in the Filter pane for this visual. I don't want the actual score to show, and I don't want it to show blank either. So, for that, I'm going to manually set the maximum axis value for the x-axis to 13. I do that by selecting the Range option under Visual for the X-axis and setting the Maximum to 13. I'll do that in the Format area of the Visualizations pane, and when I do that and have the visual selected, I can now see the result I want in Figure 6-31.

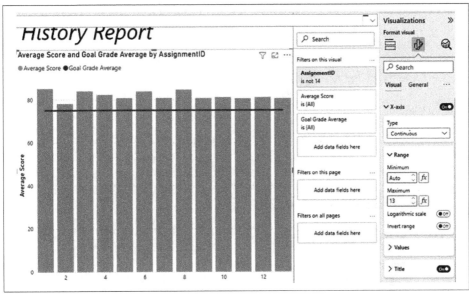

Figure 6-31. Better, much better

For interactivity, I add two slicers to the bottom-right corner of the report page so I can filter by Assignment Category and Term in the same way I add any other visual to the canvas. When I do that, I get a final first report page that looks like Figure 6-32.

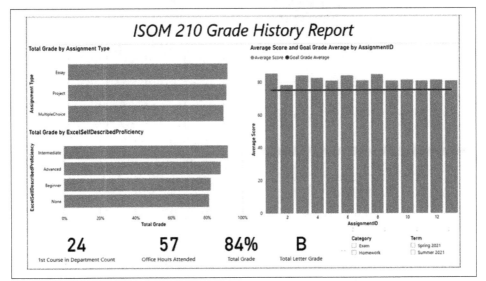

Figure 6-32. One full report page. We did it!

I'll leave you and this chapter with one conundrum that I'll let you figure out on your own. Using all the tools we've talked about, when you filter on Term, you'll notice that the 1st Course in Department Count won't filter. Identify why that's happening and figure out a way to solve the problem. You could take quite a few approaches, so get out there and experiment!

Conclusion

In this chapter, I wanted to go step by step to really demonstrate how we use the things we had talked about in the preceding four chapters. Now you should have a basic understanding of how to use Power BI Desktop to get data into the report, how to go about shaping it to your needs, building relationships and measures, and finally putting some results on canvas for users.

In the next chapter, we are going to transition a little bit to some more advanced reporting features in Power BI, which will round out the Power BI Desktop portion of this text. If you've gotten this far, I want you to know, you're doing great. You're pushing through on something new, and you should be proud of yourself for getting to this point. Let's keep pushing!

CHAPTER 7

Advanced Reporting Topics in Power BI

To this point, we have successfully loaded, transformed, and modeled data. We've built out an example report page using many individual pieces of Power BI Desktop that we discussed in the preceding chapters. In this chapter, we're going to review some of those pesky advanced topics that I said we'd address later.

The tools and topics we'll discuss here can be valuable and bring that little extra to your report that takes it from good to great or unlocks that one insight that makes the whole report click. However, using many of these functions without a firm understanding of the basics can also lead to misunderstanding exactly what you're doing or what you're looking at.

Specifically, we'll cover the currently available AI-powered visuals along with what-if analysis. I'll also discuss integration of R and Python into your Power BI setup and go over some of its limitations. These are incredibly powerful and have the ability to help you uncover facts about your data that would be otherwise buried and difficult to find. They'll also enable you to put forth scenarios to help your organization make better decisions.

AI-Powered Visuals

At the time of writing, Microsoft has put four AI-powered visuals into Power BI Desktop, and it's expected it will continue to invest in creating more AI-powered visuals to further extend Power BI's capabilities. All these visuals work in both Desktop and the service. You can find them in the Visualizations pane, shown in Figure 7-1. From left to right, the visuals are Key influencers, Decomposition tree, Q&A, and Smart narratives. Let's look at each one now.

Figure 7-1. AI-powered visuals as seen in the Visualizations pane. I promise these AI visuals have no connection to Skynet.

Key Influencers

The "Key influencers" visual is a powerful tool. It takes a value and analyzes it by a set of categories to determine varying levels of impact on a value. These categories are then identified and grouped to help you identify the relative impact compared to other categories.

You'll notice that if you try to use this visual on the dataset included in this book, it won't be very effective. I used several data randomization techniques to ensure that the data was as random as possible and used the "Key influencers" visual to test whether my data was sufficiently random. If it found correlations that could provide meaningful results, I went through another set of data randomization.

Since the data from our previous dataset is so heavily randomized, I will be demonstrating the "Key influencers" visual from a separate dataset from Microsoft known as AdventureWorks. AdventureWorks is a sample database shipped with Microsoft SQL Server. There are also many examples of AdventureWorks being connected to Power BI. In this example, I'm analyzing the count of invoices by territory name, product category, product subcategory, product description, and part number.

This visual can be split into several parts. Let's look at Figure 7-2, and we'll break down the visual from there. We're going to focus first on what impacts the count of invoices for the company. In theory, more invoices mean more sales, so figuring out what increases or decreases that count could be useful information.

We can go through the image from top to bottom and get an idea of what's going on. First, we can select either "Key influencers" or "Top segments." Currently and by default, "Key influencers" is selected.

Next, you'll see a framed question around what causes whatever we are analyzing to either increase or decrease. By default, this is set to Increase, but I selected Decrease here to show more results. Then you'll see on the left a list of selected conditions and how that specific condition impacts the value I'm analyzing.

In this case, when the subcategory is Touring Frames, the count of invoices for that subcategory is 43 less than the total average of all subcategories. This subcategory is highlighted, and you can see it farthest to the left in the column-graph portion of Figure 7-2. On the right, since the dimension in question is Subcategory, it shows me a graph that details the average number of invoices by subcategory and highlights the specific group selected. You'll notice the graph on the right is also scrollable, allowing me to see all the subcategories in this way.

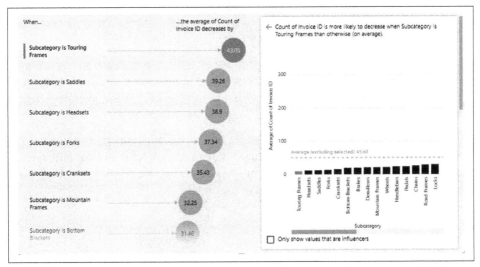

Figure 7-2. The "Key influencers" visual has so much going on. This is just one little piece.

Now let's go back to the top of the visual and select "Top segments." We can see what that looks like to start in Figure 7-3.

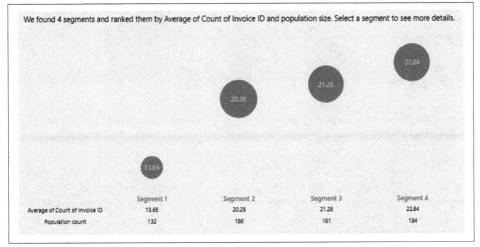

Figure 7-3. The ability to quickly see the impact of different combinations of data is very powerful

The first line is the same as before. The second line, though, is a little bit different. You'll notice that the question that frames the selection box is worded slightly differently. Instead of asking what might be causing a value to increase or decrease, it's asking when the point of analysis is more likely to be high or low. In this case, I have selected Low, but High is the default.

As the figure shows, Power BI has found four segments it thinks are interesting and worth diving into for this question; it displays a small scatterplot and details how it is organized. In this case, it's going from smallest average invoice count to highest, while also showing the count of records that make up that segment.

When you click into any of those bubbles (in this case, I'm choosing segment 2), you get to see all the details that make up that segment on the left. On the right side in Figure 7-4, you can see segment 2 in comparison to the overall value and see how much of the data is contained in the selected segment.

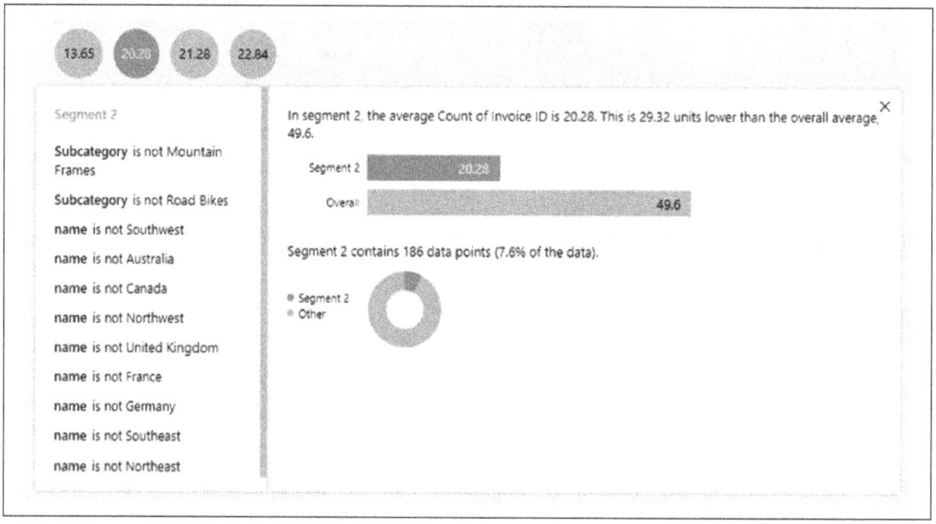

Figure 7-4. This visual works because it allows you to see the details of the categorical combination

While the visual itself is incredibly powerful, it can also be frustrating to use. As you add categories to the "Explain by" section of the Visualizations pane, the visual will refresh itself after every addition. It may struggle to find combinations of data that lead to the discovery of influencers or segments of note. It is not always more useful to keep adding categories either; the more categories you add, the smaller your population for each combination of categories gets.

Using this visual effectively requires you to really understand your data and to add some human intelligence. What does your intuition tell you should be important? Start there and see whether your intuition is validated. You'll find that to be a common theme in the AI visuals section. Human intelligence makes these things work; the AI visuals can't do it alone.

Decomposition Tree

"Decomposition tree" is significantly easier to understand than "Key influencers." For a given value, it shows you for each categorical level how that value is impacted by the values in that category. Let's return to our Cool School University dataset and put our Total Grade measure into the Analyze section of the Visualizations pane for this visual. What we see at first is pretty boring, as shown in Figure 7-5.

Figure 7-5. Is that really all there is?

This visual really shines when we add categories to the "Explain by" section. We can quickly see how that value changes based on the combination of values, and since it's a tree, we can have many "branches" to look at.

Let's first add Term from the UniversitySuppliedData table to the visual and see what happens...OK, that was underwhelming. You'll notice that the only thing different from Figure 7-5 is that there is a plus sign now next to the bar for Total Grade. When we click that plus sign, things start to happen. A small dialog box will appear with High Value, Low Value, or the name of the category. Selecting either High or Low Value will be accompanied by a lightbulb. In this case, I choose High Value, and we can see what that looks like in Figure 7-6.

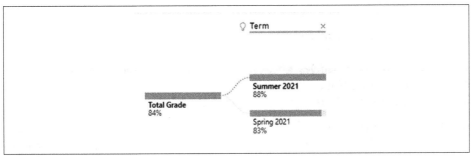

Figure 7-6. The tree begins to take shape

In our working example, we know from our work in Chapter 6 that our Total Grade is 84%, and we can quickly see that for Spring 2021 it was 83% and for Summer 2021 it was 88%. In Figure 7-6, we see that Total Grade has been broken into branches by term, Summer 2021 at 88% and Spring 2021 at 83%. The highest value for the category is always shown at the top and is organized from high to low, so that's why Summer displays above Spring. If you hover over the lightbulb next to Term, you'll get a tooltip showing that Summer 2021 is the highest value.

If you want to remove a particular branch from the tree, you can click the X button to the right of the column name on the visual. This removes the branch from the tree, but not from the visual. This is important because you can rearrange the branches of a tree at any time by removing a branch or branches and then choosing a different column order when the plus sign at the end of the tree is selected. Take note that any value in the tree is going to be reflected at whatever level the selected value of the category is and all the selected categories before it. Let's see what I mean here by looking at Figure 7-7.

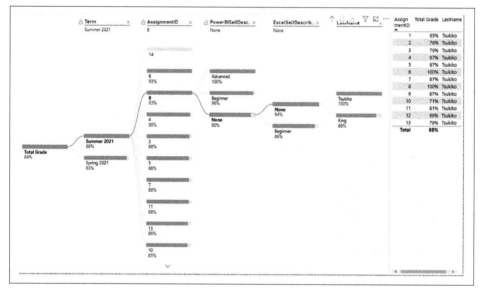

Figure 7-7. Follow the line to read the tea leaves

Take a look at the ExcelSelfDescribedProficiency category, which is second from the right. For the selected value of None, it has to go through the flow shown by the selected values, and this is demonstrated by the line that goes through each category.

So when we say that people who described their Excel proficiency as None have a 94% total grade, that is true only for people who also had no Power BI proficiency specifically on Assignment 8 who were in the Summer 2021 course. In other words, to read a data point in this visual, it's still dependent on all the parts of the visual that precede it. Each branch, when selected, shows only values that are also true for all the categories preceding it.

So, when we look at the LastName category, only two students had no Excel or Power BI expertise in the summer 2021 class for Assignment 8. Ms. Tsukiko did a very good job on the assignment and got a 100%! Mr. King didn't do so badly at 88%. At a glance, we can see that, on this assignment at least, people who had no Power BI or Excel proficiency in aggregate did better than those who had no Power BI proficiency but did have beginner Excel proficiency.

If you ever get lost reading this visual as you go through various steps, remember to follow the blue line through the categories and remember each step is dependent on the step before it.

Two other things to note for this visual. First, like all Power BI visuals, it does interact with other visuals, but only when a value on the last branch of a tree is selected. Otherwise, the visual will filter itself to show items selectable for the next category. Second, this visual has no scroll bar, but you can click and drag right to left to scroll horizontally. There is no vertical scrolling, though, so to navigate vertically you have to use the arrows like those shown at the bottom of Figure 7-7 in the AssignmentID category. Note to Microsoft: please give us easier vertical scrolling capabilities.

Q&A

The goal of the Q&A visual is to empower end users to ask questions of the data by using natural language. Power BI will attempt to take your question and turn it into a chart or set of results that answers that question.

Q&A can be powerful, but out of the box it can feel like it has a couple of screws loose. Some of the suggested questions might not seem relevant, and while Microsoft continues to improve on Q&A in seemingly every release, I wouldn't call it quite "natural language" yet.

However, you can do many things to provide just enough extra context to Power BI to help make Q&A feel more natural. Plopping down a Q&A visual into our canvas, we first see the result in Figure 7-8.

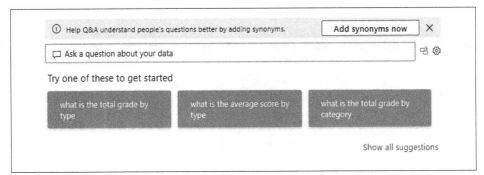

Figure 7-8. When you put a Q&A visual into your canvas, the initial suggested questions aren't always super exciting

Just looking at the suggested questions, we can see that Q&A does a good job of recognizing our field names, but those field names might not be obvious in what they mean to other users. For instance, total grade by category means, "What is the total grade by the category column?" You and I both know that column exists only in the AssignmentDIM table, but someone else might not. Further, what does "category" mean? We both know that's the descriptor for whether an assignment was homework, an exam, or extra credit. But does our audience necessarily know that?

From this example, we can see one of the issues with Q&A and the example questions it generates. At first, it has only our column names and relationships to work with. It will apply some simple aliasing where it can, but that won't necessarily get us all the way there.

However, we can still use one of the example questions to demonstrate what Q&A can provide as a result. In this case, I'll select the first question on the left, "What is the total grade by type?" In this case, Power BI generates a bar chart showing the total grade measure for each type of assignment. I can see that result in Figure 7-9. Notice that this visual interacts with all other visuals on the canvas and can be interacted with by other visuals, like anything else. So keep in mind what question you asked when you start cross-filtering across visuals with Q&A!

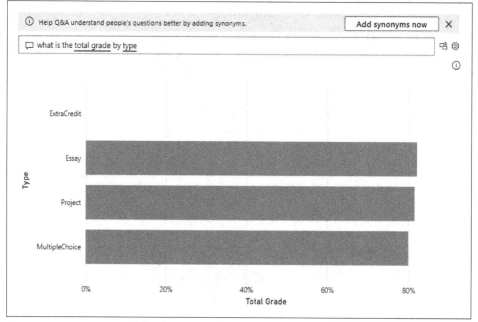

Figure 7-9. Power BI will do a good job, though, of choosing a chart type that best answers the question

Breaking down the visual itself, there will always be the option to add synonyms unless you click the X next to the button. We'll get to that in a little bit. I appreciate that it keeps the question you asked in the text bar, and it highlights the keywords it used to identify the intent of the question—in this case, "total grade" and "type." Let's say you find a result you really like from Q&A and want to make it a more permanent fixture. You can click the first button to the right of the text box to convert the Q&A visual into a visual of the type generated. The widget next to that leads you to Q&A settings. The circled "i" provides a quick tooltip when hovered over, confirming what the visual is showing.

Since the question remains in the text box, we can easily add, change, or remove a part of a question. For instance, I know why ExtraCredit shows as blank for Total Grade based on the way the measure works. I'd rather remove it. I'll add "without ExtraCredit" from the visual and voila, it's gone!

When you make additions to a question, the text box will show a drop-down that will attempt to guess your question via a search engine. This feature, as you might expect, gets better the more it is used and the better your synonyms are.

We could even add another step to this question and add something like "for last name King." Then we can see those results for students with the last name King. One of the things Q&A does well is allow you to refine your question. We started with total grade by type, removed or filtered out the ExtraCredit type, and then specifically filtered the result down again for those students who have the last name of King.

We could rename columns to more friendly names if we planned on leveraging Q&A extensively. That might help the AI more easily figure out what a column means. We can also add synonyms to certain column descriptors to help make the language easier when users type questions. In Figures 7-8 and 7-9, a button in the top-right corner says, "Add synonyms now." If we click that, it will open the Q&A setup window and automatically navigate us to the Field synonyms section, as seen in Figure 7-10. Note that it will show all the tables in the model, even the ones we have hidden in the Report view. However, by default it will remove those tables from Q&A selection.

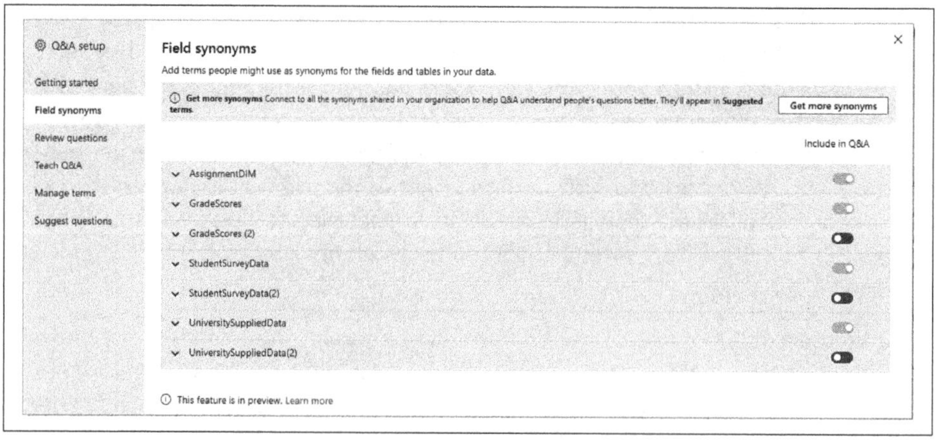

Figure 7-10. If you're going to make Q&A shine, you're going to need to spend a lot of time here in the Field synonyms section

When you choose a table, you'll see the list of columns under Name, the currently recognized synonyms under Terms, and a list of Suggested terms to the right of that. Finally, you will still see a toggle at the column level to let you include or not include that column in Q&A results. In Figure 7-11, I've selected the UniversitySuppliedData table to expand.

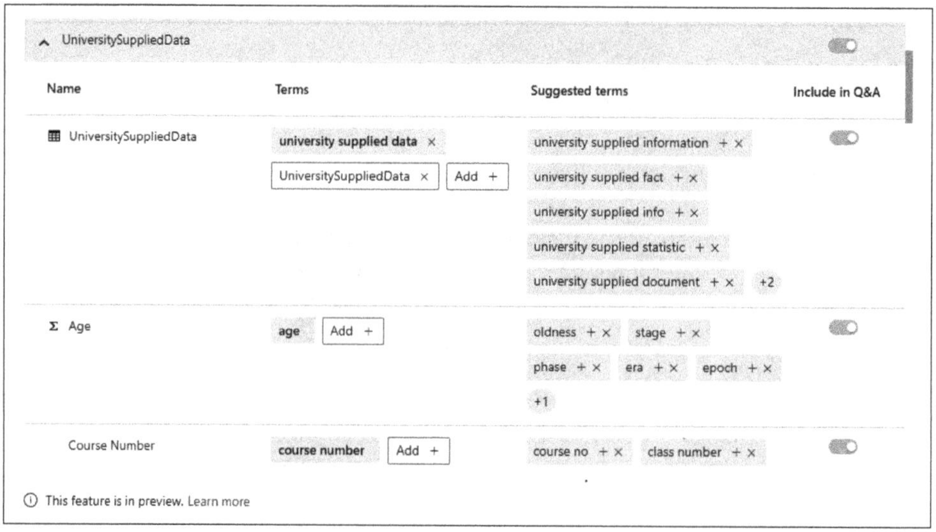

Figure 7-11. Though you can add as many synonyms as you want, be careful not to mix and match them too much

If I click the plus button on any of the "Suggested terms," that term will immediately be added to the list of terms for that column. Thinking about this process from right to left best demonstrates how this works. "Suggested terms" provides a list of possible synonyms that become Terms. When one of those suggested terms is selected, it is added to "Terms." Those terms are then the actual synonyms that Power BI will use when it encounters a question in Q&A to figure out which column it should go use to answer the question. The object referenced by a given term is shown under the Name column. Terms can reference table names, column names, or measures. You'll also notice that Power BI will have some basic terms already preset, but they're not particularly insightful. For instance, the column FirstName will have a Term preset of first name.

I would love to be able to give you advice on setting up Q&A in your own enterprise; however, language is unique to an organization. Q&A is one of those features that Microsoft continues to improve on little by little, and is committed to natural language querying in Power BI.

My suggestion before deploying Q&A is to throw as many questions as you can think of against the engine. See what results come back, add synonyms where necessary, and try again. Lots of opportunities exist for fine-tuning results, and improving Q&A in your organization is going to be an iterative process.

I want to touch on two other features of the Q&A setup: the "Review questions" and "Suggest questions" features. The "Review questions" section allows you to review every Q&A question that has been submitted across all the datasets you have access to and that has been asked in the last 28 days. Annoyingly, it shows you all the datasets you have access to, not just the datasets you have access to that have had questions asked against them with Q&A. However, if someone does have a question, you can review it and the answer Power BI provided, to check for accuracy and provide guidance on how you would have preferred the answer be given for that particular question.

"Suggest questions" allows you to put questions in front of your audience, like the ones we saw when we first opened the visual. The difference is that those are questions you have already reviewed. Think of these suggested questions as easy-to-use cheat commands for other users building reports using Q&A visuals. You know what results will be displayed when that question is selected. These can be great starting points for your organization to begin using Q&A in a bit more of a sandbox, give confidence to users about the results, and encourage exploration.

This can also be good to provide a specific set of answers to specific questions. In a single visual, users can choose suggested questions that may help them frame other visuals on a given report page. Q&A is a complicated beast, and if you want to get the most out of it, it's just like getting to play at Carnegie Hall. It takes practice, practice, practice. If you would prefer not to allow users to use Q&A against a dataset in the Power BI service, you can also disable Q&A against datasets in service.

Smart Narrative

"Smart narrative" as a visual is a bit different in that it doesn't do anything on its own. If you try to put this visual onto a blank canvas, an error message will appear, and a text box will be generated instead. However, when added to a report page with other visuals on it, the "Smart narrative" will "read" the other visuals from the data points of those visuals and construct a narrative to help "read" the data.

In Figure 7-12, you can see I took our final page from the end of Chapter 6 and made some room for a "Smart narrative." It's important to note that a "Smart narrative" visual can be cross-filtered and interacted with by any other visual on the canvas and will update its narrative accordingly! Also, because it is still inside a functional text box, you can add commentary to the "Smart narrative" that will be present regardless of filter context changes that would influence the rest of the narrative.

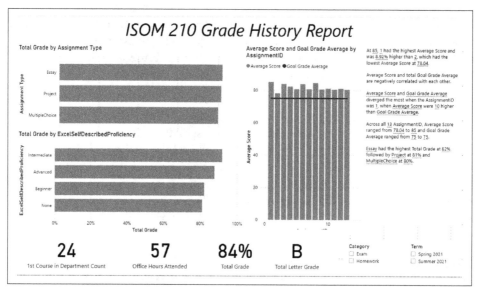

Figure 7-12. That text on the right of the page is a breakdown of all the data in the visuals on this page

The "Smart narrative" is a double-edged sword in my view. On one side, it's an absolute godsend for data literacy. This visual does a good job of breaking down the data in a way that can make it readable for nontechnical users and others who aren't as familiar with the data, and that can have so much value for report users. However, it is also quite big and clunky. At the end of the day, it's a large text box that can produce narratives so long that you need to drag them up and down to read the whole thing. Design space is at a premium, so whether or not the "Smart narrative" visual is the right choice is ultimately contextual to your audience and your design choices.

What-If Analysis

In many scenarios, you ask yourself a question that starts with two simple words: "what if." What if our production line gained 1% of efficiency? What if we had sold 200 more units? What if our students had scored 15 more points over the course of the semester? Each of these questions is the basis of *what-if analysis*. This is the practice of taking a value and modifying it by a parameterized result and seeing what changes.

What-if analysis in Power BI begins with the creation of a What-if parameter. This is done from the Modeling tab of the ribbon in the Report view, under the "What if" subsection. Click the "New parameter" button and you'll see a dialog box pop up, as shown in Figure 7-13.

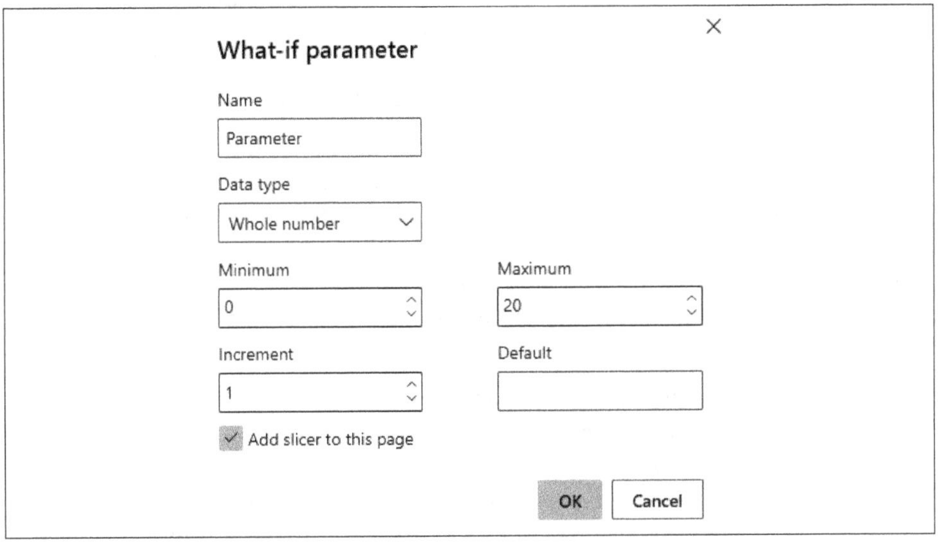

> **What-if parameter** ×
>
> Name
> [Parameter]
>
> Data type
> [Whole number ⌄]
>
> Minimum   Maximum
> [0 ⌃⌄]   [20 ⌃⌄]
>
> Increment   Default
> [1 ⌃⌄]   [   ]
>
> ☑ Add slicer to this page
>
>   [OK] [Cancel]

Figure 7-13. This is where we will build our parameter(s) that will allow us to manipulate values

Parameter Setup

The What-if parameter has several inputs that need to be managed. Name is obvious but also has a unique consequence. Whatever name is selected, a couple of objects are going to be created in the data model to support the parameter.

The finalized What-if parameter will use the GENERATESERIES statement with the name of the parameter to create a DAX-generated table. It will then create two objects inside that table. One will be an object that looks like the "New parameter" button that we clicked to bring up the dialog box. This will be a slicer that can be put onto the canvas to manipulate the value of the parameter on the report canvas.

The second thing that will be created is a measure that uses the SELECTEDVALUE function so that you can call in another measure for this parameterized value to use in other DAX functions. This will be demonstrated in a little bit.

After naming our parameter, we need to define the type of data it can be: Whole number, Decimal number, or Fixed decimal number. A *fixed decimal number* has a fixed location for the decimal separator. This can be useful in specific scenarios where rounding could introduce errors, or you have really small numbers that you are modifying, and errors could accumulate. In our case, we don't hate ourselves enough to grade scores to decimal points, so we can go ahead and choose "Whole number."

The minimum and maximum values set the first and last value in the GENERATE SERIES statement, which will create the table and values that will be utilized by the parameter. I personally like to keep the value of zero somewhere in the series. It doesn't have to be the minimum or maximum, but having zero in the series can be helpful when I want to show the baseline value without modification. In this case, I will choose –100 for the minimum and 100 for the maximum.

Next, I set the increment for the change. This describes the allowed interval for editing the value. For instance, if I chose 5, with a minimum of –100 and a maximum of 100, I could choose –100, –95, –90, ... 95, 100. I can't choose 97 or 43 or –37. If my increment was 1, I could choose any whole number value between –100 and 100. Obviously, if you are going to have a decimal-based increment, you should be using a decimal or fixed decimal data type. For the purpose of this example, I am going to set an increment of 1.

Finally, I set a default value. This is the value that will be shown when I first bring the slicer from the Fields list onto the canvas, and it will be the value that the parameter will reset to if someone uses the "Reset to default" feature in the Power BI service. When zero is selected as the default, the slicer will initially show a blank value. This is nothing to worry about and is intended behavior. We have one final selection to make, and that's whether we want Power BI to automatically add the slicer it will create to this report page.

DAX Integration of the Parameter

After clicking OK, I now have a parameter. However, that parameter doesn't do anything! That is because nothing can currently be modified by the parameter. We have to call the parameter in some value that we will bring onto the canvas. This is why the measure created along with our parameter is so important. With the slicer on the report page, we can modify one of our measures to add the value of that parameter to the total. Let's go back and review our Total Grade measure and then show where we could place the created measure from the What-if parameter in Figure 7-14.

```
1 Total Grade =
2 DIVIDE (
3      CALCULATE (    SUM ( 'GradeScores'[Score] ) ) ,
4      CALCULATE (    SUM ( GradeScores[MaximumPossibleScore] ) ),
5      "Extra Credit"
6 )
```

```
1 Total Grade =
2 DIVIDE (
3      CALCULATE (    SUM ( 'GradeScores'[Score] ) ) + [Total Grade Modifier Value],
4      CALCULATE (    SUM ( GradeScores[MaximumPossibleScore] ) ),
5      "Extra Credit"
6 )
```

Figure 7-14. The What-if parameter creates a measure that we can call, just like any other in a DAX statement

With this modification in mind, based on our dataset, I'm going to focus on the following question: What if our total grade was *X* amount higher or lower? What would that do to the relevant letter grade? For the purpose of this demonstration, I'm also going to revert the Total Letter Grade measure to display two decimal places instead of zero.

I've created a very simple page here with a term slicer, the What-if parameter slicer, and a table with the total grade and total grade letter. Let's move the grade modifier to –100 and to 100 and see what that does to our table in Figure 7-15.

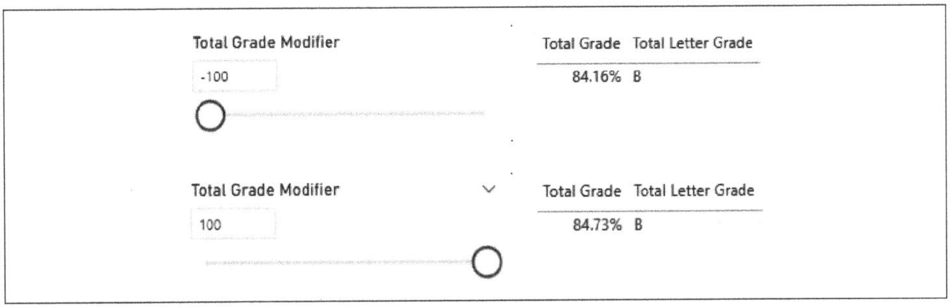

Figure 7-15. The parameter is working, but a total of 100 points in either direction doesn't seem to make a big difference

We can see from Figure 7-15 that those 100 points either way don't make or break the class. However, given that we are talking about grades, you could imagine that if we shrink the population, that difference would be more obvious. We know previously that Summer 2021 had only seven students, but their overall grade was higher. Would 100 points get Summer 2021 up a letter grade? Let's try expanding the analysis here to see what would happen in Figure 7-16.

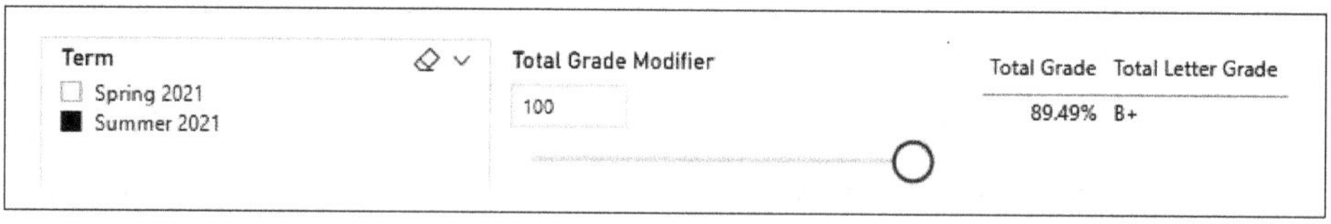

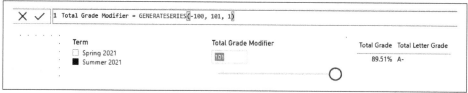

Figure 7-16. Fate is a cruel mistress. It seems they needed 101 points.

Well, if we added 100 total points of score to the summer 2021 class, they would have finished with a total grade of 89.49%, which is 0.01% away from rounding up to an A–.

Parameter Modification

However, what if we wanted to expand our parameter? What if they needed 1 more point or 10 more points? We know it's greater than 100. The good news is modifying the minimum, maximum, and increment of a What-if parameter is extremely simple. You just modify the DAX that created the table of values that are used.

In this case, we will modify the GENERATESERIES statement. This statement follows a very simple statement logic: GENERATESERIES (Minimum value, Maximum value, increment). You'll notice with a minimum of –100, maximum of 100, and increment of 1, our GENERATESERIES statement looks like Figure 7-17. We will modify the middle part of the statement to 101, just to add that one extra point to allow our parameter to go up to that value.

```
1   Total Grade Modifier =
2   GENERATESERIES ( -100, 100, 1 )
```

Figure 7-17. What-if parameters can't work without having an actual value in the data to grab, and that's what the series does for us

After that small modification to the maximum value, we can see in Figure 7-18 that, had the summer 2021 class gotten 101 more points of score, the class would have had an aggregate grade of an A–.

Figure 7-18. Don't be afraid to modify your parameters!

The ability to modify these parameters is incredibly helpful. You can also create multiple parameters and have them interact. For instance, let's say your widget factory produces 100 widgets at $10 each. You know how much revenue that is. However, you could have What-if parameters for both price and quantity and try different combinations of price and quantity to see if one is more impactful than the other, given a set of operational constraints.

What-if parameters are incredibly powerful and flexible. I've seen some crazy accountants get all the way down to the General Ledger Code level with their What-if parameters.

In baseball, you could add or subtract X number of hits and figure out what the change to batting percentage would be, for an individual or a whole team.

Personally, I have a Power BI report that estimates my total grocery spending each month, and I use What-if parameters to estimate the impact to my wallet based on possible rates of inflation. It is one of the most powerful tools in the Power BI toolbox.

R and Python Integration

R and Python are both programming languages that can be used to extend the analytics capabilities of Power BI. R has its roots in statistical programming, and Python is a very flexible scripting language. Both languages have a wide variety of applications around statistics, data visualization, data wrangling, machine learning, and more.

While learning how to program in R or Python is beyond the scope of this text, learning how and where you can integrate these functions into your Power BI work and the implications that come alongside using R and Python in Power BI are pertinent to our discussion.

Limitations of Using R and Python

I know this feels like a weird place to start, but utilizing R and/or Python comes with some serious consequences that users should be aware of. First and foremost, if you have R or Python being used either in Power Query or for visualization, you will be able to refresh a dataset utilizing these tools only with a personal data gateway, which must be installed and actively running on the machine at the time of refresh.

The Power BI Data Gateway is a tool that can be installed to allow access to on-premises data from the Power BI service. It can also be used in "personal" mode, which allows the gateway to run on your local machine. For R and Python, refreshes must be done using a personal data gateway, as it's your machine that is known to have the necessary libraries or packages to run the request. The Power BI service does not have installations of those languages in a place that can be accessed universally by datasets. From the perspective of Power BI Desktop, this is just an annoyance. However, for the dataset in service after publishing, it can be a significant limitation.

Next, it's important to understand that Power BI does not support every R library or Python package. When you are doing development on your local machine, you have access to all the resources you have locally installed.

For instance, if you had every R library ever known to exist on your local machine, Power BI Desktop can use those locally just fine. However, after publishing, the Power BI service does not have access to the entire universe of, in this example, R libraries. Microsoft does introduce support for additional R libraries and Python packages in each release update of the Power BI service, but they're not always well publicized.

To see a list of currently supported R packages and Python packages, you'll need to go to Microsoft's official documentation. You can find the list of supported R packages at "Create Visuals by Using R Packages in the Power BI Service" (*https://oreil.ly/YXKRQ*) and the list of supported Python packages at "Create Visuals by Using Python Packages in the Power BI Service" (*https://oreil.ly/ASnan*).

It's also worth knowing that "Data source settings" for any R data source must be set to Public, and all other steps in a Power Query editor query must also be set to Public. This can be done by choosing File → Options and settings → Data source settings, then choosing the Edit Permissions button with the relevant data source selected. At the time of writing, Python also has a known limitation: you cannot use Python scripts in reports using the Enhanced Metadata feature.

Enabling R and Python for Power BI

The first thing we must do to use R and/or Python in Power BI is to make sure Power BI knows where the relevant home directories are so that it can call those libraries and packages when they're used. To do that, go to File → Options and settings → Options. That will bring you to the full options/settings list for Power BI Desktop.

Several advanced settings are available here, but what we care about are the R scripting and Python scripting settings. Power BI Desktop does a good job of identifying the home directories for these languages when they're installed. However, if they are not autodetected, you'll have to navigate to them inside the Options window. Note that in both of these settings, a hyperlink will take you to the relevant Microsoft documentation for installing R or Python. Once that is done, you're good to go.

R and Python in Power Query

First, I'm going to look at using R and Python scripts to modify data, and then we can discuss R and Python as their own data sources.

R and Python scripts can be found in the Transform section of the ribbon in the Scripts subsection, which is farthest to the right. Clicking either button will bring up a dialog box where you can put your relevant R or Python script.

Make a mental note that an R or Python script goes into the query's applied steps in order, like everything else. This has the advantage of being able to be done at any point until the R or Python script is called, and both R and Python will support calling the data in the step before that transformation as "dataset," for the purpose of referencing the data in your relevant script.

R and Python also do not need to be terminal transformations. You can have Power Query transformations occur both before and after an R or Python script is called. This can be helpful when you might find a very specific data transformation difficult to do in the Power Query UI, or when a transformation would require some complicated M.

You can also use R or Python scripts as their own data sources. If you choose "Get data" and search by "script," you'll see both R and Python script options. In scenarios like this, where you may already have a well-defined script that you have developed from the relevant language's IDE, you can just copy and paste that script into the dialog box that appears. This will call the R or Python script that will probably contain a link to some source data, run that script, and display the results as a completely new query. Those results are then fully modifiable in the same way as any other Power Query table in any future transformation steps, and that can include, again, a script transformation that uses either or both languages in sequence.

R and Python Visuals

R and Python visuals are also supported in Power BI Desktop, assuming you have the relevant languages installed. The first time you select Visual from the Visualizations pane, you will get a warning dialog asking if you want to enable script visuals.

Script visuals give you the ability to make custom visuals utilizing either language in a way that can really expand your analysis beyond the visualizations that might normally be available in Power BI—and even those that could be available through the Power BI custom visual options.

These visuals are also fully interactive with other visuals on the report page and slicers. Other cross-filtering from other visuals can, in fact, modify R and Python visuals as well. When you first open an R or Python visual, you will be asked to drag fields into the Values area of the Visualization pane. Power BI will use the fields that are dragged into the visual to define what will be the "dataset" for the visual. We can see what that looks like before and after fields are added in Figure 7-19.

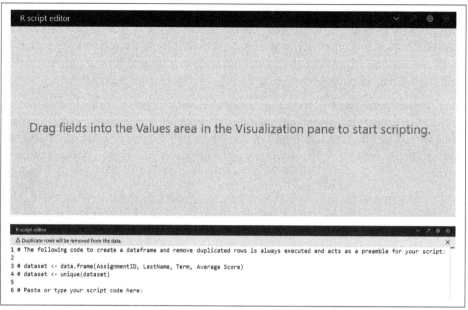

Figure 7-19. Power BI will try to give you a head start on R and Python visuals by defining the "dataset" from your field selections

You'll also notice that, for both R and Python visuals, you will get an alert noting that duplicate rows will be removed from the data. After you have put in your relevant scripts and modified them to reference the "dataset" that you've built in the Power BI interface, you can click the Play button farthest to the right in the script editor bar to run the script. You can click the menu arrow to minimize the window. The arrow pointing up and right will open your relevant language's IDE, so if you need to edit the script, you can do it in a more friendly editor.

Conclusion

In this chapter, we went over some more advanced analytics topics in Power BI Desktop that you can use to extend your analysis. Utilizing AI-powered visuals, what-if analysis, and even R or Python can be tools that help your data consumers get to the information they need quickly and accurately.

This chapter concludes our section on the Power BI Desktop. From here, we will move to an overview of Power BI service and everything that goes into sharing the wonderful reports you'll develop.

CHAPTER 8

Introduction to the Power BI Service

Now that you've completed the previous chapter, you have a beautiful report filled to the brim with insights. You're ready to share your creation with the organization to help make the big decisions...but how? You share by using the Power BI service.

Power BI is more than just the Desktop authorship tool we've been discussing thus far. It's an ecosystem of products, and in this chapter, you'll find out about the second part of that ecosystem, the Power BI service. The *Power BI service* is the software-as-a-service (SaaS) portion of the Power BI infrastructure that allows end users to share reports with one another, manage access to workspaces, create reusable data elements for other report users in the forms of dataflows, and create collections of report elements for broad distribution in the form of apps.

In this chapter, you'll learn the basics of the Power BI service. How do you log in? How do you navigate around? What's a workspace? Why do workspaces matter? How do you use the Power BI service to share reports? There's much to unpack, so let's get started!

The Basics of the Service: What You Need to Know

Initially, you can log into the service (*https://oreil.ly/HrrWE*) and enter your Microsoft account (or employer account) credentials. Everybody can access the Power BI service with a "free" license. That free license gives you access to "My workspace." In this personal development space, where you can publish reports and review how they look and behave in the service.

After providing your credentials, you'll be taken to a home page that looks something like Figure 8-1.

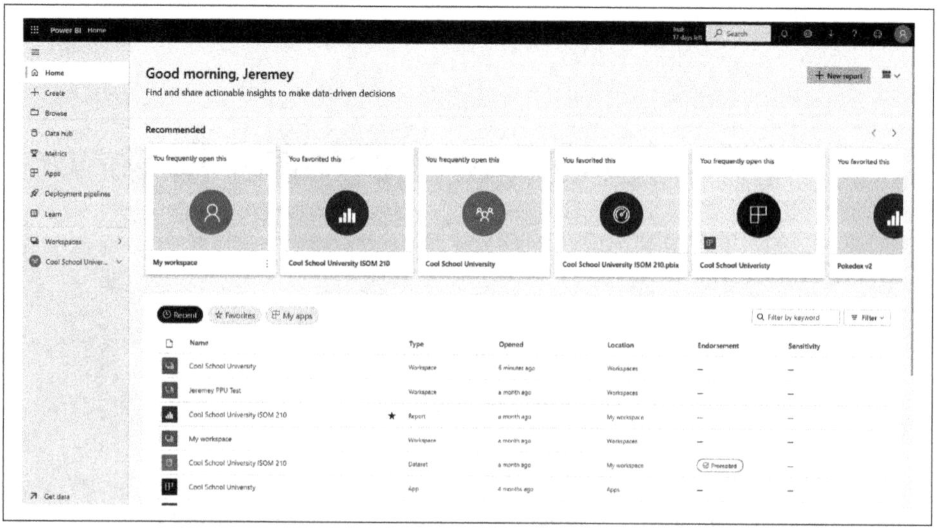

Figure 8-1. The Power BI service home page

You'll notice a ton going on here. There's a navigation bar on the left, a Favorites and Frequents listing in the middle, and underneath that, a link to recent elements and apps you have access to (we'll discuss the context for what apps appear here a little later). At the top right in the darker bar, several options enable searching for objects you have access to, creating new reports, and settings controls. This first look is also the same look you'd get if you were to click the Home link that's at the top of the menu on the left side.

The good news is that everything you really need to access at first can be obtained from that left-hand menu, called the Navigation menu, so let's walk through those areas and get an idea of the most important objects there.

The Navigation Menu

Figure 8-2 shows the Navigation menu up close. In the dark bar at the top, you'll see what looks like a nine-dot box, the Power BI title, and another link to Home.

The nine-dot box is quite convenient. If you click it, a shortcut list will appear to take you to other Microsoft services you might have access to. For example, you can go to Outlook, OneDrive, Word, Excel, PowerPoint, OneNote, SharePoint, Teams, Sway, and other Microsoft products you might have under your Office 365 license. This can be helpful when you're working in Power BI and just need to quickly get to another part of your Office suite. It can also be convenient when you're building something like a dataflow and need to reference where an object might be that you want to pull in from SharePoint or OneDrive for Business.

That Home link will do the exact same thing as clicking the Home button that's shown below, next to the house icon (in the lighter part of the menu). Remember, Microsoft wants to give you a million ways to do something, even if they're literally pixels apart.

Directly beneath that nine-dot box in the Navigation menu, you'll see a hamburger menu icon that will minimize the Navigation menu or expand it, based on your viewing needs. When it's condensed, you can still see the icons of the Navigation menu and use them to get around. When expanded, you'll get explanations of what those icons mean. Personally, as someone who really struggles with remembering icons, even when they're as relevant as Microsoft has made them here in the Navigation menu, I will just leave the menu expanded. I condense it only when I'm looking at a report page and need some extra space. With that in mind, let's dive into the Navigation menu and look through these options, starting with Home.

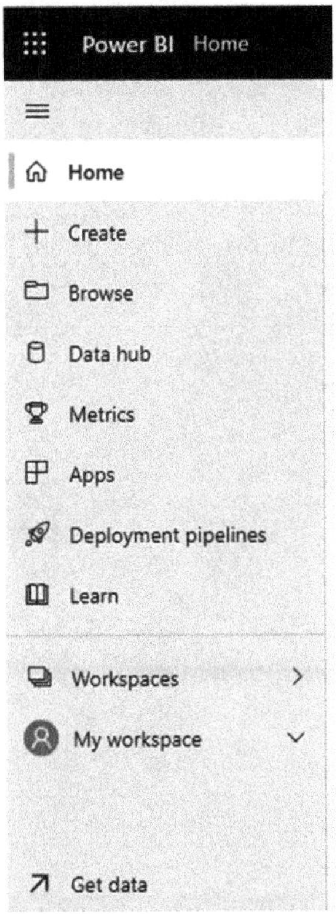

Figure 8-2. Here's a close-up of the Navigation menu, fully expanded

Home and Browse

The Home section contains quick links to objects in the Power BI service that are recommended to you, objects that you've accessed recently, objects that you've favorited, and apps that you have access to.

As shown in Figure 8-3, at the very top of this page is a nice greeting and a button (called "New report") to create a new report, which will take me to the same section as the Create link on the Navigation menu. Next to that is a combination ellipses and hamburger menu icon that will allow me to choose either the simplified or expanded layout. The expanded layout doesn't really look much different, except it has some useful learning links at the bottom of the page. Everything you see in this section uses the simplified page layout.

Along the top, you can see a list called Recommended, containing recommended objects. These can be workspaces, reports, datasets, apps, pretty much anything. Also included in this list can be data elements that are promoted by your organization, such as promoted or certified datasets and apps to which you might have access.

Below the recommended objects is a collection of recently accessed elements, favorited elements, and apps. I can toggle between the views by simply clicking the relevant button. I can also search the lists by keyword, and the Filter button lets me choose specific types of objects to look for, things I've opened in a given time frame, or I can filter by endorsement status.

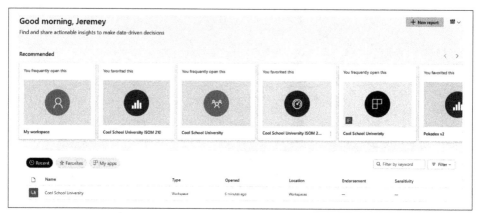

Figure 8-3. Home is designed to help you feel at home in the Power BI service

This layout is very similar to what you might see, for example, in a SharePoint list. I can see the names of the content I've favorited. I can see the type of element, whether it's a report or a dashboard, the owner of that element, its endorsement status, and any sensitivity labels on that element.

In the Favorites list, you can see where Power BI still shows those items as starred, even though that feels a bit redundant. Well, that same functionality exists in the same unmarked column in Recent. If any recent objects are also in your Favorites list, you will see those elements starred.

The Browse section of the Navigation menu is, in context to the Home section, pretty redundant. It shows you a list of objects that you have access to, and they are broken into subpages for Recent, Favorites, and then specifically items that have been shared with you. As you can see in Figure 8-4, Microsoft is nothing if not persistent in giving you too many ways to do the same darn thing.

		Name	Type	Opened	Owner	Endorsement	Sensitivity	Workspace
		Cool School University	Workspace	7 minutes ago	—	—	—	Workspaces
		Jeremey PPU Test	Workspace	a month ago	—	—	—	Workspaces
		Cool School University ISOM 210 ★	Report	a month ago	Jeremey Arnold	—	—	My workspace
		My workspace	Workspace	a month ago	—	—	—	Workspaces
		Cool School University ISOM 210	Dataset	a month ago	Jeremey Arnold	⊘ Promoted	—	My workspace
		Cool School Univeristy	App	4 months ago	—	—	—	Apps

Figure 8-4. Seriously, Microsoft, do we still need this? Not sure that we do. Home already looks so nice!

Create

Power BI offers a way to build reports in the service itself. Honestly, it's one of those things that exists, but the use cases for doing it in the web versus downloading Power BI Desktop for free and using that to generate a report aren't very common.

If you can use Power BI Desktop for authorship, you should. With that in mind, the Create tab will give you two options. You can manually enter or paste data into a table sheet, or you can pick another published dataset in that workspace and create another report based off that dataset. We can see what this interface looks like in Figure 8-5.

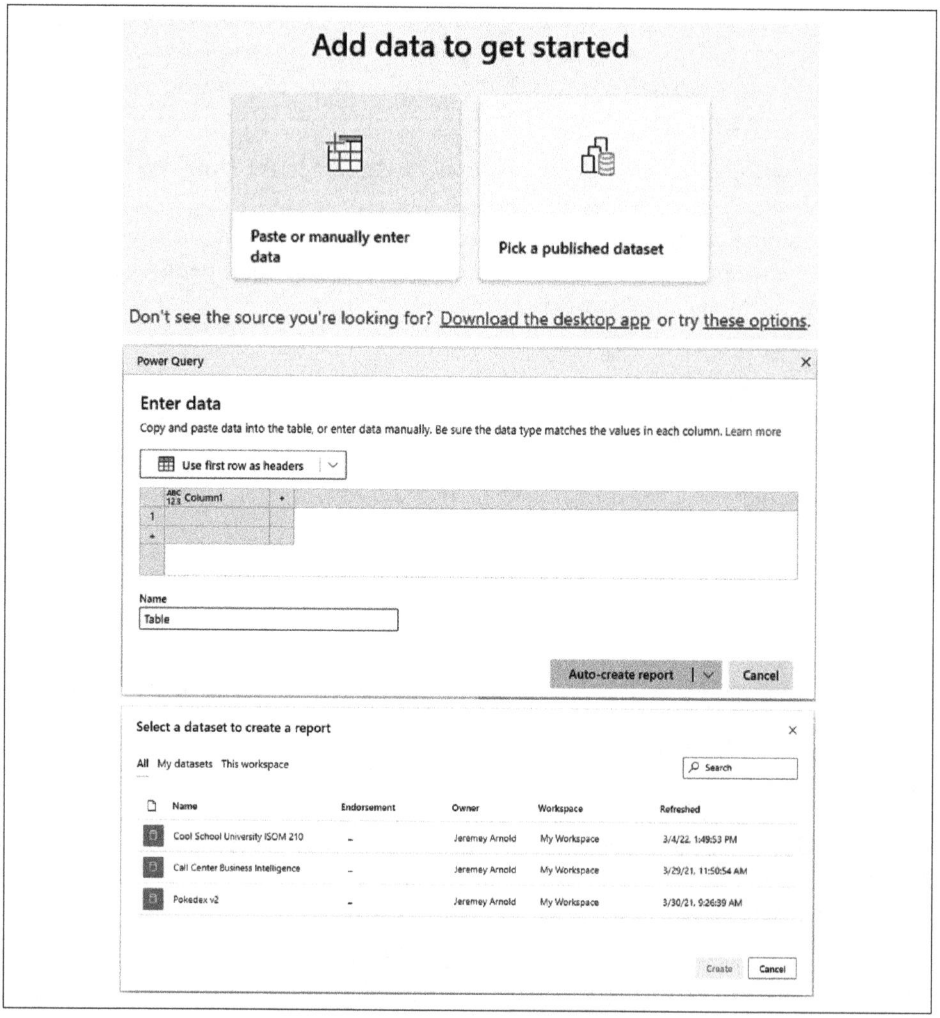

Figure 8-5. The first screenshot shows the two options for Create. The next shows what happens if you click the manual data entry option. The third shows what happens if you select "Pick a published dataset" to build a report on.

Data Hub

In the "Data hub section," you can see a list of recommended datasets, a list of all the datasets you have access to, and the specific list of datasets that you have authored. As of the time of writing, a new feature in preview called Datamarts is also visible here if you have Premium Per User or Premium Per Capacity licensing.

You'll note that Microsoft makes some hyperlinks available in this view that will send you to their documentation if you have questions on specific elements on this page regarding dataset discovery and explaining what exactly a dataset is.

With each dataset, a vertical three-dot selection brings up a menu that gives you an expanded list of options for that dataset. We can see what that looks like in Figure 8-6.

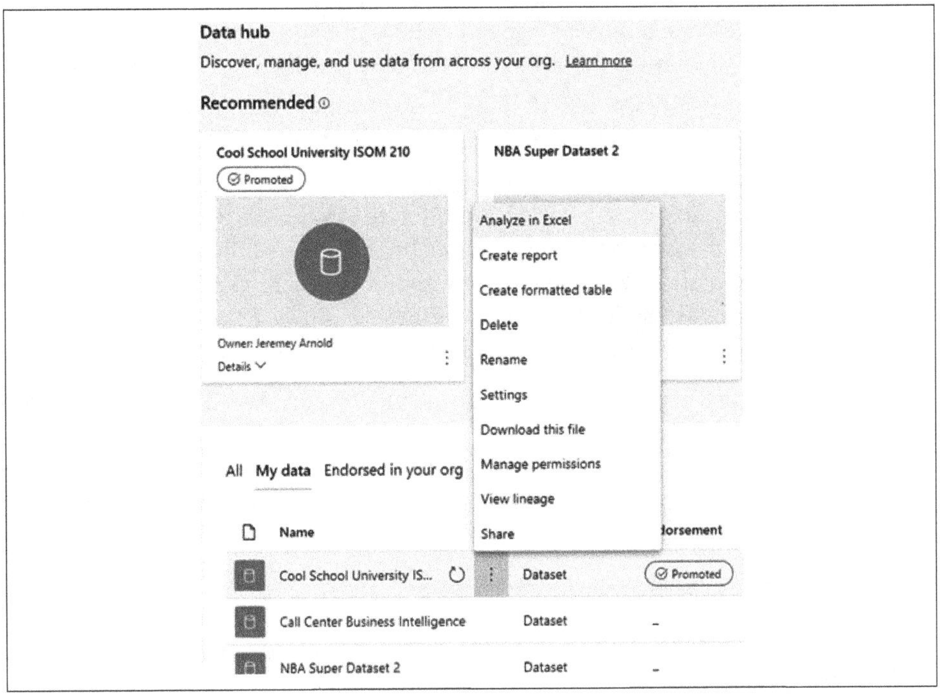

Figure 8-6. The Data hub is the place to go to view and manage datasets

You can do several things with a dataset from this menu. I'm going to approach them a little bit out of order, putting settings last because that's really its own section.

The first option we see is Analyze in Excel. The first time you do this, Power BI will ask you to install an update to Excel to read the file format. Once that is done, Power BI will generate an Excel worksheet that will already have a live connection setup to the dataset it originated from.

This is very similar to connecting to a Power BI dataset to create a report from Power BI Desktop. The data is opened in a pivot-table format, and you can put fields into rows and columns and insert measures into the Values section, just as you would any other pivot table. This is helpful to users who may know how to leverage the data model you have created, but aren't yet comfortable with Power BI Desktop (in which case, might I suggest a copy of this book for them?). Or maybe the user just needs some quick pivot-table analysis in Excel. The advantage of this function, from an Excel perspective, is that the only data stored locally is the data that appears in the cell itself—because the core of that data is in the cloud.

"Create report" will take you to the web report authoring experience, where you will see all the tables and measures in the dataset. You can use them to build a report with as many pages as you need, and that report will exist in the Power BI service. One word of caution: the web authoring experience does not allow you to edit a dataset. If you are missing a measure or need to add a table or something, you can't really do that from the web authoring experience. You'd have to open the original dataset, add your relevant data elements, and then republish that dataset back to the service.

"Create paginated report" will create a Report Definition Language (RDL) file that will have all the necessary connection information to create a pixel-perfect report, a la SQL Server Reporting Services, to be hosted in the Power BI service. Paginated reports for the Power BI service are not authored in Power BI Desktop but are authored in Power BI Report Builder, which is a different software package. You will see this option available in only Premium Per User or Premium Per Capacity workspaces.

"Manage permissions" will allow you to see all the objects for which you have the ability to add or remove users. You can see who has direct access to a report, dataset, or workbook. You can add users manually from this interface and see which users have requested access but whose requests are still pending. See an example in Figure 8-7.

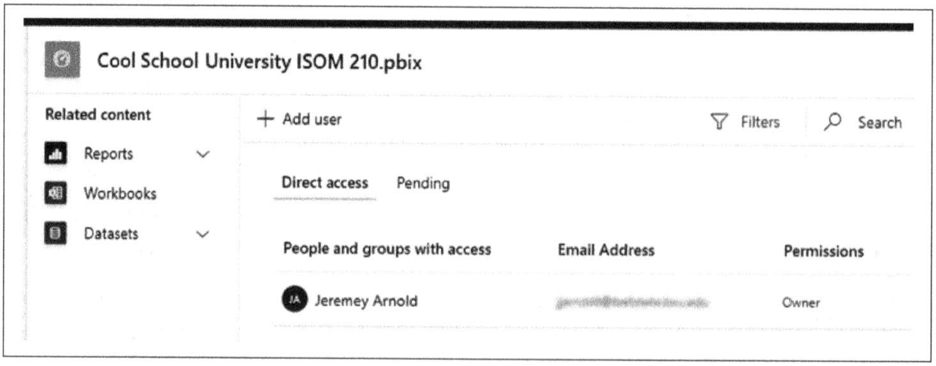

Figure 8-7. Good access management is critical to keeping data secure. "Manage permissions" lets you see who has access, add users, and see who has requested access but is still waiting.

"Chat in Teams" will create a link that is shareable to a person, group, or channel in Microsoft Teams. Users can then access the dataset via Teams, bringing them to the appropriate location in the Power BI service. You can also share reports and report pages in Teams. Microsoft Teams can be a great way to embed analytics into your organization in a framework that users will already be familiar with. This opens the door to using Teams as a channel to discuss the results of a given report or dataset and gives you, the author, the ability to provide quick insights, address questions, or make improvements based on user feedback.

"View lineage" opens a new browser window where you can see all the data elements inside a given workspace and their dependencies. For instance, if I had a dataset that utilized a SQL Server instance, that SQL Server would show up before the dataset and then all the reports on that dataset would follow, and then any dashboards that were created from report elements would also be shown.

In my personal workspace with the datasets I currently have, they're all based on flat-file data, so there's no element before the dataset. We can see what that lineage view looks like in Figure 8-8.

The other thing you can do from this view is create a number of other elements by using the New button. This will allow you to use web-based design tools to create new elements directly into a workspace or to upload PBIX files directly into a workspace. This can be used for reports and paginated reports, scorecards, dataflows, and even datasets. If you have an opportunity to use Power BI Desktop instead of the web authorship tool, I would always recommend doing so. For things like dataflows and scorecards, though, this is where you'll create those.

In my opinion, this is a strange location for this functionality to live, especially for items better suited to Power BI Desktop, but it's the single most cohesive place that these options exist from a web authorship perspective. At the time of writing, Microsoft does plan to provide a web authorship tool for paginated reports, and at that time, this option may push you to the web authoring for said future paginated report.

Clicking any dataset will show you a list of tables and columns in that dataset. "View lineage" will allow you to see how data elements flow from one item to another, showing you potential impacts that would result from making a change to a dataset, even beyond your single workspace!

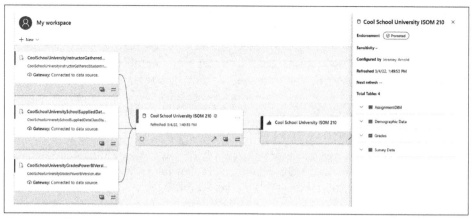

Figure 8-8. "View lineage" will help you see what data came from where and what is using it now

Settings

The Settings selection on a dataset will take you to a properties page preselected to the Datasets portion of the Navigation menu at the top of the page. You'll see a list of all the datasets in the workspace on the left. On the right, you'll see several properties options for the currently selected dataset that are very important to the management of your dataset(s). Figure 8-9 gives us a look at this page.

The first option, which is the "View dataset" hyperlink, takes us to the dataset's workspace page, which is an area we'll discuss when we get to Workspace navigation. The second option, "Refresh history," opens a pop-up inside the page that will show you the dataset's refresh history, indicating whether it was successful; and if there was a failure, it provides a reason for that failure. Some failure messages are helpful. Some are not. It's still a Microsoft product, and Microsoft's error messages can be hit-or-miss in terms of their helpfulness; they're notoriously unfriendly when it comes to troubleshooting in Windows. Next, we can create or update the dataset's description.

For data sources that are not in the cloud or more specifically in Azure, you will most likely need a data gateway installed to facilitate that dataset's refresh. For example, let's say I have my Power BI dataset refreshing from a couple of Excel files on my company's network drive. The Power BI service doesn't have access to my network drive.

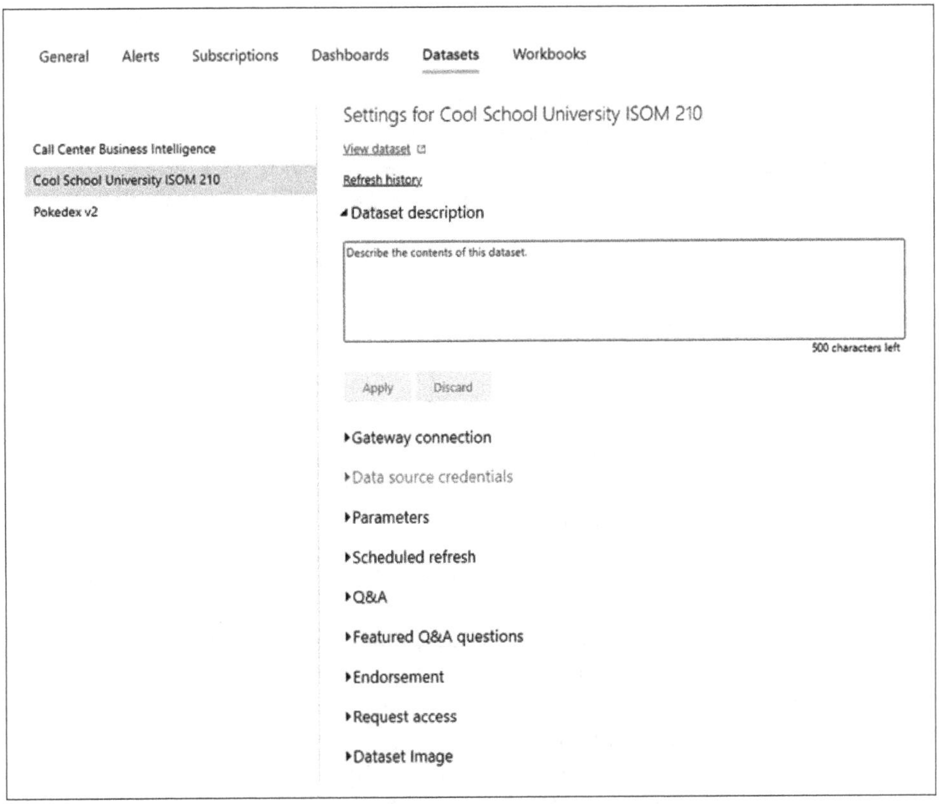

Figure 8-9. Dataset configuration options are plentiful

A data gateway acts somewhat like a virtual private network between the Power BI service and the locations allowed by the data gateway to facilitate Power BI being able to get the data for refreshes. Going over each data source and whether it requires a gateway would take a long time, and admittedly Microsoft would be the best and most up-to-date source for that.

If you need to check whether a data source requires a data gateway, go to "Power BI Data Sources" (*https://oreil.ly/8WpPq*). Gateways will typically be managed by your IT or security team, so if your organization is already using an enterprise gateway, reach out to the relevant stakeholders to see if you need to get a certain data source added to it.

Microsoft does make a personal version of the data gateway available for download. This version runs on your local machine, and assuming your machine is on and the gateway is running at the time of refresh, that will also work. Take note that all R and Python data sources and transformations require the use of a personal data gateway, not an enterprise one. This is because the Power BI service needs to run the relevant

R and Python scripts from your machine since, presumably, your machine has all the necessary packages and libraries.

Next, although grayed out in Figure 8-9, "Data source credentials" would be where you configure your credentials required to access the data. In this case, let's say you were pulling data from an on-premises SQL Server and that SQL Server instance was configured in your data gateway; you would use this section to provide the relevant credentials so that Power BI would know what credentials to use to pass through the gateway and onto the original data source.

A Power BI file when uploaded will generally keep the credentials in place that were used in Desktop, but that doesn't mean that's what you want. For example, you may want to transfer the credentials used for refresh to a service account that has been set up. Or you may need to change credentials when someone has left the organization or for myriads of other reasons. Power BI will do a good job of telling you if something needs to be checked here, so if you are having refresh issues, it never hurts to double-check your data source credentials.

Parameters are straightforward. If you have parameters in your dataset, you can configure those parameter values here. One use case is that I like to parameterize my server names and database names. If something should happen and I need to quickly repoint my Power BI dataset to a backup server, or the name of a database gets changed, I can come into these settings and basically hot swap those connections, refresh the data, and move on with my day. All your Power Query parameters for a given dataset can be managed and have their values updated here. When those parameter values are updated, it will push a refresh to accommodate the newly updated data state.

"Scheduled refresh" is where the real magic happens in the Power BI service for me. This is where you will configure what time and how often your Power BI dataset will refresh against its source data. You can set up to 8 scheduled refreshes in nonpremium environments and up to 48 refreshes a day in premium capacity environments. You set your time zone, whether it's daily or on specific days of the week, and you save those settings. Just because you set up refresh doesn't mean it will work. Make sure you've successfully refreshed your dataset in Power BI Desktop first and make sure all your settings are correct for the dataset in service before setting up a scheduled refresh.

We talked about Q&A quite extensively in Chapter 7. Q&A allows you to turn on or off Q&A functionality on the dataset. It also allows you to share your synonyms with everyone in the organization. Likewise, "Featured Q&A questions" allows you to put featured questions in front of your audience when they view reports based on this dataset.

The Endorsement feature allows you to identify a dataset and highlight it across the organization. Microsoft makes three levels of endorsement available: None, Promoted, and Certified. None is the default setting. When a dataset has no endorsement, it will show up in search results, but that's it. When a dataset is promoted, it will show up in search results, and that result will be promoted in the search context. You can also choose to make that dataset discoverable, which means users who don't have access to that dataset will be able to discover it and request access themselves. Finally, a dataset can be certified. A *certified dataset* is one that has been reviewed, and this is a sort of "source of truth" label. By default, an individual doesn't set a dataset to Certified status. That is done by processes in your organization. Each organization will have its own criteria for when a dataset can be labeled Certified.

"Request access" will let you determine how users can request permissions to access content related to the selected dataset. You can have a request emailed to the dataset owner, or you can have an automatic response providing a set of instructions for the follower to get access.

Finally, Dataset Image allows you to choose a nice picture that will show off the dataset in the places where it is discoverable. This image will be available and represent this dataset everywhere in your organization where a dataset can be discovered.

Metrics

Metrics are a relatively new feature to the Power BI service. They allow you to create trackable KPIs or goal metrics by using data in the Power BI service. You create scorecards that show the performance of a given metric over a given time period.

Metrics are always going to be connected to a specific user or business case, so I don't want to get too into the weeds with this. If you think you might have a use case for metrics, I recommend just trying it out. Microsoft recently enabled working with metrics in your personal workspace, as well, so try to work on creating some goals for yourself before expanding into this functionality for other parts of the organization.

Apps

An *app*, in the context of the Power BI service, is a collection of packaged content that can be distributed to a broader audience. Apps are created inside a workspace and then, when they're ready, can be published to a collection of individuals, a Microsoft 365 group, or an entire organization. Apps can also have different permissions than those in a workspace, making user management a bit easier since the app's permissions are managed in one location.

Users can make apps from a workspace. Many apps also are available for you to use, called *template apps*. These apps are collections that others have put together and shared so that you and others in your organization can use them.

In Figure 8-10, we can see the initial Apps view, which will first appear empty. We can then add either a template app or an organizational app and view the content from that application. We can use the yellow "Get apps" button in either location to access the list of available apps that we can bring into our workspace. In my example, I've created an RLS Test application that will be an organizational app, and the others are template apps.

We will walk through the installation of the template app using Microsoft's COVID-19 US Tracking Report template app. Notice that in the "All apps" section, organizational apps are always listed first before template apps, but in both groupings they're not really organized in a meaningful way to me. You'll note there is a place where you can choose to select only endorsed apps. This can be helpful if you're looking for a collection of data that has been endorsed inside your organization quickly.

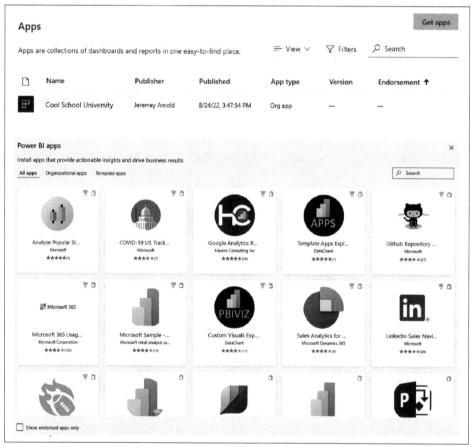

Figure 8-10. Apps are a great way to curate content and get ideas for yourself

Installing the application is as easy as clicking the appropriate box and being taken to the relevant page in AppSource (Microsoft's application and custom visual portal). Some apps may have licensing involved, so you'll want to check that in the description, but in most cases, there will be a big Get It Now button.

In the case of Microsoft's template apps, they will have a pop-up before installation that will ask you for some information for marketing purposes. This does not have to be associated with the same information as your Power BI account itself, so if you're uncomfortable, feel free to use a throwaway email.

Once the app or apps are installed, they'll show up here. Accessing them is as simple as clicking the link under its name. Each app will have a list of information, including the publisher, the date it was published, the type of app, the version number if relevant, and its endorsement status. Once an app is installed, you can look at the reports that came alongside that app. I enjoy looking at some of the template apps for design ideas for my own personal work, so don't be afraid to borrow clever ideas!

Deployment Pipelines

Deployment pipelines are a Premium Per Capacity–only feature that allows you to designate Development, Test, and Production environments for a given Power BI workspace. This can be a tool used by developers to help with issues like version control and user testing.

Workspaces can either be created or assigned to support a pipeline, but as mentioned before, all such workspaces must be in Premium Per Capacity.

Deployment pipelines are typically managed by either workspace- or tenant-level administrators, or whichever group inside an organization manages the Premium Per Capacity tenant. If you happen to be on a Premium Per Capacity tenant and have a need or desire to establish a pipeline, work with your relevant administrator to get that put together or ask to have work added to an existing pipeline.

Learn

Learn is a small learning portal where Microsoft gives you links to training resources, Power BI documentation, and some sample reports to get you started. In Learn, you can also join the larger Power BI and Power Platform communities.

I cannot speak highly enough of the Power BI community. Many great users take time to create resources, answer questions on forums, promote new ideas for the product, and create events for practitioners to share what they've learned so others can learn from them as well.

Publishing Your Work

Now that we've discussed where and how you'll navigate the Power BI service, we need to get content in here so that others can learn from our data! We've dealt with the first half of that Navigation menu, but the things in there really matter only if we get content into our workspaces.

To publish your work, you will take your PBIX file from Power BI Desktop and can either use the Publish button in Power BI Desktop from the Home ribbon or upload a PBIX file to the Power BI service from the Navigation menu. You may have seen the "Get data" button at the bottom of Figure 8-2. When we click that button, we see the page in Figure 8-11.

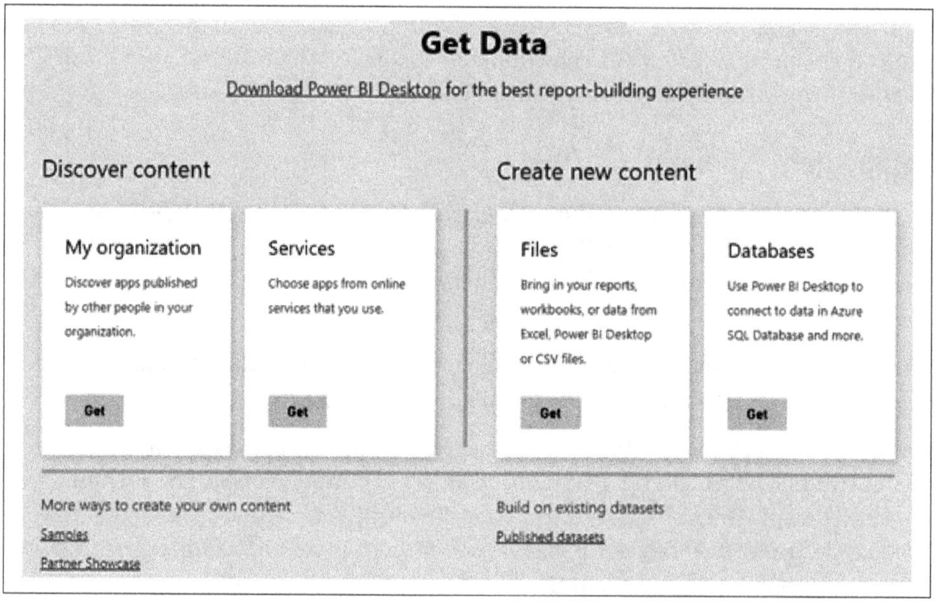

Figure 8-11. You can get data into service from the Power BI Desktop or from Power BI service

In Power BI Desktop, you will see a menu that shows a list of workspaces you have access to, and you'll choose which workspace to publish the report in.

In the service, it's more of a pull-up function than a push-out function. You'll upload the PBIX file from the workspace that you wish to add the dataset and/or report to. On the left, we see the Discover content functions that will allow you to see your organizational apps and other template apps that can be plugged right into the workspace.

On the right side is a Files option that you can use to upload your PBIX file.

The Databases & More option allows you to work on creating a dataset from a connection to Azure SQL, Azure SQL Data Warehouse (which is now Azure Synapse, and I don't know why Microsoft hasn't updated this; my guess is because almost no one uses this), SQL Server Analysis Services, or Spark on Azure. In Figure 8-12, we'll see what service looks like when I select File, because that's really what you'll use this option for 99% of the time.

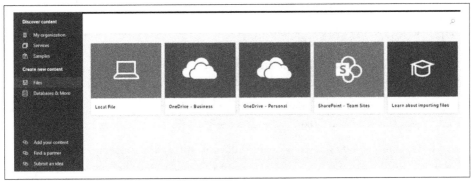

Figure 8-12. Uploading files? This is where you'll be.

From here you'll see a couple of options. Local File, in this case, means your PBIX file that you generated from Power BI Desktop. The OneDrive links allow you to create a dataset in the Power BI service that's connected to either your OneDrive for Business or OneDrive personal accounts.

From a refresh perspective, these sources are convenient because they do not require a data gateway to refresh. However, I still suggest building your report in Power BI Desktop using OneDrive sources, as opposed to doing that here. Likewise, the same is true for the SharePoint option. Note that in scenarios where you might be using OneDrive or SharePoint for version-control purposes, you can still upload PBIX files as well via those channels, and that can be a convenient use case for these nonlocal file options.

When Local File is selected, you'll see your classic Windows Explorer window open. Navigate to the appropriate file and upload it. After that, the dataset will appear in the workspace navigation area for the selected workspace (which you can see under Workspaces if you look back at Figure 8-2).

One other point: whenever a dataset is uploaded to a workspace for the first time, it also will automatically create a blank dashboard with the same name as the dataset. So you see that getting our Power BI work into a workspace is pretty simple, but what actually is a workspace and why do they matter?

What Is a Workspace?

A *workspace* is simply a place where Power BI data assets are held. Datasets go into a workspace, reports go into a workspace, dashboards go into a workspace. A workspace can be used as a place to send people to get content, and it can also be used as the basis for an app that you would send users to for content. When we publish datasets and their reports to the service, we are publishing them to these workspaces.

My Workspace

Everyone who logs into the Power BI service will have a personalized "free" workspace. You need to know about some important limitations of this workspace.

First, while you can share content that is in your personal workspace, both you and the users you share with are required to have at least Power BI Pro licenses.

Second, it's generally considered a best practice to not share content out of your personal workspace permanently, since access to that workspace can be an issue if you should ever leave the organization. Also, you cannot make an app out of content in your personal workspace. Sorry, you can't use this to get around Microsoft's licensing.

The other thing you cannot do is create a Power BI dataflow. The best use for one's personal workspace, in my opinion, is to view it as a personal test environment. You build your report, you think it looks good in Power BI Desktop, you publish it to the service, and you look at it there and make sure all the things are behaving the way you want. Does the report still look good with different screen dimensions? Does the navigation of the report flow the way you want when you don't have Power BI Desktop's extra functionality? These are questions that you can answer from your personal workspace. You can also test your scheduled refresh in this workspace, which can be helpful before moving that dataset into a more permanent home in a shared workspace.

Shared Capacity Workspaces

In a *shared capacity workspace,* people who have Power BI Pro or Power BI Premium Per User licenses can share Power BI data elements with users who also have access to that workspace.

Creating a workspace is a very simple process. When you click the Workspaces button in the Navigation menu, a pane will appear to the right of the Navigation menu, showing you the list of workspaces you have access to.

In this case, I've created two workspaces to go along with "My workspace." One is a Premium Per User workspace, and one is a normal shared capacity workspace.

Some features work only in a Premium Per User workspace. Premium Per Capacity workspaces will have a diamond symbol next to their names, so you can tell if it is a Premium Per User or Premium Per Capacity workspace, as opposed to a typical Pro license shared workspace. Get a quick look at that in Figure 8-13. At the bottom of that list, you'll see the option to create a workspace.

The workspace that is created will show you options in alignment with your licensing. In my example, I'm taking advantage of the 60-day free Premium Per User trial so I can demonstrate the creation of both types of workspaces.

When you go to create a workspace, a pane will appear on the right side of the page. It will have a place to put the workspace name and description, alongside an image to describe the workspace.

The advanced section of this pane also has several settings. We can choose who will be on the contact list for this new workspace, attach a OneDrive location for file hosting for the workspace, and identify which license mode is attached to the workspace (in this case, Pro, Premium Per User, Premium Per Capacity, or Embedded).

Embedded and Premium Per Capacity will be grayed out unless your organization has that licensing in place. Premium Per User will also be grayed out if you don't have a Premium Per User license.

You can choose to identify the workspace as being used for the development of a template app, and you can allow contributors to update any app that comes from this workspace. This can be good when you have multiple people working in development of a given Power BI solution and you want to have more than one person who can deploy the updated app.

It is important to note that Pro and Premium Per User workspaces can be accessed in a licensing hierarchy. For instance, if I have a Pro workspace, users with either Premium Per User or Pro licenses will be able to access it and the data elements inside. However, with a Premium Per User workspace, only people with Premium Per User licenses will be able to access that workspace. This rule does not apply to organizations with Premium Per Capacity licensing, as that allows for an infinite number of readers inside an organization to any workspace made on its premium capacity node.

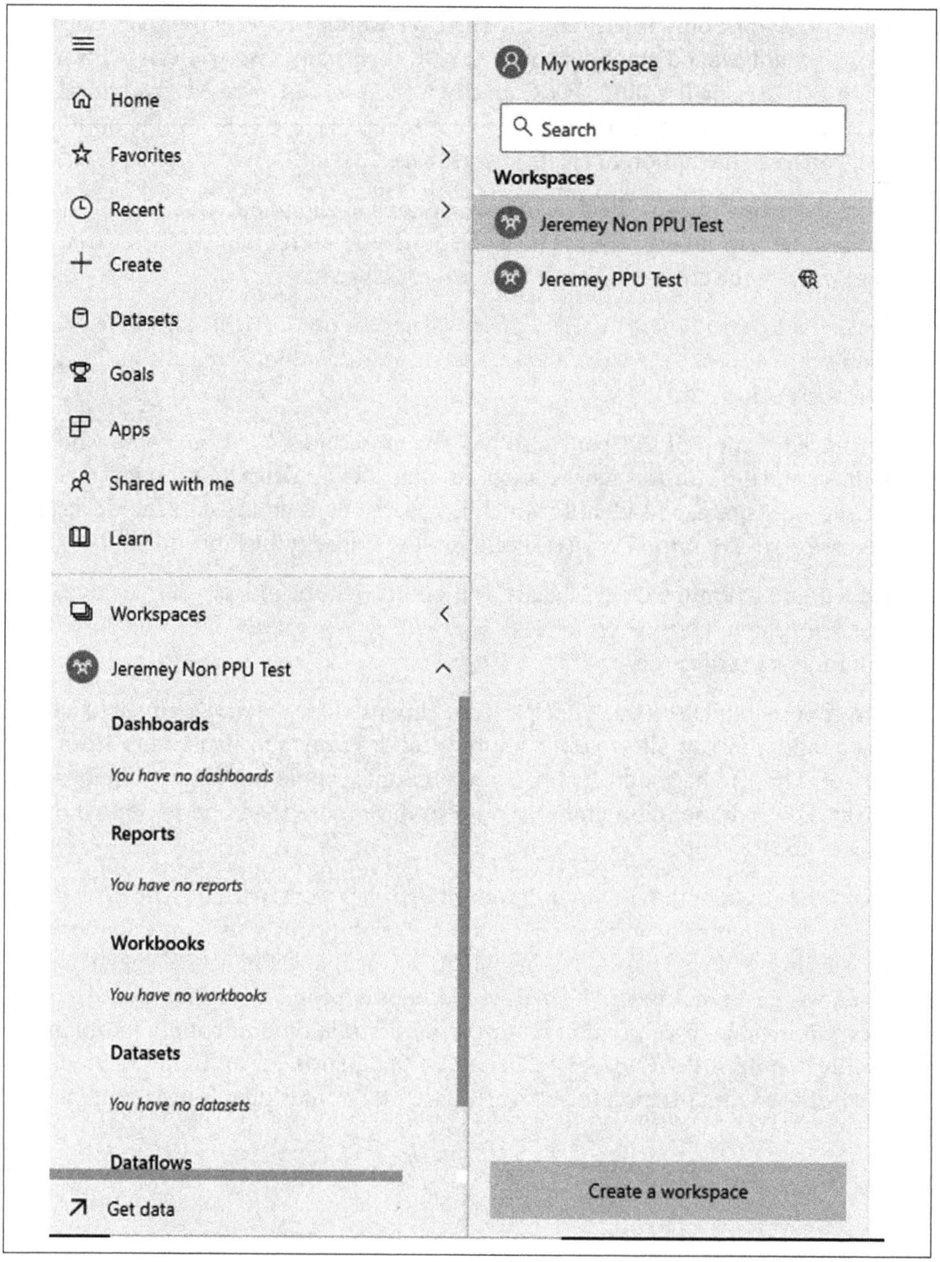

Figure 8-13. Here you can see how to navigate to a workspace and where to go to create a new workspace

Dataflows in Shared Workspaces

With an understanding of what a shared workspace is, we can now discuss the creation of dataflows in a workspace. A *dataflow* is a shared data element that is stored in a workspace that can be called as a data source for report development in Power BI.

Think of this as an ETL process that gets data from somewhere and does some transformations but creates a data element that can be used for further analysis outside a specific model context.

There are two types of dataflows nowadays. There are what I'll call classic dataflows and streaming dataflows. Any workspace that has one type of dataflow cannot have the other type of dataflow in the same workspace. This may change, but as of the time of this writing, streaming dataflows are still in preview.

A *classic dataflow* is a collection of tables that are created in the Power Query in Power BI service. You'll find the option to create a dataflow in the Get Data section. It's a new option under the "Create new content" section that wasn't there when we were looking at that page in my personal workspace. A Power BI dataflow does not have all the same data sources available as Power BI Desktop does. We can see what data is available to Power Query Online in Figure 8-14.

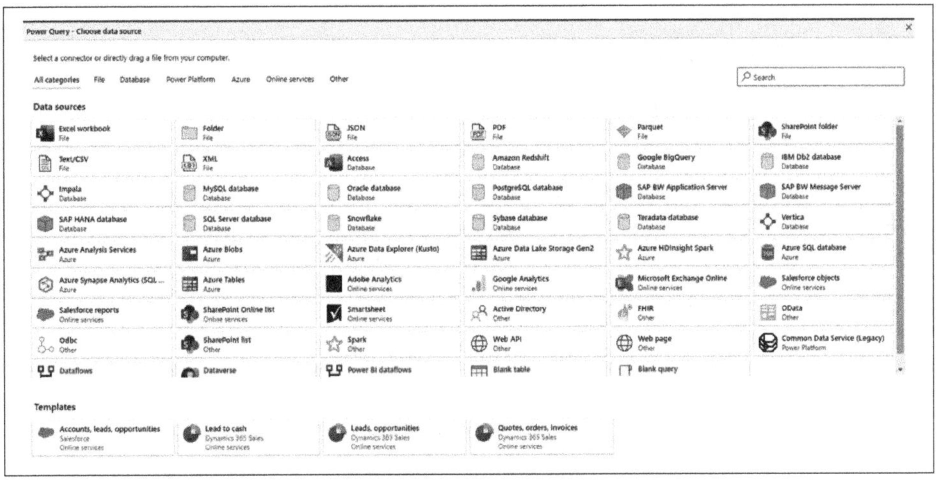

Figure 8-14. Dataflow generation using Power Query Online

It is a pretty good list of common data sources, and Microsoft does add new data sources to Power Query Online from time to time. It can be nice to have a set of transformations or pieces of a data model that aren't locked behind a single dataset from a Power BI Desktop file. And it is nice to have reusable data elements that other people in the organization may be able to leverage for their own analyses. Classic dataflows can be used on Pro licenses.

Streaming dataflows require at least a Premium Per User license. Reports shared from streaming dataflows can be consumed only by users with a Premium Per User license or in a Premium Per Capacity environment.

A streaming dataflow allows Power BI to call either an Azure Event Hub event or an Azure IoT event. It allows you to consume data from either of those sources and do transformations with them in real time so you can do "real-time" reporting on data coming from these scenarios. While this is a cool feature, being limited to Azure Event Hubs and Azure IoT Hub does limit its functionality, and there's a little more setup for this type of event. I personally hope that they expand the number of options before going to general availability and that they make these easier to use.

Putting Your Data in Front of Others

So, while we can put our data into a workspace, we still need to get it in front of people. To do that, we have a couple of options. We can bring users into the workspaces we create. We can create an app. We can link reports to Teams or to SharePoint. We can also embed report elements into a website or into an application if we are using Power BI Embedded. If you want to embed reports into an application, I recommend working with an application developer who will be able to help walk through those technical hurdles. Otherwise, let's get sharing.

Adding Users to a Workspace

The easiest way to get someone to see our data is to invite them into our workspace. Doing that is easy.

In Figure 8-15, we can see the view we get when we select a workspace from our workspaces list. In this case, you see my non-Premium Per User workspace I created. You'll see in the upper-right corner an Access button. Click it, and a pane will appear on the right that allows us to add or remove users and identify the role they play in the workspace.

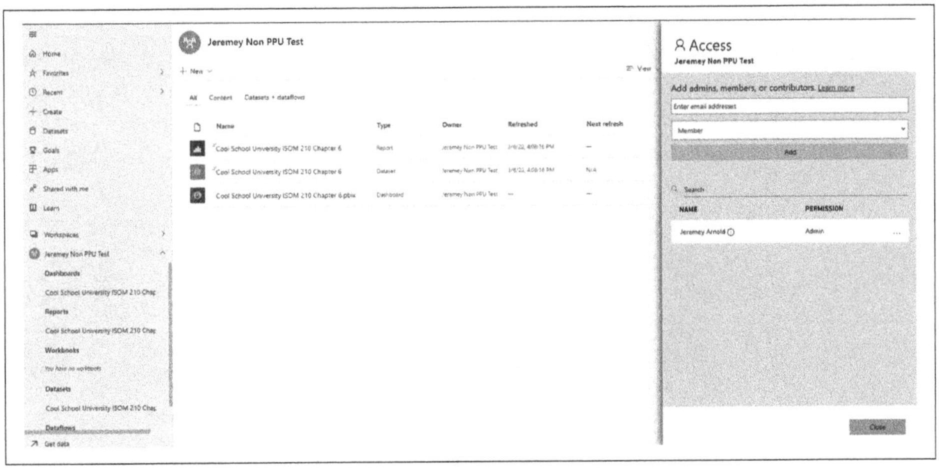

Figure 8-15. Adding additional users is elementary

You will also see an area to add people or groups via email addresses. This is nice because in an organizational setting, Power BI can pretty seamlessly integrate with your active directory instance, letting you search for people in your organization and confirm their email addresses. Click Add, and they're in.

This also works with security groups if you have a group of people you want to add to a workspace in bulk. You can add a user at four levels: Admin, Member, Contributor, and Viewer. Each role has certain levels of permissions, with Admin being the highest and Viewer being the lowest.

If you'd like, you can review what each workspace role can do at "Roles in Workspaces in Power BI" (*https://oreil.ly/z0zH4*). However, my general rule of thumb is that the person who creates the workspace is the administrator. Anyone else who does development in the workspace is a member. Anyone who is there to read reports is a reader. I don't tend to use the Contributor option much, but if you do find a really good use case for that, I'd love to hear about it!

Sharing via a Link or Teams

You can also send out a shareable link to a data element from that data element itself! So, if I look into the shared workspace where I placed my report, I can see a number of options above the page of the report I am currently looking at.

Not everyone who sees the report will have all the options here, but from a sharing perspective, I think it's worth highlighting both Share and Chat in Teams.

Share will create a link that someone can use to view the data element as though they had the viewer role.

Chat in Teams will first, if necessary, have you sign into your account and then create a link to the report page and allow you to share that to a person, group, or channel in Teams. This is useful when you are working on development and want to get feedback or you have really critical KPIs that you want to have an open communication channel on. Chat in Teams is awesome for quick collaboration. We can see what both of these dialog boxes look like in Figure 8-16.

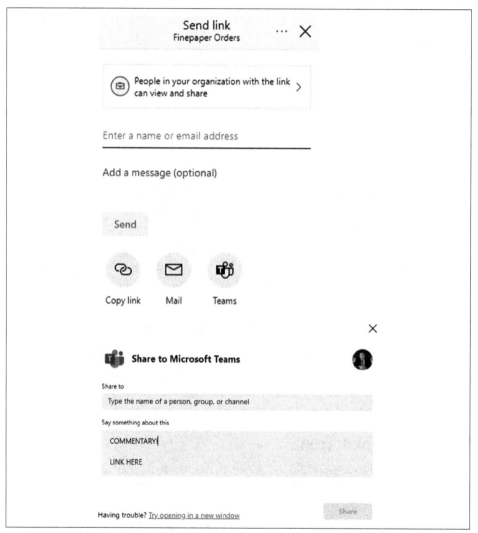

Figure 8-16. Sharing is caring, and you can do that using a link or via Teams

Sharing via SharePoint

If you want to share a data element to a SharePoint page, that's also quite simple. On any given report page, look to the left of Share and Chat in Teams, and click the File option. That drop-down menu has options under "Embed report" for SharePoint online, embedding a report in a website or internal portal, publishing to the web as a public report, or using the Developer Playground for Power BI Embedded testing. We can see this in Figure 8-17.

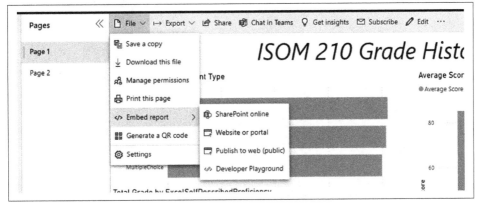

Figure 8-17. Share via SharePoint by choosing File → Embed report

The SharePoint option will give us a website link that we can use to embed in our SharePoint site. This can be done with a Pro license or higher. You'll then go to the relevant SharePoint site you want to add this to and follow a couple of steps.

Note that this feature works only on modern pages in SharePoint. Once we have the link, we can create a new modern site page, select Power BI from the drop-down menu, add the report, provide the copied URL into the Power BI report link, and then publish!

Creating an App

We've discussed apps a couple of times in this chapter, and creating an app is very simple. Select your workspace that has the data elements of your future app. You'll see, on the far side of the workspace items, a toggle that lets you choose whether it should be included in the app.

Datasets are not shared in apps; only reports and dashboards that use that dataset will be included. The app still goes back to the dataset for its information, but it hides the dataset itself from app users. In the upper-right corner, once you have your items selected, click "Create app," and that will take you to a page like that in Figure 8-18.

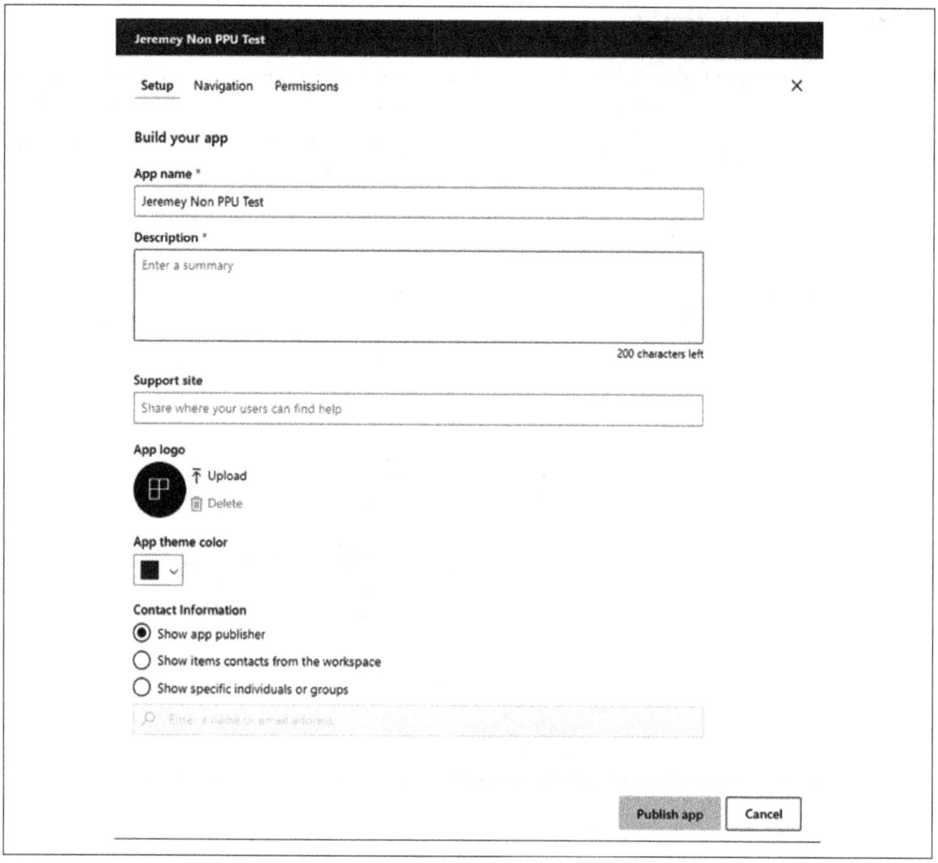

Figure 8-18. From here, we can set up our app and include helpful navigation information and control access

There are controls to choose the app's name, enter a description, create a link to a site where end users can get help or read documentation, determine app navigation settings (I really like the default navigation of the navigation builder so I tend to leave this alone), and set permissions around who can access the app. Is it the entire organization? Is it a specific group of users? Who can access the underlying datasets with build permissions? Can they make copies of reports? Can users share, and finally, should this app be installed automatically? You might want to discuss some of these settings with someone responsible for data governance in your organization, as they may have policies in place that will help guide your decisions.

Conclusion

In this chapter, we started with the navigation of the Power BI service and discussed some of the features for management inside that navigation. We then discussed how to take those datasets and reports we publish and put them in front of other users so that they can share the insights we are gathering.

Next, we're going to discuss some best practices around workspace and app management. We'll also dive into the details around Power BI licensing and when it makes sense to consider Pro versus Premium Per User versus Premium Per Capacity.

CHAPTER 9

Licensing and Deployment Tips

Congratulations! Your report was a huge hit. You took disparate data from different sources, brought that data together, and provided insights from that data that pushed your organization forward. You are keeping your PBIX file up to date, adding new reporting features and measures, and maybe even correcting the odd error or two.

Then you finally experience what every business intelligence professional both hopes for and inevitably dreads. You unlock the imagination of the organization. Now they want you to spread the Power BI gospel across the organization so that other parts of the org can not only leverage what you've built, but also build things for themselves.

First, take a deep breath. Next, let's talk through key questions that will help you put the pieces in place to empower your organization on its larger Power BI journey. What kind of licensing structure should we pursue? What's Pro versus Premium? When does Premium capacity make sense? How do we manage our workspaces and our apps? How do we assign users to roles we created for RLS? How do we make sure our database administrators (DBAs) don't kill us by having a crazy dataset refresh schedule!? Let's talk about it.

Licensing

A *license* itself is a simple idea. It's a purchased agreement that allows you to use a service for as long as you continue to pay for it. Some products have different levels of functionality inside that service, and you may choose to pay for one level of functionality or another. Power BI licensing can be broken into three major categories for most users: Pro, Premium Per User, and Premium Per Capacity.

Pro Licensing

Remember what you get for free. Power BI Desktop is free. Your own private workspace in the Power BI service is free. Your limitation is that you just can't share anything from that workspace. The inability to share can leave some smaller enterprises in a bit of a pinch.

Every user who wants to be able to share their data products in the Power BI service will need a Pro license. In addition, every user who wants to use the data products that have been shared with them will need a Pro license.

Pro licenses, as of the time of writing, for *normal businesses* (those that are not in a government cloud or nonprofits) cost $9.99 per user per month. So, call it $10 per month, or $120 per year per user.

If, in an ideal world, you'd have 10 users and 1 content creator, you're looking at a little over $1,300 for 12 months of coverage. That cost is not insignificant. Certainly many enterprises are looking for ways to cut costs, but Power BI's pricing model, especially for Pro licensing, is very competitive compared to its major competitors like Tableau, Qlik, or Domo.

That doesn't change the fact that it can be tempting to just keep using Excel. Remember that Power BI is more than just an individual component; it's a platform of products built on top of the most powerful analytics engine in the world. Don't undervalue that in your workflow!

If you're in that situation, I recommend doing a real check of who needs to have access to Power BI reporting and, if needed, separate those reporting needs into groups of people who might use department-wide access, if that's feasible based on security needs.

Power BI Pro for *nonprofits* is currently $3 per user per month, a price designed to encourage utilization in that space and help Microsoft look good, for sure.

Power BI allows *individuals* to purchase Power BI Pro licensing. Plus, Power BI gives every user a 60-day free trial at the Premium Per User licensing level, which has all the Pro features. Leveraging that deal might be a way to test who in the organization would most often leverage the Power BI service.

You should be aware of some key restrictions in Power BI Pro licensing:

- Power BI file size limit of 1 GB.
- Eight maximum refreshes for a dataset per day.
- No integration to Azure AI tools.
- No access to deployment pipelines.
- No XML for Analysis (XMLA) endpoint read/write access.

- Total workspace storage cannot exceed 10 GB across all workspaces and cannot exceed the number of Pro licenses times 10 GB.
- Cannot deploy paginated reports.

Premium Per User Licensing

Let's say, for sake of argument, that Pro licensing wouldn't be a problem. In what cases does a Premium Per User licensing scheme make sense? Premium Per User is designed as the middle ground between the Pro licensing and Premium Per Capacity levels. Premium Per User licensing is twice as expensive as Pro licensing.

So, when does Premium Per User make sense? First, do you have a need for any of the items listed in the preceding bullets (that show which features of the Power BI service are limited in a Pro license)? If you do, that's probably a case where Premium Per User makes sense. You can fit a lot of data into a 1 GB size PBIX file.

You may have use cases where that's not enough in a single model. There is a limit of 10 GB for an entire workspace, but most of the time users don't have 10 separate 1 GB files. They usually have a single massive dataset that might be more than 10 GB itself that causes this to be an issue, and this large model support is supported in Premium Per User workspaces.

If you are in a case where DirectQuery can't cut it and you need up to 48 refreshes per day, then Premium Per User is an option there as well.

If you are working in an environment where you have machine learning models in Azure Machine Learning studio or have models running in Azure Cognitive Services and you want to put those results directly into your data model from those services, then, at the least, you'll need a Premium Per User license.

Do you want to use deployment pipelines to manage your PBIX models in a way that's more consistent with continuous integration and continuous deployment (CI/CD) principles? Do you want places to work in development before going to testing and finally production? In this scenario, you would need at least a Premium Per User license.

Do you want outside software to be able to connect to your Power BI data model that you have in service? Do you want to be able to edit a dataset in service without having to mess with a PBIX file? In those cases, you would need XMLA endpoint access, and that can be done with read access or both read and write access. You can't do read and write unless you are in at least a Premium Per User workspace.

If you have paginated reports currently in SQL Server Reporting Services, you can host those reports in the Power BI service. Hosting RDL files requires at least a Premium Per User license.

Here's the catch. If you have a Pro license, you cannot access a Premium Per User workspace. You can't even get around this, for instance, by using an app, because if a given report uses a dataset that is housed in a Premium Per User workspace, that specific report won't work. Microsoft saw that loophole before the release went out. Microsoft does let you add users with Pro licenses to subscriptions, however, so if you have email subscriptions that send a PDF of the report pages, these can be shared with Premium Per User and Pro licensees alike, though they will be static.

Again, in any scenario where you're using Power BI Pro and Premium Per User licenses together in your environment, make sure you ask the right questions to get the users the appropriate licensing based on their needs and to minimize your spending.

Premium Per Capacity, the Big Boy

The final licensing structure I'm going to discuss in this chapter is Power BI Premium dedicated capacity. Premium Per Capacity consists of all the Premium Per User features along with its dedicated compute and dedicated memory. What does that mean? It means the processing cores, the memory, and hard drive space used in the Azure data center are set off to the side and can't be used by anyone but your organization.

Technically, the Power BI service is a generally shared-compute service. That means that Power BI has however many thousands of processors and thousands of GB of RAM that exist in a compute cluster. Therefore, depending on demand in that compute cluster, things can go faster or slower. By pushing your Power BI instance to Premium Per Capacity, you are putting aside Azure resources that cannot be touched by anyone else.

The analogy I like to use when describing this is the difference between a cable modem and fiber optics directly to the home. In a cable modem, your connection goes to a central hub, and all the people who connect to that hub technically share the internet pipe (however large it is) to that hub. When you have fiber directly to your house, it's yours and it belongs to only you. You're not sharing that with anyone else.

Premium Per Capacity comes in different tiers of investment. The licenses for Premium Per Capacity go from P1 to P5. P1 starts at about $5,000 per month. Premium Per Capacity allows you to share Power BI content with anyone, including people not even in your organization, without the need to purchase a user-based license. I would note that your content creators still will need their own separate Pro license.

In addition, Power BI Premium doesn't exclude you from utilizing Power BI's shared capacity with the normal licensing structure. In other words, you can have both Premium Per Capacity workspaces (with all the functionality Premium Per Capacity brings) alongside what I call "regular" workspaces (which users can access with user-based licensing) in your organization's Power BI tenant.

Premium Per Capacity is really designed for enterprise business intelligence at scale. Everything that you can do in a Premium Per User workspace can be done with a Premium Per Capacity workspace. It is also one of the two ways to license Power BI Report Server, which is the analogous on-premises version of the Power BI service.

If you are part of an organization that, for some reason, simply cannot do a cloud-based solution, you can still leverage Power BI and sharing with the assistance of the on-premises product. The other way to license Power BI Report Server is to license SQL Server Enterprise Edition with Software Assurance.

Beyond the Premium Per User workspace, Premium Per Capacity has the following additional features available:

- Ability to share Power BI content with anyone, including people outside your organization if allowed
- Access to Power BI Report Server on premises
- Up to 48 refreshes per day for a given dataset
- 400 GB model size limit (which is *a ton* of data)
- Multigeography deployment for international companies
- Bring your own key (BYOK) functionality
- Autoscale capacity availability
- 100 TB maximum capacity storage

We don't need to go through every feature on this list. For example, if you know you need BYOK functionality, then you already know. But if you don't know what BYOK functionality is, you probably don't need to worry about it.

Is Premium Per Capacity right for you?

The ability to share content with, in theory, an unlimited number of users gives you the opportunity to consider whether Premium Per Capacity makes economic sense. The following is my idea of the formula a nongovernment for-profit organization can use in making such a decision:

Power BI Cost/Month = (Number of Pro License Users × 9.99) + (Number of Premium Per User License Users × 19.99) + Opportunity Cost of Premium Per User Features for Non-Pro users + Opportunity Cost of Premium Per Capacity Features

You'll notice that I hit on opportunity cost twice. The *opportunity cost* is the invisible cost associated with not having access to those features. For instance, what does it cost your organization to *not* be able to manage Power BI datasets with XMLA endpoint connectivity? What does it cost your organization to *not* have multigeographic redundancy management? These are questions I can't answer for you. But your organization should think fully through those opportunity costs before deciding if Power BI Premium is the right choice. You can't do a proper return on investment calculation without thinking through the opportunity costs.

It's not simply about the bill you pay Microsoft. It's about the bill you pay Microsoft, plus the costs of having to manage these opportunity costs.

Small business licensing example

Let's work through this formula for both a small business and a 10,000-employee multinational company.

For the small business, let's say you have 10 users. One is a data scientist who wants to be able to integrate some insights from their Azure Machine Learning model directly into Power BI, and those results need to be seen by 2 of those 10 people.

This means we need seven Pro licenses and three Premium Per User licenses. So, we go through the math here and get something that looks like this. I'm going to round the numbers, for ease of math:

$(7 \times 10) + (3 \times 20)$ + Opportunity Cost for Pro Users Not Having Premium Per User Features + Opportunity Cost for Not Having Premium Per Capacity Features

In this case, let's say that two of those users should also probably have Premium Per User licenses, and the opportunity cost for those users is twice the Premium Per User licensing fee. And our organization isn't large enough to really worry about most of the Premium Per Capacity features, but some governance things would be nice if they were universal, so let's say that is $100 a month.

Now our formula is $(7 \times 10) + (3 \times 20) + (2 \times 40) + 100$ = a bill of $130 from Microsoft for the month and a full cost, including opportunity costs, of $310 per month. You can see that we're nowhere near the point where getting Premium Per Capacity licensing makes sense.

Multinational organization licensing example

Now let's look at our multinational company. Out of 10,000 employees, we believe about 3% would use Power BI in some capacity. Out of those 300 employees, 10% would use Premium Per User capabilities. That means so far, our formula looks something like the following:

$(300 \times 10) + (30 \times 20)$ + Opportunity Cost for Pro Users Not Having Premium Per User Features + Opportunity Cost for Not Having Premium Per Capacity Features

Before we consider opportunity costs, we're at $3,600 for a bill. If our opportunity costs are greater than $1,400, Premium Per Capacity makes sense. We've already identified we're an international company, and assuming some of our users aren't in the same locations, we really should consider multigeographic redundancy and deployment management. Is that worth $1,400 by itself? Probably, in that case. With 300 users, should we have some sort of CI/CD-based deployment strategy to prevent data from being siloed? Maybe leverage deployment pipelines? What if we didn't need the Premium Per Capacity stuff, but just the Premium Per User stuff? Well, 300 users at Premium Per User is $6,000 per month, which is above the $5,000 cost of a P1 capacity node.

Obviously, this is a simplified model framework to help you think about whether Premium Per Capacity makes sense. The difficulty is admittedly in figuring out those organizational opportunity costs. However, if you can think through your use cases as an organization, you can usually come up with a reasonable estimation that will help you fill in the blanks in your organization's calculus.

As a quick overview, Table 9-1 neatly puts together the general features that are available at each licensing tier.

Table 9-1. A comparison of the different levels of Power BI licensing features

Feature	Power BI Pro	Power BI Premium Per User	Power BI Premium Per Capacity
Mobile app access	Y	Y	Y
Paginated reports	N	Y	Y
Unlimited sharing	N	N	Y
Report server license inclusion	N	N	Y
Model size limit	1 GB	100 GB	400 GB
Model refresh limit	8/day	48/day	48/day
Azure ML integration	N	Y	Y
XMLA read/write	N	Optional	Optional
Deployment pipeline	N	Y	Y
Multigeo deployment	N	N	Y
BYOK	N	N	Y
Autoscale functionality	N	N	Available as add-on
Maximum storage	10 GB/user	100 TB	100 TB

Workspace and App Management

Regardless of which licensing structure you decide is best for your organization, you'll need to add users to workspaces and to apps that you create, as well. I will be demonstrating all the functionality here with a Premium Per User license.

Workspace Generation and Access Control

In Chapter 8, we briefly showed the interface for workspaces, but let's go into a little more detail here. There are a couple of ways to access a workspace. From the Home menu screen, Workspaces show up as a type of object that can appear in your Recent list, as shown in Figure 9-1. Also, on the menu on the left, a line divides Learn from the Workspace Management navigation.

If I click the menu arrow next to Workspaces, a second gray vertical box will appear, showing the list of workspaces I have access to, and a "Create a workspace" button will contextually appear, if I have the ability to create one, that is.

The most common scenario where you wouldn't be able to create a workspace would be if you were on Premium Per Capacity and the tenant administrator disabled this functionality.

Second, take a look at the vertical menu arrow on the line beneath that Workspaces line. It shows you the workspace you are currently in, and when you click it, it details all the dashboards, reports, workbooks, and datasets in that workspace. We can see what this looks like in my personal workspace example, shown in Figure 9-1.

Here, you can see that I'm currently in "My workspace" and have a couple of datasets. Along with the details of what's in the workspace shown, there is a scroll bar because you can't see all the objects in the workspace from here.

Another way to see all the elements inside a workspace is to select a workspace on the right side of the menu under Workspaces, as shown in Figure 9-1. That will take you to a workspace landing page that shows all the various data elements stored in that workspace.

Now, we can get into workspace generation. You'll note in my previous example that I don't have a Cool School University workspace. I've been working in my personal workspace on the dataset, as you can see it in the list of objects in Figure 9-1.

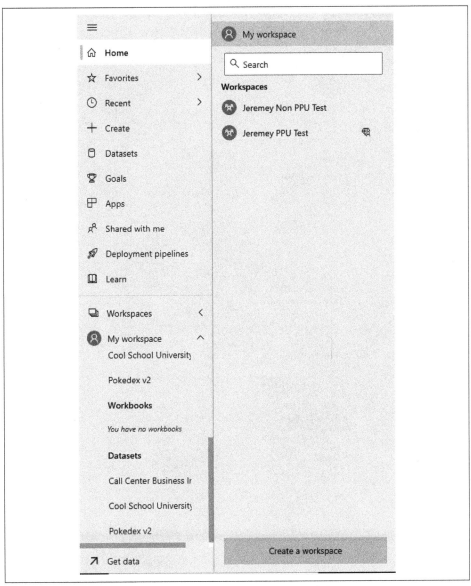

Figure 9-1. Workspace navigation from the main menu in the Power BI service

So, let's create a new workspace using that yellow "Create a workspace" button. When you click that button, a new pane opens on the right side of the screen, detailing the workspace creation options. By default, the advanced options are not shown, so you will need to click the Advanced menu arrow to show these options. We can see this in Figure 9-2.

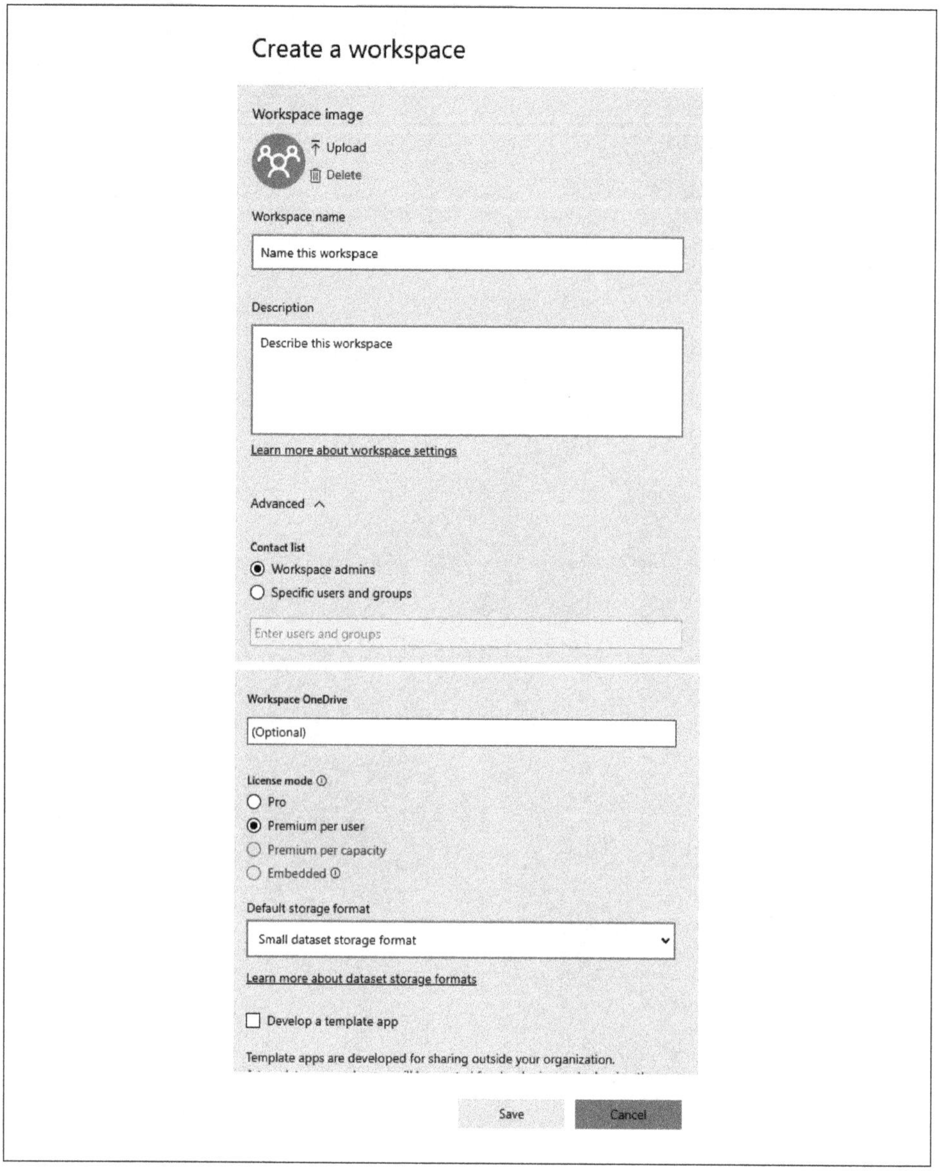

Figure 9-2. Here are all your workspace creation options

In looking at Figure 9-2, going from top to bottom, we can see there's an option to upload an image for the workspace. You can provide a description of the workspace for users.

Then we get to the Advanced settings. First, you choose who is to be contacted with requests for access to a workspace. You can also define a Workspace OneDrive location for file storage, the license mode of the workspace, if the workspace will generate a template app, and finally if contributors can update the app generated from the workspace, if one exists.. Most of the time, workspace administrators will be the people you want notified for access requests. However, in Premium Per Capacity environments, the tenant administrator can exercise greater control over workspaces, and the organization may have all such requests routed to an IT group or tenant administrator in such circumstances.

We can set a OneDrive for Business location, to be used by the workspace as a place to store documents. You can't, however, just use your personal OneDrive. That would be too convenient for private users, wouldn't it, Microsoft? So what you really target here is the Microsoft 365 group's SharePoint document library.

This group should be created outside Power BI first. You can, in fact, create a group like this from OneDrive for Business, but the ability to create Microsoft 365 groups can be restricted in your environment. If it is restricted, reach out to your IT department or SharePoint administrator for additional details on linking OneDrive and your new workspace.

Next, we have the "License mode" selection. For our purposes, this will be the most important selection, since it determines the functionality our workspace will have. In the previous example, I have two options available to me: Pro and Premium Per User. I don't have Premium Per Capacity because that's outside my personal budget.

If you choose Premium Per User or higher, one additional element appears that was not previously there at all, in what can only be considered inconsistent design language. You are asked to choose a default storage format for your datasets. You can choose either the small dataset storage format, which is the default for all Pro workspaces and can't be changed, or the large dataset storage format. If you plan to have data models in excess of 1 GB, make sure you have "Large dataset storage" enabled.

Next, you can choose whether this workspace will be home to a template app. A template app is developed for sharing content outside your organization. If you have a need to develop a template app, I highly recommend beginning with Microsoft's documentation for template apps at "What Are Power BI Template Apps?" (*https:// oreil.ly/I8AT7*).

The final choice is also important if you plan to use elements from this workspace in an app eventually. We will discuss access levels and controls after this, but this question is asking whether someone in a contributor role should be able to edit an app that is powered from this workspace. That is a data governance question for the workspace administrator and/or tenant administrator to answer. In some cases, like in development, you may want to enable that function so that you can make changes quickly. But you may want to turn it off when it goes into everyday production to minimize the number of people who could disrupt operations with accidental edits.

Once everything is filled out, that Save button will turn yellow and the workspace is created. You'll note that Pro workspaces do not have a diamond next to them. Premium Per User and Premium Per Capacity workspaces will always have that diamond next to their names to help users identify the kind of workspace it is.

Managing Users in a Workspace

I've created a Premium Per User workspace titled Cool School University, and now I need to add users to it. From the landing page of any workspace, toward the upper-right corner of the page, are options for View, Filters, Settings, Access, and Search. Access is what we're looking for. When we click that button, a pane similar in form to the Workspace Generation pane slides in from the right, and that's where we can add users. We can see this pane in Figure 9-3.

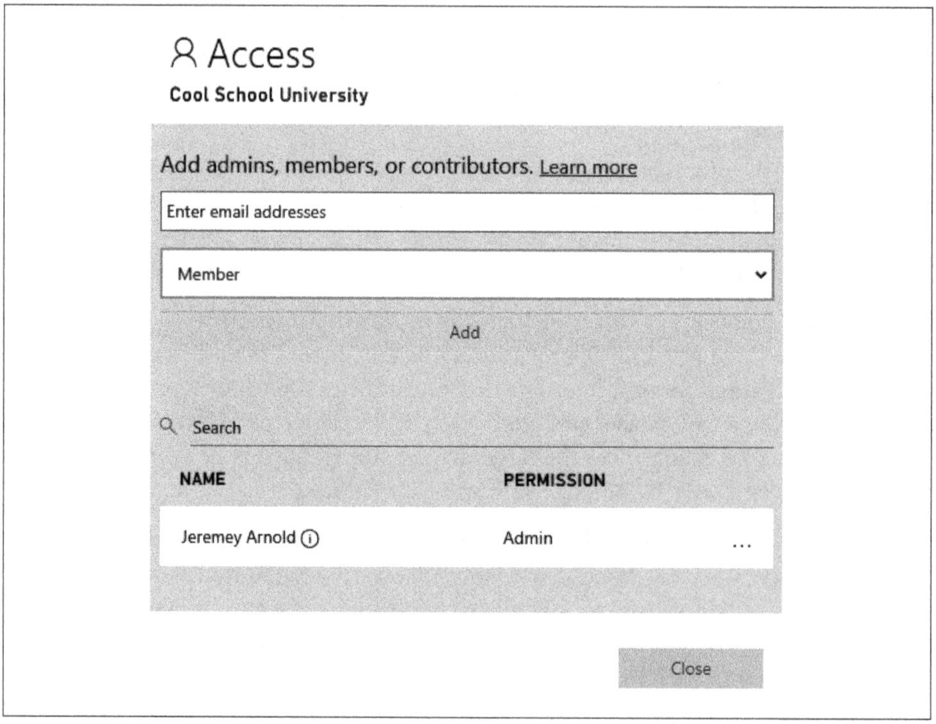

Figure 9-3. The workspace Access control pane

Power BI works very neatly with an organization's active directory instance such that if your organization is using Windows or Azure Active Directory, Power BI can and will search for users as you type their email addresses or Microsoft 365 groups if you have them, as shown in Figure 9-4. Yes, you can add entire groups into a workspace with a couple of clicks.

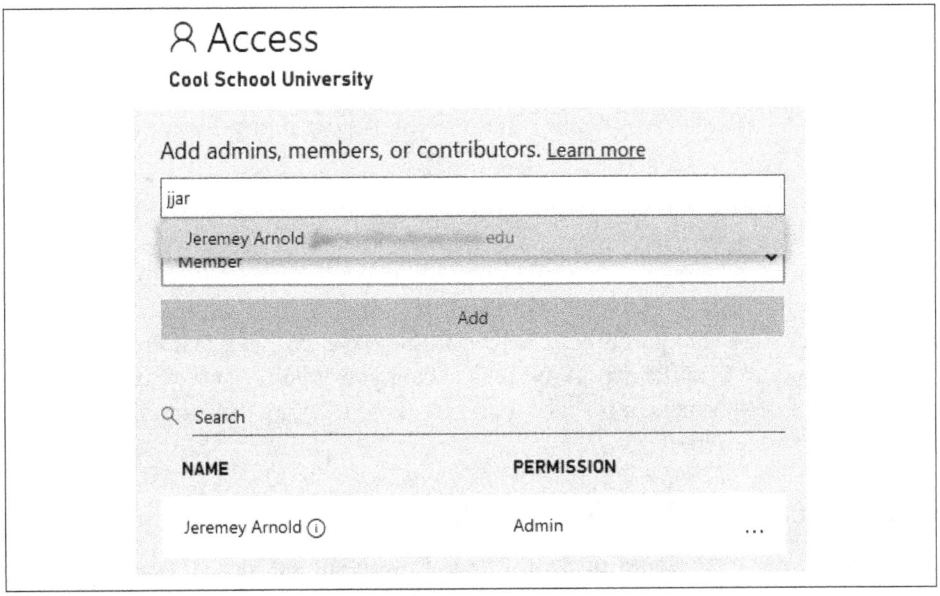

Figure 9-4. Active Directory puts in the work for you by searching for and filling in names or groups as you begin to type them

You can also add multiple people at once by typing multiple emails. Notice that line beneath the email address? That's where we determine the level of access to the workspace a user will have. Four roles can be assigned to users in a workspace: Admin, Member, Contributor, or Viewer. These roles are hierarchal in nature, so someone in a lower role can't affect the user access of someone in a higher role. For instance, a Member can't kick out or remove an Admin from a workspace, but the Admin can kick out the Member. Only Admins can remove other Admins.

Admins and Members can do things that either impact users in a workspace or modify workspace elements that are used outside the workspace. Contributors can work on things inside of the workspace but generally don't have the ability to interact with the way external viewers interact with workspace data elements. Viewers can only see objects in a workspace and cannot make any edits to any objects in the workspace.

My advice when managing workspaces is to have at least one service account, an account that does not belong to a user, but to the organization at large and for whom the credentials are owned by a limited number of people. This service account should be included as an Admin in all workspaces, even if it's not generally used. If for some reason the only Admin of a workspace left the organization, you would have to go through the Power BI Admin API at that point to promote a new Admin to the workspace. I think that's a bit annoying.

However, your organization may have data governance protocols that will help you determine the best course of action for you and your organization in this regard. The most important thing is to have some way or method in place so that, if necessary, you can regain control of a workspace in the event of a personnel disruption.

With that wonderful segue, let's quickly discuss how you remove a user or change their role in a workspace. In Figure 9-5, to the right of the listed permission, you see an ellipsis, three dots. Click that, as a button, and a small pop-up appears that will show a list of roles you can reassign to a user. At the bottom of that list, you'll see Remove. If you click Remove, they're gone. If you click another role, that user is moved to that role. That part is easy, maybe a little too easy, given that Power BI does not even bring up a confirmation message asking you if you're sure you want to do this. However, if you make a mistake, you can easily fix it, as you can see from how easy as it is to add users.

Adding Users to Roles for RLS Implementation

You have your workspace set up with the users who should have access. Now you need to add them to RLS for each dataset in the workspace that has different roles defined. This is pretty simple to do, as the hard work is really in defining the roles in the first place, as we discussed earlier in this book.

From a workspace's landing page, hover over the dataset you want to add users or groups to for RLS until you see a vertical three-dot ellipsis menu appear next to the dataset name.

Click the ellipses and go to Security. When you do that, if you have roles defined for your Power BI dataset, you'll see the list of roles and the current members of those roles in the dataset. You can add users or Microsoft 365 groups.

One thing to remember, if a user belongs to more than one group, Power BI will treat them as though they have full access to whatever combination of data would be present in between the multitude of roles, much like a SQL outer join.

Figure 9-5 shows the simple RLS user addition interface, and just as with adding users for the workspace, Power BI will attempt to find users as you type in the appropriate email or group name.

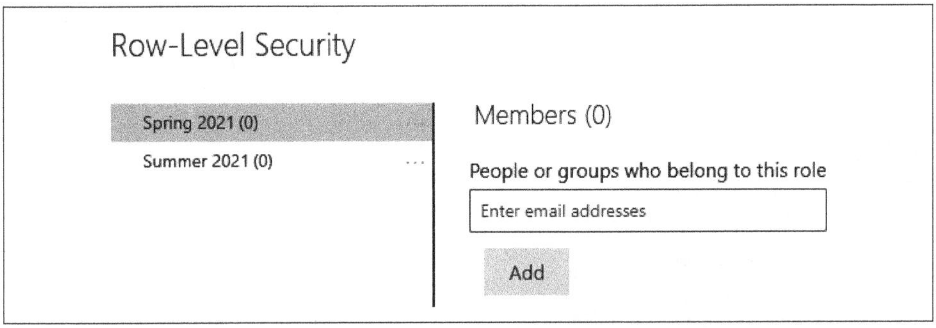

Figure 9-5. Get those users in the roles they belong by assigning RLS

App Creation and Management

At some point, you may want a way for users to interact with your data elements that you've created without adding them to the workspace directly. You can do this by adding them to an app that is powered by a workspace.

From our workspace landing page, a big, yellow "Create app" button is in the upper-right corner. Let's start there and see what we get in Figure 9-6.

Here, in this first Setup page, we have several options. We name our app and provide a description, and we can provide a link to a support or documentation website where users can get help with using the app, provide a logo for our app, pick the app's theme color, and finally we can show contact information for who should be contacted about access to the app. This should all feel familiar at this point, as this is in line with our workspace creation experience.

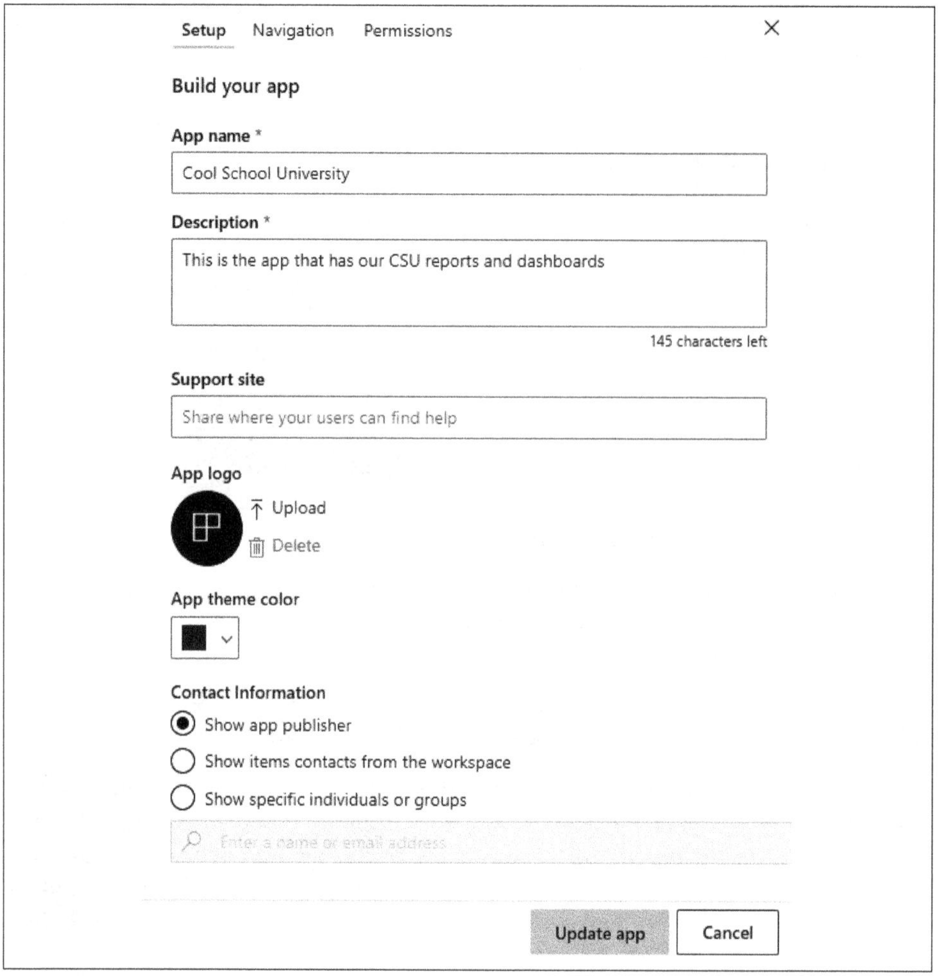

Figure 9-6. The birth of an app starts with the "Create app" button. Some might call this app setup.

However, you'll see some other items we should manage before clicking that "Publish app" button. Next to Setup, we have Navigation and Permissions. Let's tackle those in order, starting with Navigation, as seen in Figure 9-7.

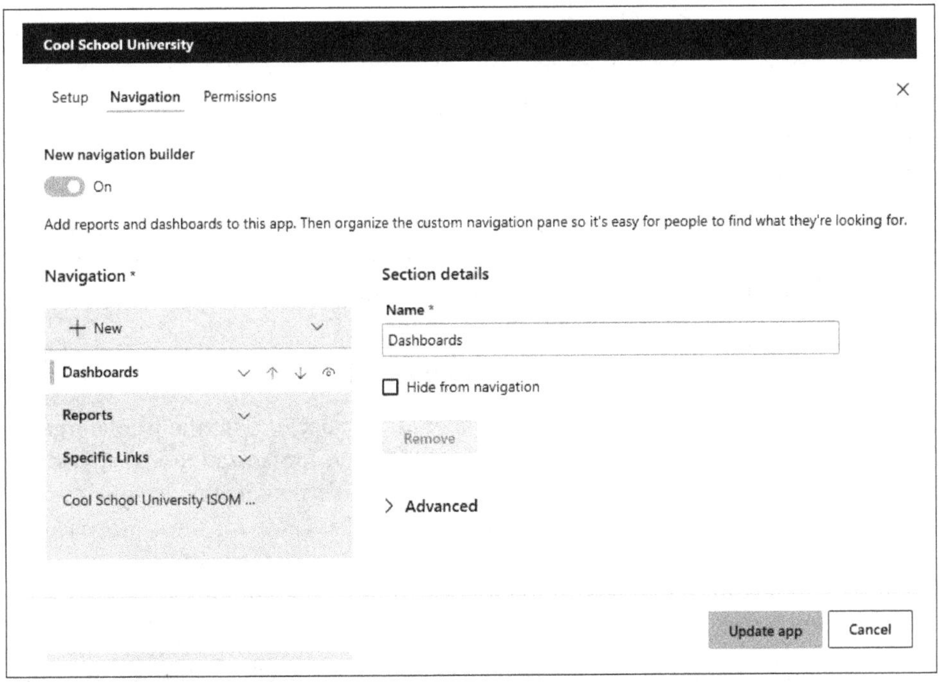

Figure 9-7. Help users help themselves with good navigation

The first thing we see is a on/off toggle to let us choose whether we want to use the New navigation builder. At some point, the old option, I imagine, will just go away; if you are starting new with apps, provide your users a consistent experience and just leave this setting alone.

In an app, we do not include any of the underlying core data, only the data products. We don't include datasets or dataflows in an app, for example, but we do include reports and dashboards.

You will see on the Navigation pane on the left that all the dashboards and reports that exist in the workspace are put into the app by default. In this case, I have a generic dashboard that was created when I uploaded my PBIX file, and I have the actual report itself. The gray menu on the left that shows what those elements are. You don't really *remove* items from an app so much as you *hide* them. You can hide items that you don't want included by clicking the little eye next to the up and down arrows. If it has a line through the eye, it will be hidden.

Navigation becomes useful when you click that +New button and can either add a section or a link. A *section* is like a display folder. You cannot have a multilevel folder structure—no folders within folders here. A *link* gives you the ability to define a link to a web page, either in Power BI or not, and what the browser behavior should be to open it.

When you create a section, the area on the right in Figure 9-7 will give you places to name the section and give you the opportunity to hide the section from navigation.

When you create a link, you name the app element, provide the URL for the link, determine how that link should be opened when selected, and then choose a group for the element to fit in for navigation.

OK, so at this point, you have your navigation set up all nice and neat. Now you need to figure out who should be able to access the app *and* what underlying permissions are granted by having access to the app and the datasets that power the app behind the scenes. That's a lot to take in, so take a moment.

We can see the Permissions window in Figure 9-8.

As you can see, first you must decide who should have access. Is it the whole organization? Is it specific individuals and/or groups in the organization? In this case, *groups* refer to Microsoft 365 groups. Power BI also notes that anyone who has access to the workspace will have access to the app. That makes sense for the same reason a workspace Admin isn't affected by RLS. A workspace administrator can just go download the PBIX. Anyone who has access to the workspace could just go to the workspace and see the material.

Next, we choose whether people who have access to the app will be able to connect to the underlying dataset and if they'll be able to make copies of the reports in the application in their own workspaces. These two selections are hierarchical. If you don't have access to the app's underlying datasets, you can't copy reports. But having access to the datasets doesn't mean you can copy reports. One is necessary, but not sufficient.

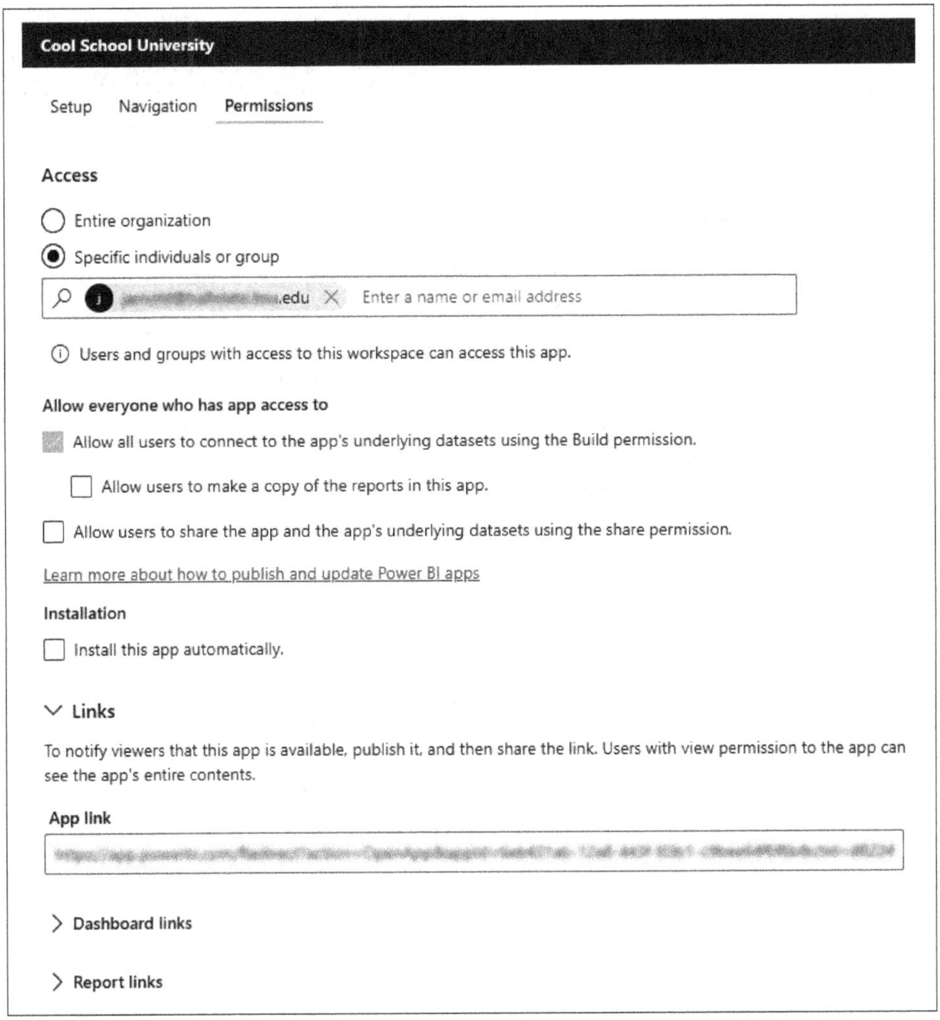

Figure 9-8. The Permissions window marks the last step before publishing

Next, we must choose whether we want users to be able to share the app and the app's underlying datasets with the share permission. It's odd to me that this also isn't hierarchical. Generally speaking, I leave this option off and try to have a location where users can request access to the app from the team that owns the app, as opposed to things being shared with no guardrails.

Finally, there's a link to extra Microsoft documentation and a choice of whether this app installs automatically for users who would have access to it. I don't mind having automatic installation turned on, as that can be really convenient for end users.

After this, we can publish the app! The app will usually take between 5 and 10 minutes to get packaged, and then it will appear in the Apps section in the Power BI Navigation menu. If you need to update the app, come back into the workspace that hosts the app, and you'll see that "Create app" button has changed to "Update app." That's it. You now have an app!

The Golden Dataset(s)

At some point, as you manage your Power BI deployment, you are going to accumulate a lot of data elements. As those data elements increase, you have computational concerns. If you are in a world where every report is powered by its own dataset and each of those datasets is refreshing, that's a lot of moving parts!

Heaven forbid you have that many datasets refreshing against enterprise databases...because if those datasets are of any size at all, you might give your poor DBA an actual heart attack! How much of the data between those datasets is replicated for no reason?

These are questions that, when the Power BI service really came into its own, a lot of analysts who were using Power BI and pushing this space forward didn't have really good answers to. But we have a thousand Excel workbooks floating around, so why is this any different?

The problem is that, at some point, data elements become mission critical. We need to manage them like mission-critical assets. So, to look at how we needed to manage this problem, we needed to go back into Power BI's past and remember what it is under the hood. It's Analysis Services. How would we manage an enterprise-wide Analysis Services deployment? We would create a core master dataset or a small number of datasets that we could manage. Doing that would minimize the computational burden on other parts of our data pipeline.

We can do the same thing with Power BI by creating that master dataset, or golden dataset, or whatever you want to call it. The fewer times we can make big data requests of our databases, the better off we are. The fewer places we must manage RLS, the easier it is to manage. The fewer datasets we must manage, the more we can feel comfortable pushing out our best data elements in front of our data consumers, knowing there's a higher chance of being able to answer the questions users want to ask. We do that by making the data easier to find.

Does this mean you must have one dataset to rule them all? Not necessarily. You could certainly organize data into a data-mart-type structure, creating a small number of datasets that are highly curated to answer specific types of questions but are still reusable data elements.

A good example of this goes back to RLS. In a Power BI dataset, you establish the roles that exist and define those roles in DAX. If you have three similar datasets, that means you have to manage those roles in three different locations; you have to remember to go into Power BI service, find the dataset in the Workspace landing page, hover over the dataset until the ellipses menu pops up, click that, go into security, and make sure to include the people or groups into those roles you've defined. What happens when you forget to do it once and one of the datasets isn't updated? That means someone sees data they shouldn't.

You could definitely see this being a larger issue in, say, a Premium Per Capacity environment where you might have hundreds or even thousands of report viewers who could be in dozens of groups for which you're trying to manage access.

Does this mean that when your organization gets large enough, you should stop considering Power BI for ad hoc spontaneous analysis? Of course not! Hopefully, you'll be able to leverage your dataset, or small numbers of datasets, to get to the answers you want to find more quickly. However, sometimes you have to go outside the box to look for data.

Microsoft recommends in large Premium Per Capacity environments that customers split their business-mission-critical capacity from their ad hoc exploratory capacity. I think this is a good idea and easy enough to do with workspace management, even in nonpremium environments.

Encourage your users to connect to datasets in the Power BI service as data sources in Power BI Desktop when they start building reports of their own. This will reduce dataset bloat. I have seen too many organizations with dataset bloat decide that Power BI was just too complicated of a tool to use. It's because they didn't have good governance practices in place and eventually got to a point where users lost track of all the resources they had available.

Conclusion

If you've gotten this far, I genuinely hope that this text has helped you feel more confident in your use of Power BI Desktop and, in these recent chapters, the Power BI service. We've discussed licensing, workspace management, app management, and general deployment strategy to help you stay in front of problems.

In our tenth and final chapter, I'd like to expose you to some third-party tools in the Power BI ecosystem. These tools will be helpful when you try to troubleshoot issues and speed up development. Hopefully, they'll give you a leg up on your Power BI development and management journey.

CHAPTER 10

Third-Party Tools

To this point, everything that has been discussed in this book has been relevant to a specific part of the Microsoft Power BI ecosystem, usually Power BI Desktop or the Power BI service. Now we're going to step outside that realm.

As you grow in your Power BI skill set or come across new development requirements, you might eventually find some parts of Power BI that aren't as easy to manage as you'd like. Things like exporting data from Power BI aren't as straightforward as they could or maybe should be. Version control has always involved tedious PBIX files, and while Microsoft may have better internal solutions in the future, it too is currently not as easy as it should be. At some point, you may want a little more granular control over where you put your measures when they're created, or you may want to have them automatically generate in the display folder you've created for them.

The purpose of this chapter is to tell you about some great options that will improve your use of Power BI. Power BI is really a great ecosystem, but no software or service is perfect. Thankfully, independent developers inside the Power BI community have gone above and beyond to create completely free tools that can provide very real quality-of-life benefits in your Power BI journey. There's software to streamline your development experience, manage data models, help with version control, format your DAX properly, and more.

In this chapter, I'm going to highlight some of the most popular external tools used by the Power BI community. I'll give you a brief overview of their functionality and discuss ways you can use them. I don't plan to give exhaustive explanations for every tool. My purpose is just to get you started in learning how to use them in your workflow. You'll be glad you read this final chapter.

Just think, soon you will graduate from Cool School University and make me so proud. But let's keep working for now.

Get to Know Business Ops

For most tools, you can try to find each individual piece or extension, download that extension, install it individually, and manage stuff. I'm lazy and don't mind admitting it. With that in mind, *PowerBI.tips* makes an external tool manager called Business Ops that is completely free to download (*https://oreil.ly/tP7Rr*).

This site does all the hard work of collecting a ton of third-party tools, bringing them into one place, and allowing you to quickly install and configure the ones you are interested in. It's consistently updated when newer versions of the external tools it links to are also updated. This is important in helping you stay current as development improvements are made to those other external tools we'll talk about later in the chapter.

The download itself comes as a ZIP file, with the installer located inside the ZIP file. Once the installation is complete, you'll see an interface like the one shown in Figure 10-1. On the Home landing page, you can see the release notes for the version of Business Ops you've installed. The code is completely open source, so if you want to go to its Git repositories, you can.

Business Ops will allow you to install a ton of Power BI add-ons, easily access learning tools, create Power BI themes, use a gallery for custom visualizations outside of AppSource, and find links to some of the best DAX resources on the planet.

Figure 10-1. Business Ops will save you time in installation and management of your Power BI external tools

Add External Tools, Remove External Tools, and Modify Display Order

From here, we can go to Add External Tools to see the list of external tools that Business Ops has curated, then get those packages added so that Power BI recognizes them as external tools. You do this via a very simple checkbox interface, as shown in Figure 10-2. This page is quite long, and while the scroll bar on the right side of the application isn't the easiest to see, I promise you it's there. I personally like to navigate this with my mouse scroll wheel.

This chapter focuses on the ALM Toolkit, Tabular Editor, DAX Studio, and Bravo. When you have all the tools you want to add, click the blue "Add External Tools" button in the bottom-right corner and let Business Ops take care of the rest.

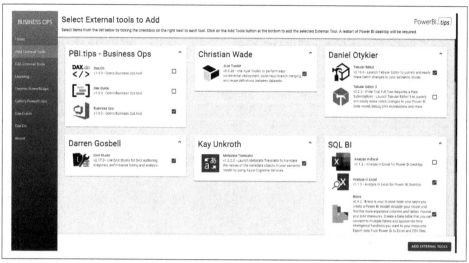

Figure 10-2. Tool installation is so easy with Business Ops

One inconvenient aspect is that the software add-ons, like the ones we are discussing, get installed into the same folder where the Business Ops software is installed. Business Ops also won't make separate entries in your Start menu for these software installations, which is different than if you installed them manually from their individual installers.

I get around this by opening a blank Power BI file after the external tools are added and using those external tools to force open those pieces of software. Then, in the Windows taskbar, right-click and select Pin to Taskbar.

If you want to create individual shortcuts for your desktop, go into Windows Explorer, navigate to the software inside the Business Ops directory, and make a shortcut to the software, as you would normally in Windows.

Under the Edit External Tools section, you can modify the relative order in which the tools appear in the External Tools part of the ribbon in Power BI Desktop. You can also remove components from the list altogether.

When you install external tools, a JSON file is generated for each tool. Clicking the pencil icon allows you to modify the filename. The tools in Power BI Desktop are shown in alphabetical order, left to right. By default, each JSON file starts with a three-digit code that sets the initial order.

In Figure 10-3, I've modified five of the items to have five-digit codes and gave them numbers that will put them in front. I give the ones I edited five digits so that I know I've edited them. By giving them five digits, assuming the first three are zeros, they will always appear before the first autogenerated three-digit code.

You can also remove items from your External Tools list if they were installed via this software. Do this by clicking the trash can next to the pencil/Edit button. If you remove something by accident, you can go back to Add External Tools, and everything you already have there will be grayed out. You can just select the tool you want to recover and add it again.

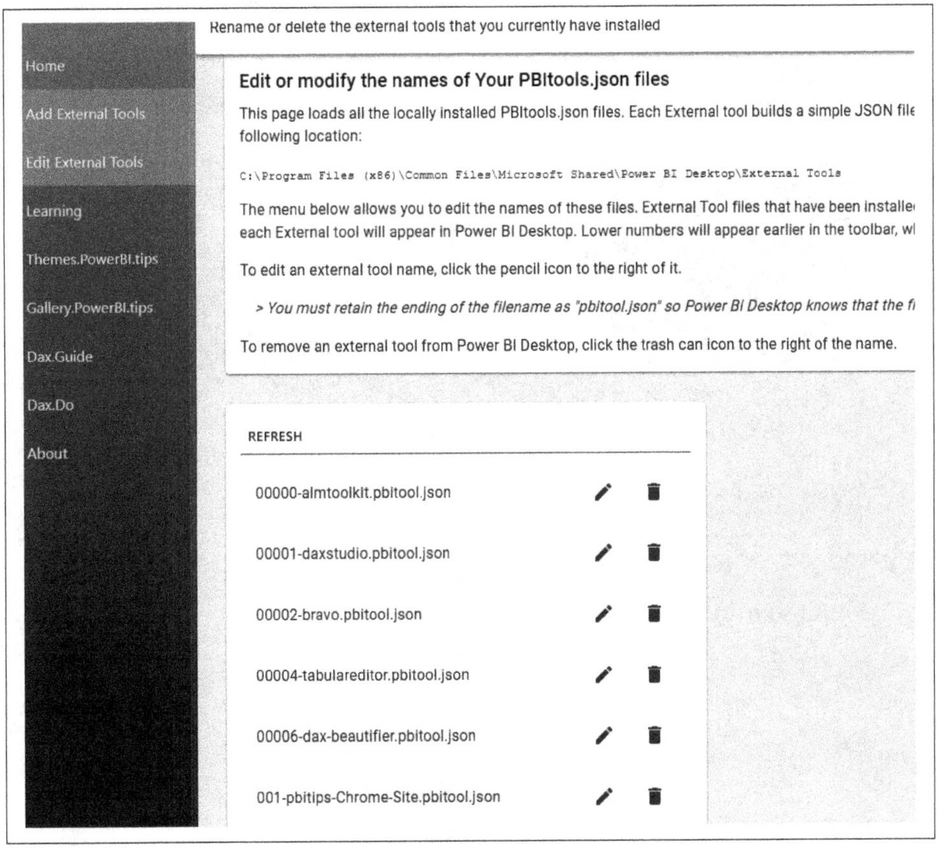

Rename or delete the external tools that you currently have installed

Edit or modify the names of Your PBItools.json files

This page loads all the locally installed PBItools.json files. Each External tool builds a simple JSON file following location:

`C:\Program Files (x86)\Common Files\Microsoft Shared\Power BI Desktop\External Tools`

The menu below allows you to edit the names of these files. External Tool files that have been installed each External tool will appear in Power BI Desktop. Lower numbers will appear earlier in the toolbar, wl

To edit an external tool name, click the pencil icon to the right of it.

> You must retain the ending of the filename as "pbitool.json" so Power BI Desktop knows that the fi

To remove an external tool from Power BI Desktop, click the trash can icon to the right of the name.

Home
Add External Tools
Edit External Tools
Learning
Themes.PowerBI.tips
Gallery.PowerBI.tips
Dax.Guide
Dax.Do
About

REFRESH

00000-almtoolkit.pbitool.json

00001-daxstudio.pbitool.json

00002-bravo.pbitool.json

00004-tabulareditor.pbitool.json

00006-dax-beautifier.pbitool.json

001-pbitips-Chrome-Site.pbitool.json

Figure 10-3. Removing tools and managing their order is simple

Learning, Theme Generation, Visual Generation

The Learning section has additional resources about topics we touched on briefly earlier in this book, like "Quick measures" and some things that we touch on later in this chapter and in Appendix B. The Learning section also contains links to documentation and training videos for the additional external tools we'll discuss later in the chapter.

The custom theme generator is incredible! You can put together a theme of colors and custom visual settings that you can set at the global or individual visual level. Then you can import it as a custom theme in Power BI Desktop.

This function will also give you the hex codes for all the colors you choose so that you have those for future reference. Let's first look at the color palette generator in Figure 10-4.

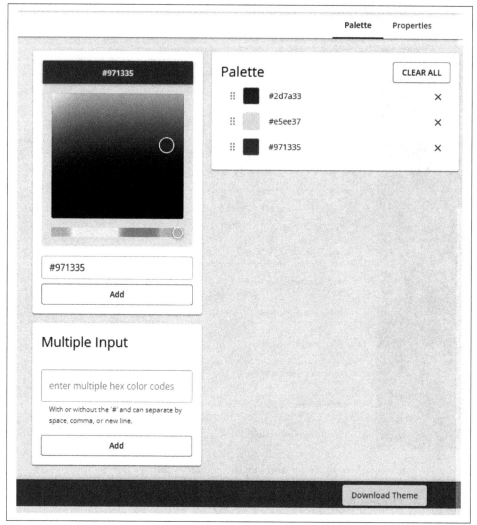

Figure 10-4. The palette generator offers a quick and easy way to pick colors for your reports

On the left, you see a color sliding scale that allows you to go from red all the way to violet and then back again to red in the red, orange, yellow, green, blue, indigo, violet color order. At any point on that bar, the square for the selected color range will show you a variety of lighter and darker shades to pick from, along with the hex code for the currently selected color. If you happen to already know your hex codes, like if your marketing department gave you your organization's hex-code color scheme, you can enter those codes directly in the input section at the bottom.

In Figure 10-5, we can look to add preselected formatting options on either a global or visual-by-visual basis as a part of our custom theme.

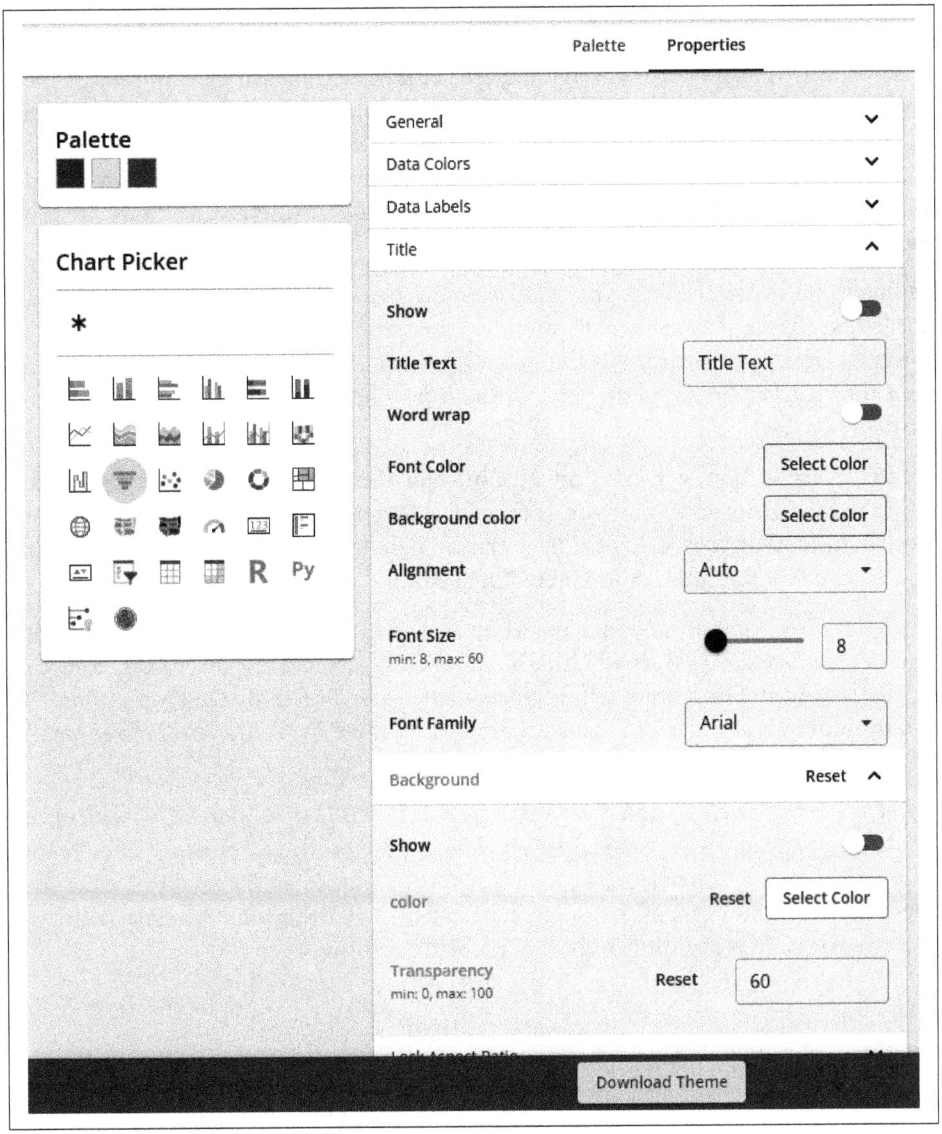

Figure 10-5. Custom themes add a whole new level of visual control to Power BI

Here you can see that the colors I chose previously from Figure 10-4 are still present. In this case, I have the funnel chart selected, and you can see the variety of formatting options I have on the right. For any value you've modified, the text of that category and the changed options in that category will display in blue text.

In this exercise, I've modified the background portion of the formatting options by specifically changing the background color and the transparency level. The * in the Chart Picker will apply changes made there to all the visuals where applicable. When you have your colors and your custom formatting the way you want them, you can download the theme as a JSON file and import the theme into your report in Power BI Desktop. Do this by going to the View portion of the ribbon and, in the Themes drop-down, select "Browse for themes." You'll navigate to where your JSON file is on your computer, select it, and that's it!

It's important to know that if you make changes to a visual's base formatting options at the theme level, they can still be modified as an individual visual on your canvas in Power BI Desktop. This is more about accelerating a change when you know how you want the visual to behave a majority of the time when it's different from the default formatting preset.

In the Gallery section, you can find a list of color themes that have already been generated in the Palette section. If you click a color theme in this portion, it will bring up a small example Power BI Report page that will show you what the theme looks like against visuals. I find this feature incredibly helpful.

The Charts section shows you a list of custom visuals that have been created with Charticulator, a do-it-yourself visual creation tool created by Microsoft. You can download and import these custom visuals into your Power BI Desktop report. Do this by adding it as a custom visual by importing the PBVIZ file. We can see this in Figure 10-6.

The Create My Own option will open a fully functional version of Charticulator inside the application. Note that this is technically a *fork* (or a copy of the code repository) of Microsoft Charticulator, as Microsoft has made some small UI edits. But anything you build in this version of Charticulator will behave in the exact same way as if you had built it by going to the Charticulator website.

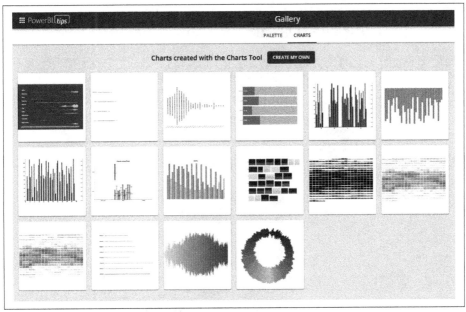

Figure 10-6. Some additional custom visuals and a direct route to Charticulator

Additional DAX Resources

Business Ops links directly to two additional fantastic DAX resources, DAX Guide and DAX.do, both courtesy of the folks at SQLBI.

DAX Guide provides a list of every DAX function and includes its syntax, the kind of values that function returns, real coding examples written with DAX best practices, and, for many functions, a YouTube video in the upper-right corner that has even more details on the function in a friendly video format.

On the home page of DAX Guide, as shown in Figure 10-7, we can select a specific group of functions to look at or learn about the most recent DAX functions that were released and when. As someone who works with DAX in more contexts than just Power BI, the ability on the left to see which products a particular DAX function will work in is a lifesaver!

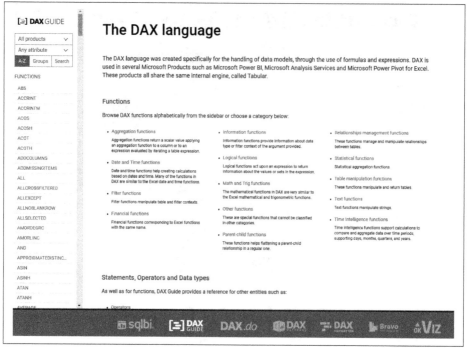

Figure 10-7. DAX Guide is an amazing combination of knowledge accessibility and real-world examples

DAX.do, on the other hand, is a full-featured DAX playground that allows you to manipulate and move around certain elements to fit your preferred testing style. The playground comes with two data models that you can switch between, Contoso and the DAX Guide models. DAX.do has drag-and-drop functionality from the column list. It identifies which functions you are trying to use and will show you a drop-down list of those functions to bring up their DAX Guide pages. You can see your results, and when you write a query with an error, you'll get an appropriate error message.

Figure 10-8 shows DAX.do and its component parts. DAX Guide and DAX.do have their own websites, so if you would rather engage these tools from a browser, you can.

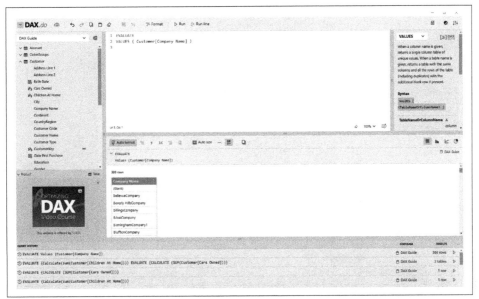

Figure 10-8. Premade documented data models where I can practice DAX? Sign me up!

With Business Ops giving us access to a wide range of third-party tools, I want to highlight some of the most useful ones in the next section. In particular, I'll cover a DAX editor, a dataset editor, and a tool for reviewing dataset health and easy measure generation. First, let's talk about DAX Studio, the preeminent DAX querying tool.

DAX Studio

DAX Studio is a SQL Server Analysis Services–based (SSAS) tabular model query tool. It allows you to write DAX queries against a data model and get results. When it is opened directly from the External Tools portion of Power BI Desktop, it will automatically connect to the Power BI dataset it was launched from. You can also use this to query datasets that are in the Power BI service if you have the XMLA endpoint enabled to do so. Let's look at the interface in Figure 10-9 and discuss what is available.

We won't go over every option here, but there are a couple key things to find. First is the large Query window in the center of the screen. That's where you write DAX and get results back. At the bottom, you can see the results that were returned. On the left, you see my list of tables and columns, along with any display folders I have.

Along the top of the ribbon are options to run a query you write, cancel the query that's being evaluated, clear the in-memory cache, and determine an output format for your results.

Figure 10-9. DAX Studio is more than a simple querying tool, as you can see from its interface

I'll skip over the Query Builder for a moment, and you can see that classic clipboard functions are made explicit in this ribbon. There is a DAX format option. If you attempt to format a DAX statement that is invalid, it will display a very lengthy complaint in the results window.

You can make things uppercase, lowercase, comment something out, uncomment something back in, and swap the delimiters to use either commas or semicolons. Merge XML is useful if you plan to use DAX parameters while querying, but it is not something I find myself using very often. Find and Replace are self-explanatory.

The Trace functionality is awesome and will be incredibly useful when you start to investigate why specific DAX queries might be taking longer than you'd expect. Is that visual taking longer than it used to? Use the Performance analyzer, get the query run by Power BI Desktop, copy it into DAX Studio, clear your in-memory cache, turn on Query Plan and Server Timings, and look to see if specific portions of the query are taking longer than others. Make sure you clear your cache before each run-through, as once the results have been run, that query pattern is placed into memory, which will speed it up.

You can see along the bottom, beneath the query results, a list of tabs showing Output, Results, Query History, All Queries, Query Plan, and Server Timings. The latter three tabs will appear only if you have the trace options selected in the ribbon.

All Queries cannot be enabled if Query Plan or Server Timings are enabled. All Queries can be useful when you want to know how many queries are being generated to get to a specific result.

My personal favorite function in DAX Studio is the Query Builder. In fact, the query shown in Figure 10-9 was generated by the Query Builder. I've been working on an NBA dataset recently and wanted to know, in this case, how many regular season games and how many points my favorite player of all time, Reggie Miller, scored in the regular season for each season he played.

You can see in Figure 10-10 that you can put columns and measures in the top portion of the Query Builder, and in the bottom half you can choose columns to filter by and the filter conditions. A section toward the bottom is for ordering the results.

As you bring in elements into the relevant areas, you can click Edit Query to generate the query in the Query window for you to view. This is a couple of great uses. Let's say you have a dataset in service, and an end user wants to extract a very specific collection of data. They could use DAX Studio, connect to the dataset in service, and use this Query Builder to get back the information they're looking for.

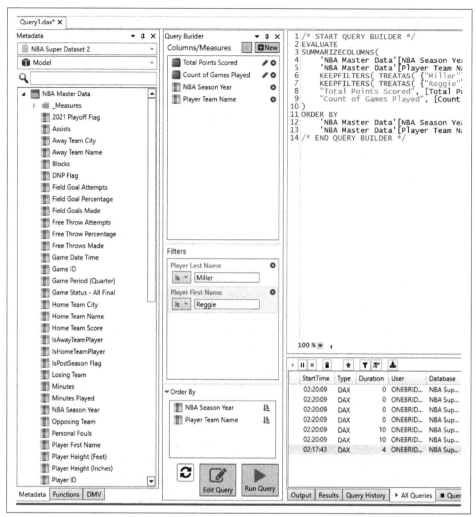

Figure 10-10. The Query Builder is totally a cheat mode, and I love it

Another cool use I've found is that this feature is great for DAX practice, especially with table functions. Often in Power BI we create measures designed to get specific values, but we don't necessarily work with the functions that return a table as its product. This gives us an opportunity to work with some of those functions in a way that doesn't impact our dataset itself. It also allows us to make manual edits and see what happens. It's a great learning tool in that regard.

Tabular Editor

Before I say anything about Tabular Editor, it's important to note there are two distinct versions of Tabular Editor, called Tabular Editor 2 and Tabular Editor 3. *Tabular Editor 2* is the original, open source solution that was developed. The same people who built Tabular Editor 2 built *Tabular Editor 3*, adding a lot of quality-of-life functionality, a nicer user interface, and some other things.

I'll be discussing Tabular Editor 2, which is the free, open source version. Currently there is no functionality in Tabular Editor 3 that can't be done in Tabular Editor 2, but it just might require some extra work.

As with DAX Studio, when we access Tabular Editor from the External Tools list, it will automatically connect to the Power BI data model that we have running. Tabular Editor is a no-frills, simple-to-use editor for any SSAS tabular model, just like the one that Power BI data models are built on top of. Let's take a look at the interface in Figure 10-11.

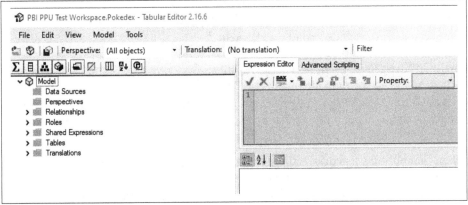

Figure 10-11. The no-fuss, no-muss layout of the free, open source Tabular Editor 2

At the top, we can see the classic Windows menu navigation: File, Edit, View, Model, and Tools. Beneath that we see three symbols. The first is an open folder that will allow you to open the files that Tabular Editor creates when you save a copy of the model metadata in Tabular Editor, which is a BIM file. These BIM files are basically a very large XML file, and some organizations manage their Power BI datasets entirely in Tabular Editor using BIM files. These can be source controlled, put into repositories, and are very small-sized files compared to their PBIX alternatives.

Next to that is an image of a transparent cube. This brings up the dialog box in Figure 10-12. In the Server section, we could put any analysis services database we have access to in the server address. This includes datasets currently in the Power BI service if you have XMLA read abilities enabled. Remember, this does require at least

Premium Per User licensing. If you have a Power BI dataset currently open in Power BI Desktop, you can choose one of those to connect to with the "Local instance" selector. In either case, you can choose whether you use Windows or Azure single-sign-on credentials or, if you need to pass a specific set of credentials, you can identify those credentials by choosing Username and Password and providing the appropriate information.

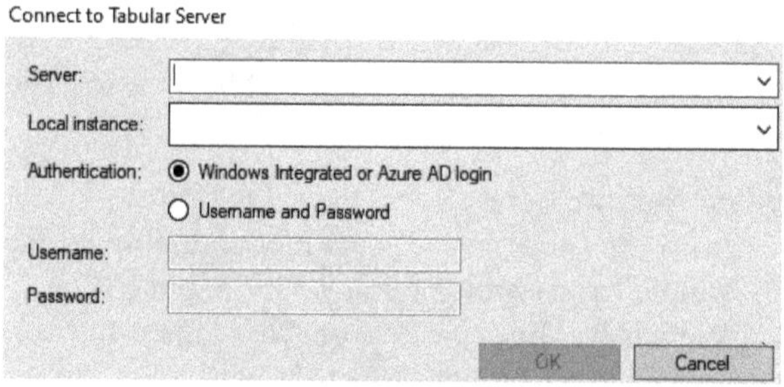

Figure 10-12. This dialog box pops up if you click the transparent cube in Tabular Editor 2. If you need to connect to a dataset in the Power BI service or an SSAS Tabular instance somewhere else, this can be a way to do it.

Finally in that group, we have what looks like a disk save icon. When this button is clicked, all the edits you made in Tabular Editor will be saved back to the database it's connected to. If that's your Power BI data model, all the measures you add, remove, or edit are going to get pushed all at once. You added some new relationships? Those will get added, too. Did you create new roles? You get the idea.

When that button gets clicked, the state of Tabular Editor will be pushed back to the system it's editing. Before you make changes to a Power BI dataset, whether that's locally or in service, make sure you have a backup. Have a Power BI Template (PBIT) file or a BIM file set to the side in case you make a mistake and need to roll back to a previous state because you modified something you didn't mean to change.

This does, however, come with an advantage. Let's say you want to create many measures for your data model. In Power BI Desktop, you must create them one at a time. Sometimes the interface is a little slow. You create the measure, but there's an error in the DAX, and you must go fix it. When the measure is ready, you want to add it to your display folder for organizational purposes, but you must do that one at a time too. That's a pain. Tabular Editor allows you to push multiple modifications to the data model at once. And while you're working on stuff, it doesn't affect the data model until the changes are saved.

Some things have a bit higher of a learning curve in Tabular Editor than they do in Power BI Desktop, though. As a result, I recommend a hybrid approach to using Tabular Editor until you feel more comfortable with the details that are needed to create many of these elements outside of Power BI Desktop.

On the Model Navigation pane on the left, you can see all the details of your model, and we can see that interface in Figure 10-13.

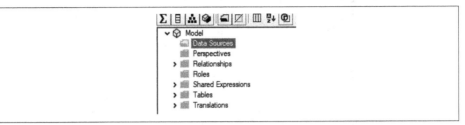

Figure 10-13. The underlying elements of the data model are shown in the Model Navigation pane

For any dataset that originates from Power BI Desktop, you won't be able to modify or even see the Data Sources. Perspectives have a very limited use case in Power BI, where they can be used with individual visuals if the Personalize Visuals option is turned on. Otherwise, they do nothing. You can create them, and they can exist in the data model, but Power BI doesn't support their functionality beyond the scope listed previously.

Basically, anytime you want to create a new element related to a portion of the data model, you right-click that element, and you'll see a contextual menu appear. I try to avoid managing relationships in Tabular Editor because I prefer a more visual way to see how all the tables fit together. However, you can create new relationships here if you like. If you're building a data model from scratch, you'll want to get used to this.

With Tabular Editor, we can also manage roles for RLS, and we can add measures, display folders, and other calculated items. Shared Expressions shows the list of what parameters exist in the dataset, and Translations shows what language or languages are supported by the dataset.

Creating Roles

Roles are what's required for RLS to work. We've talked about roles previously, and making them in Tabular Editor isn't terribly difficult. Using Tabular Editor also allows you to go beyond simple RLS and add object-level security (OLS) to a given role as well, controlling which objects in the data model a certain role can access.

In my Cool School University dataset, I have two roles that I made in Power BI Desktop and opened in Tabular Editor. In my NBA Master Dataset, I have two roles that I made completely outside of Power BI Desktop. They accomplish the same goal.

Let's look at my NBA dataset and use that to discuss making a role from scratch in Tabular Editor. I want to create a role that will show only the data for my favorite team, the Indiana Pacers, and one role that will show the data for everybody else. I'll right-click the Roles folder and select "new Role." The first thing I'm asked to do is to name the role. In this case, I'll call it "Pacers Only." Now, once that role is created, it doesn't do anything until it's defined. Just as we define roles using DAX in Power BI Desktop, we do that as well in Tabular Editor.

We can go look at the Properties pane in Figure 10-14 for the Pacers Only role. We care about the Security section and, specifically, the Row Level Security section. I want to add a DAX statement pertaining to a specific table—in this case, NBA Master Data. Given that this is player-level data, I want this role to display data only for players who were Pacers for the time they played for the franchise. The dataset in question has player information for each individual game, including their team affiliation, so I can define that as saying where the player's team name is the Pacers, and that will return data for players only for the time period in which they were members of the Indiana Pacers. That's easy enough to set up in DAX, and you can see where I've defined that.

Now, if I wanted to say that this Pacers Only role could see only certain tables, I could apply that at the table level here as well, in the OLS (Object Level Security) section, by changing the behavior for any table from Default to None. If I need column-level control for OLS, though, I need to go to the column specifically and change the role's OLS status to None.

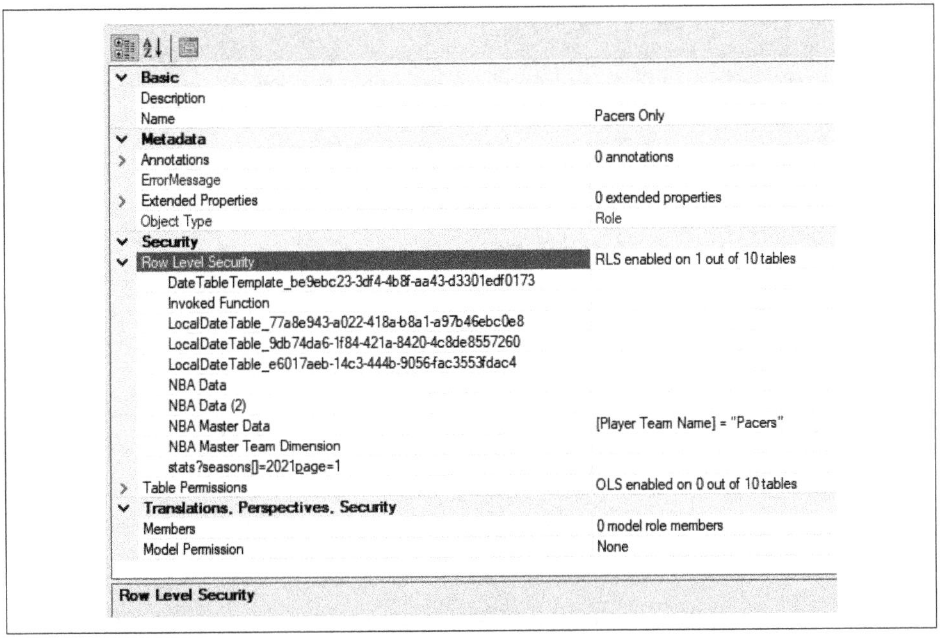

Figure 10-14. Implementing roles for RLS is pretty intuitive both in Tabular Editor and Power BI Desktop. Tabular Editor just gives you the extra power of OLS implementation as well!

Now that I have my first role created, knowing I want to create a role that is basically the same (except it's for a role that's all the teams except the Pacers), I can right-click my Pacers Only role, duplicate it, rename it, and then modify the RLS statement. In this case, I'll change [Player Team Name] = "Pacers" to [Player Team Name] = Not "Pacers."

Table and Measure Management

Here we get to how Tabular Editor can save every Power BI developer time and frustration: the creation and management of DAX-created elements. If you have calculated tables, calculated columns, or measures in your model, Tabular Editor can make your life better almost instantly. I'm going to focus on the Grades table from the Cool School University dataset. We can see this example in Figure 10-15.

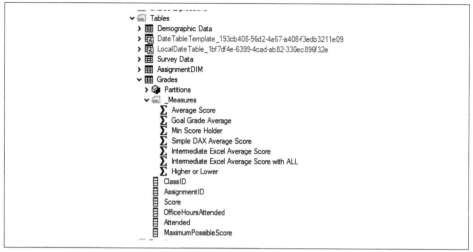

Figure 10-15. Tabular Editor can make seeing and managing your tables and measures in Power BI so much faster

If I right-click any table in my model, I can create a new measure, calculated column, hierarchy, data column, or data partition to split the table into multiple sections. If you have Incremental Refresh enabled, you'll see that Power BI takes care of creating the time-based partitions for you. I can choose to hide the table, duplicate it, or see the table's dependencies as well.

If I right-click a column, I can create a new display folder, measure, calculated column, hierarchy, or data column or set up a relationship from a given column to a different column. If you do manage relationships in Tabular Editor, this can also save you a ton of time.

You can also Ctrl+click to select multiple elements at once. Let's say you create 10 new measures using the expression editor on the right; you can deploy them all at once with the click of a button. You want to move a set of measures to your newly created display folder? You can do that. It's incredible how much faster Power BI Desktop seems to adopt those changes when they're pushed to it from Tabular Editor as opposed to when you do those things in Power BI Desktop itself.

Something Tabular Editor 2 doesn't do on its own, though, is version control, and it doesn't really keep a good history of changes you've made. This is critical because, no matter how good you get at this, you'll make a mistake sometime and need to either undo it or modify it. And you know that change could have happened multiple deployments ago. In this scenario, I would want to use a tool like the ALM Toolkit.

The ALM Toolkit for Power BI

The *ALM Toolkit* has a simple and useful purpose: identify what is different between two Power BI datasets. When the ALM Toolkit is chosen from Power BI Desktop, the source system will automatically choose the Power BI file you have open. If you aren't opening this from Power BI Desktop, you'll need to provide the source file (or the file in its current state) and the target file (the file that, in theory, you want to push the changes to). We can see that interface in Figure 10-16.

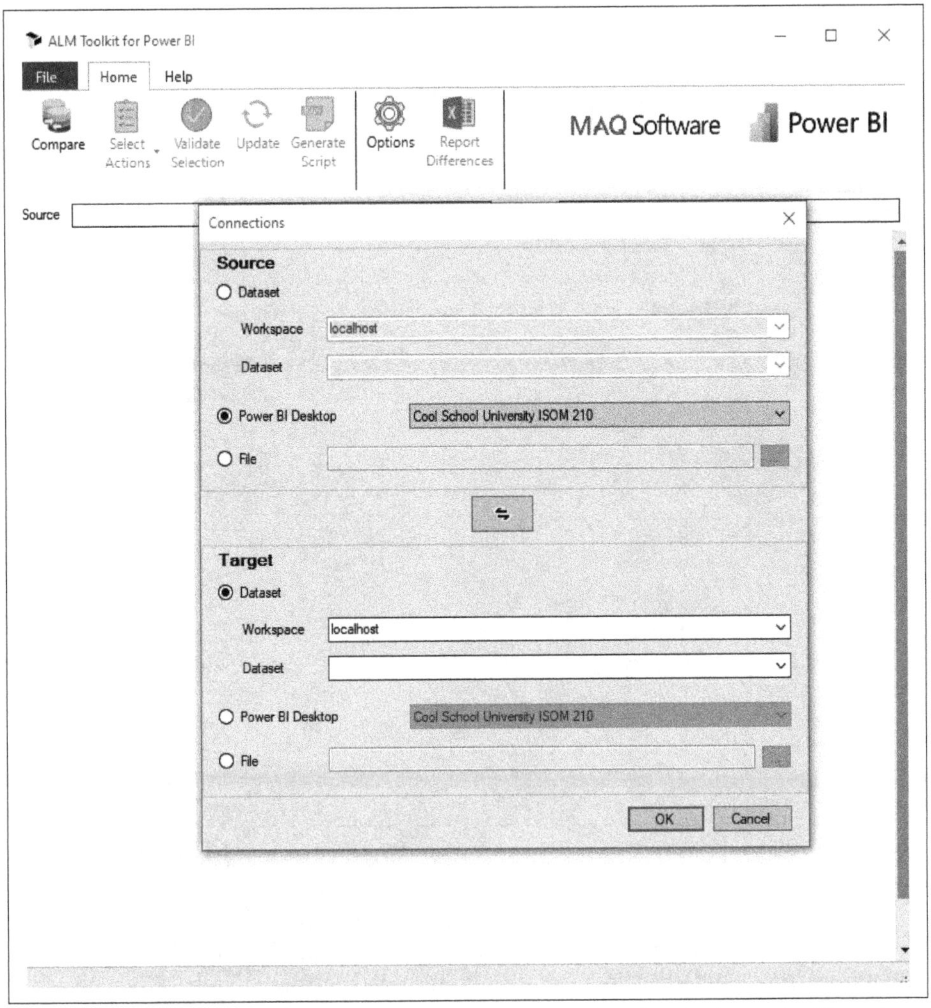

Figure 10-16. Remember, we want to take the source and push it to the target file

You'll notice a couple of options for where you can get the source and where you can point the target. The Dataset option allows you to point at a workspace in the Power

BI service, and, after you validate your credentials from a pop-up window, it will provide you with a list of all the datasets in that workspace.

Before deployment pipelines came about, it wasn't uncommon to have a development workspace with a development version of a dataset. You'd use the ALM Toolkit to push metadata changes from your development dataset in the Power BI service to a production dataset in the Power BI service in a totally different workspace.

The File option can be used only against PBIT files saved from Power BI Desktop or a BIM file from Tabular Editor. So, in this case, I'm going to compare my Cool School University ISOM 210 PBIX file to a PBIT file I made from this same dataset. I've made sure to make one change—in this case, removing a measure that was useless—so that we could easily see what changed and how that's displayed. You can see that in Figure 10-17.

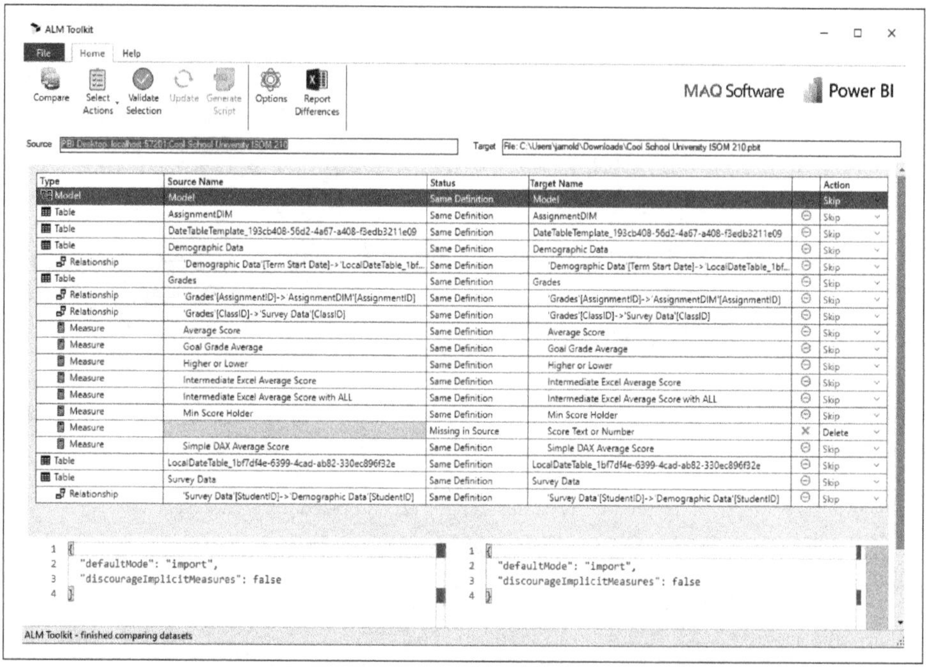

Figure 10-17. Doing this type of side-by-side metadata element comparison when you have two files is a lifesaver

I don't know about you, but I'm bad at remembering what I changed in a Power BI data model from day to day. Before I start doing any work on a Power BI Desktop file, I've gotten into the habit of saving a copy of that file as a PBIT. Now I have the PBIX I'm working with and a PBIT that contains all the metadata information. I'll make whatever changes I want to make (in this case, as shown in Figure 10-17), removing the Score Text or Number measure, and confirm that I haven't made any other unintended changes.

You can see that the ALM Toolkit identifies changes across all the metadata in an Analysis Services database. You can also see what changed with a code-line comparison, like what you would see in, say, GitHub. Figure 10-18 shows what that looks like.

On the left, in the source system, you can see no lines of code because I removed them, and that shows as a delete action. On the right, however, you see, in JSON script, what was removed, including, importantly, the expression, which for a measure would be the DAX statement.

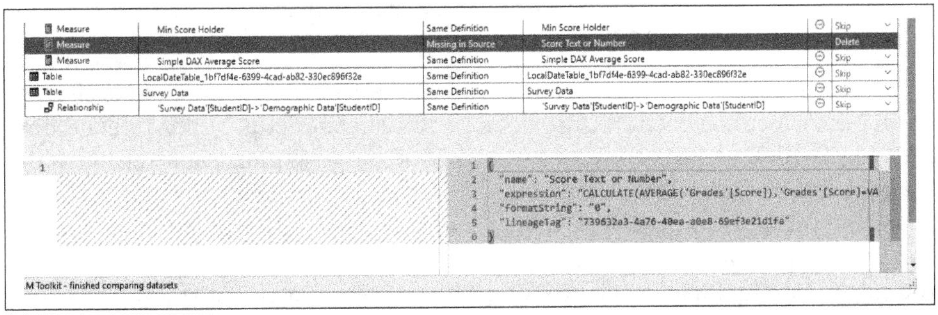

Measure	Min Score Holder	Same Definition	Min Score Holder	⊖	Skip	⌄
Measure		Missing in Source	Score Text or Number		Delete	
Measure	Simple DAX Average Score	Same Definition	Simple DAX Average Score	⊖	Skip	⌄
Table	LocalDateTable_1bf7df4e-6399-4cad-ab82-330ec896f32e	Same Definition	LocalDateTable_1bf7df4e-6399-4cad-ab82-330ec896f32e	⊖	Skip	⌄
Table	Survey Data	Same Definition	Survey Data	⊖	Skip	⌄
Relationship	'Survey Data'[StudentID] -> 'Demographic Data'[StudentID]	Same Definition	'Survey Data'[StudentID] -> 'Demographic Data'[StudentID]	⊖	Skip	⌄

```
1                                                          1  {
                                                           2    "name": "Score Text or Number",
                                                           3    "expression": "CALCULATE(AVERAGE('Grades'[Score]), 'Grades'[Score]=VA
                                                           4    "formatString": "0",
                                                           5    "lineageTag": "739532a3-4a76-40ea-a0e8-69ef3e21d1fa"
                                                           6  }
```

M Toolkit - finished comparing datasets

Figure 10-18. Code-level change detail management at your fingertips

In the Action section, I can choose whether I want to deploy that change or "skip" that change. A change that is skipped is ignored in the deployment of the metadata update from the source location to the target location. Maybe I changed a relationship to test how that would change a measure's behavior and forgot to change it back? This would catch that. I deleted an extra measure by accident, but I don't remember which one? This would catch that. I made an update to a calculated column and realize that the result is all wrong now, but I don't remember what the DAX was originally? This would catch that. I really can't express enough just how valuable this type of side-by-side metadata comparison is for your own sanity.

After you have the changes in place and ensured you have the list of changes you want to push, before choosing to validate the selection, make sure you capture the report differences. Report Differences will generate an Excel version of the table that you see in the software itself. This matters because this gives you an automatically generated change log. What does this allow us to do?

Let's say on April 24, I create the Excel file for the changes we saw earlier. I saved the Excel file with a date, so I know when the changes happened. Then I make some changes on May 1, June 1, and eventually it's September. In September, someone is trying to build a report on this dataset and comes to me and says, "Hey, wasn't there a measure for determining whether the score was in a text or number format around 61?" I can say that I removed it months ago, and when that person says that they need it for something, I can go check my change log, find the original code, and reimplement it easily.

A change log can also be helpful if you are in a scenario with multiple developers and you might be making changes to a data model that could have impacts on other people's work. "Oh, hey, I made a change to calculations X, Y, and Z" doesn't have to put you in a tailspin of worry when you find out that change broke something. It's not a problem anymore because you can identify what changes occurred and isolate the change that broke the functionality you needed.

Every good piece of software has a change log when it gets updated. Treat your Power BI dataset like a good piece of software, and maintain a change log. Make it easier on yourself to do with the ALM Toolkit.

Once you have your log in place, choose Validate Selection to see a list of the changes it will push. Once you click OK, the Update and Generate Script buttons will become available. Update will push the change automatically, overwriting a new version of the file if it was a file that was the target location. Generate Script will generate an XMLA script that you can run in something like SQL Server Management Studio or another tool that will push that change. I recommend using the Generate Script method when you might have multiple people working with a given dataset and you want to confirm all the changes with other people. It can also be helpful if you want to keep a secondary log of the XML that was pushed as code to create the changes from the source to the target.

So we've talked about a tool to get tools, and a tool to modify our dataset, and a tool to do version control and change logging, but it would be nice to have a tool that would help us accelerate our development and give us high-level information about our dataset. This is where the newest tool in the third-party Power BI landscape comes in handy. That would be Bravo, from the folks over at SQLBI.

Bravo

Bravo is a user-friendly tool designed to help you get information to quickly optimize your model. If you open Bravo from Power BI Desktop, like all the other external tools we've seen, it will open the tool in the context of the current Power BI Desktop file being used. You can sign into the Power BI service from the tool and see information about datasets in Premium workspaces as well.

Analyze Model

The first thing you'll see in Bravo is the Analyze Model window, shown in Figure 10-19. We can use this to get very quick information about how large our dataset is, how many columns it has, and, more importantly, how many columns are not referenced within the model. It is important to know that Bravo cannot see if any reports that are dependent on the dataset might use one of these columns. But Bravo can help you figure out where to start looking if you can remove columns from your data model. This will help make the model both smaller and more efficient.

There's even a nice visual to show how much of the model is taken up by specific columns or, in my example, a collection of smaller columns. If I click the smaller columns collection in the columns list, the visual will break out those columns as well. Anything highlighted in yellow is currently not being used in the model and may be a candidate for removal. There's a search option and a filter option, both of which can be helpful if you have a model with many columns. There is also an option to download a VPAX file, which is a file used in software called VertiPaq Analyzer that is also made by the folks at SQLBI. I like to use Bravo to identify columns that I can remove, and I'll keep a record of those column changes using the ALM Toolkit to deploy those changes to an updated PBIT or BIM file when I'm ready to save my changes.

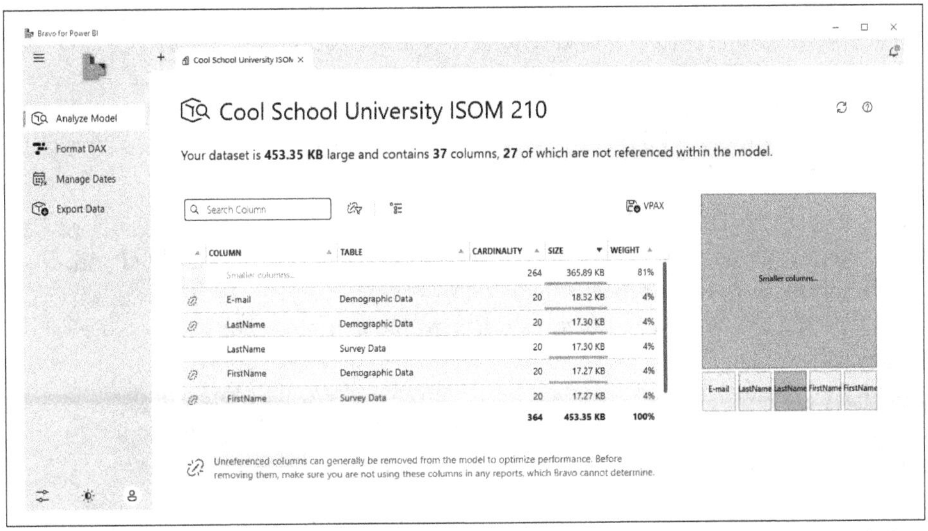

Figure 10-19. The first thing you see in Bravo is the Analyze Model window. Bravo helps make your model healthier and easier to understand, and solves some real annoyances.

DAX Formatting

If you get Bravo for nothing else, the Format DAX page is an absolute godsend. You can see all your measures, and by clicking Analyze Now, that script will be read by the DAX Formatting service. It will tell you how many of your measures have errors and how many measures you have that aren't formatted as the DAX Formatting service suggests. You can choose individual measures, or you can select all and have them mass formatted. If you click a measure, a window to the right appears that will show you both the current format and a preview of the formatted DAX. If you have a reason that you have a specific measure formatted a certain way, you can leave that one alone and fix the others. With something like Bravo, there's no reason to have unformatted DAX, and when your DAX is formatted and someone else's isn't, I promise you, you'll look better.

Manage Dates

Bravo can create a date table for you and create a ton of time intelligence measures based on measures you already have in your model. This feature can save you so much time as dozens of properly formatted measures get created to accelerate your development. However, there is a catch. First, you cannot have auto date/time enabled in your Power BI data model and, second, you cannot have another table already identified as your date table. Bravo will tell you if you can use the Manage Dates features with your current data model. If you can, then you can quickly create a date table with set time intervals, your language of choice, even which country's holidays to add to the model. I do hope in the future they will add the ability to have multiple countries' holidays.

If that was all this thing did, that would be enough to be awesome. It gets better. The time intelligence section will ask if you want these measures to be enabled and, if so, do you want time intelligence built for all of your measures or a subset that you choose? In Figure 10-20 you can see a quick example of how deep the measure rabbit hole goes in Bravo. It will also create the display folders for you, which is incredibly useful. In addition, if you want to get better at DAX, there are some wonderful examples of how to write DAX using time intelligence functions that you can use to help push you along in your DAX journey.

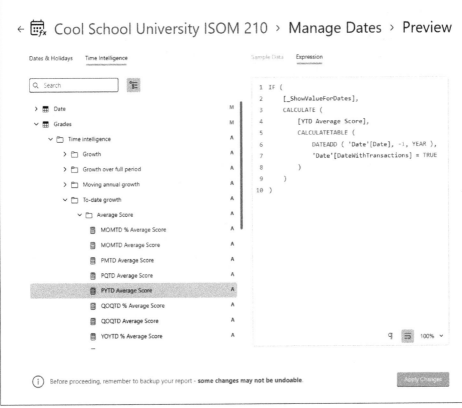

Figure 10-20. Manage Dates is feature-rich and incredibly helpful. Seriously, where was this when I was learning Power BI?

Export Data

The last thing that Bravo can do is provide an export of data from a table in a data model. It's as simple as clicking the box or boxes you want for the tables you want to export and choosing whether you want to export that data as an Excel spreadsheet or a CSV file. Bravo can also provide you with an export summary page if you want additional details around what data was exported. When the export is complete and the file is saved, Bravo even visually gives you a link to click to take you straight to the file.

Now, it is still exporting to either Excel or CSV, so it can't export an infinite number of rows. If you have a process that is requiring you to get millions of records from a table, you're probably better off using an Evaluate statement in DAX Studio and exporting the results from there. However, if your table isn't millions of rows deep, Export Data can be a really great way to export data from a table in your data model.

Conclusion

Well, we've reached the end of the road. We started with zero knowledge of Power BI and went all the way through learning how to use Power BI Desktop and the Power BI service. Then we ended here, with tools to accelerate and empower your Power BI development.

The Power BI ecosystem is wide and deep. Microsoft is going to continue to push the Power Platform forward, and Power BI will be the data cornerstone of that process. If you've read through this book and feel confident enough now to build that report, to bring together that data, to help a user get access to a workspace, or to set up a robust development pipeline, then I feel like I've accomplished something.

And you should feel like a proud graduate of Cool School University. You've worked hard, put in your time, and now you've elevated your skill set. With this, you can impress your colleagues and make an impact on your organization. Knowing Power BI will enable you to provide data analytics in a visual output that technical folks and business users alike can understand and make smarter decisions with.

I can't say I know where Power BI will be going in the future, but I know I'm excited to see it. I hope you're now ready to take on whatever data challenge lies ahead. A wise man in exile once told me that the end of learning is the beginning of death. Data is the oxygen that allows us to learn in the 21st century. Never stop learning. Good luck and Godspeed.

Commonly Used DAX Expressions

In this appendix, I will go over the syntax of some of the most commonly used DAX functions in Power BI. These are organized by section, then alphabetically within that section. For each function, there will be a brief description of the purpose of the function, the syntax of the function, and then an example using that syntax.

This is not an exhaustive list of all the functions in the DAX language. That can be reviewed at "DAX Function Reference" (*https://oreil.ly/NaAtD*).

As with many things, DAX is a prime example of the Pareto principle: 80% of all the problems (outputs) can be solved with 20% mastery (inputs).

Aggregation Functions

AVERAGE

Definition

Returns the average (mean) of all the numerical values of a column.

Syntax

```
AVERAGE ( [ColumnName] )
```

Example

```
AverageScore = AVERAGE ( GradeScore[Score] )
```

AVERAGEX

Definition

Calculates the average (mean) of a set of expressions evaluated over each row of a table.

Syntax

```
AVERAGEX ( 'TableName' , <expression> )
```

Example

```
AverageScorePercentage = AVERAGEX ( 'GradeScores', 'GradeScores'[Score] +
    'GradeScores'[MaximumPossibleScore] )
```

COUNT

Definition

Returns the number of records for a column that are not blank.

Syntax

```
COUNT ( [ColumnName] )
```

Example

```
CountOfStudents = COUNT ( 'UniversitySuppliedData'[StudentID] )
```

DISTINCTCOUNT

Definition

Returns the number of distinct values for a given column.

Syntax

```
DISTINCTCOUNT ( [ColumnName] )
```

Example

```
CountOfStudents = DISTINCTCOUNT ( 'GradeScores'[StudentID] )
```

MAX

Definition

Returns the largest value in a column.

Syntax

```
MAX ( [ColumnName] )
```

Example

```
HighestScore = MAX ( 'GradeScores'[Score] )
```

MAXX

Definition

Returns the largest value for an expression over each row of a given table.

Syntax

```
MAXX ( 'TableName', <expression> )
```

Example

```
LargestScoreAndOfficeHours = MAXX ( 'GradeScores', 'GradeScores'[Score] +
    'GradeScores'[OfficeHoursAttended] )
```

MIN

Definition

Returns the smallest value in a column.

Syntax

```
MIN ( [ColumnName] )
```

Example

```
LowestScore = MIN ( 'GradeScores'[Score] )
```

MINX

Definition

Returns the smallest value for an expression over each row of a given table.

Syntax

```
MINX ( 'TableName', <expression> )
```

Example

```
LowestScoreAndOfficeHours = MINX ( 'GradeScores', 'GradeScores'[Score] +
    'GradeScores'[OfficeHoursAttended] )
```

SUM

Definition

Adds all the numbers in a given column.

Syntax

```
SUM ( [ColumnName] )
```

Example

```
TotalOfficeHoursAttended = SUM ( 'GradeScores'[OfficeHoursAttended] )
```

SUMX

Definition

Returns the sum value for an expression over each row of a given table.

Syntax

```
SUMX ( 'TableName', <expression>)
```

Example

```
TotalEffectiveScore = SUMX ('GradeScores', 'GradeScores'[Score] +
  ('GradeScores'[OfficeHoursAttended] * 20) )
```

PRODUCT

Definition

Returns the product (multiplication) of the numbers of a column.

Syntax

```
PRODUCT ( [ColumnName] )
```

Example

```
ScoreMultiplication = PRODUCT ( 'GradeScores'[Score] )
```

PRODUCTX

Definition

Returns the product (multiplication) of an expression evaluated for each row in a table.

```
PRODUCTX ( 'TableName', <expression> )
```

Example

```
BonusScoreMultiplication = PRODUCTX ( 'GradeScores', 20 *
    'GradeScores'[OfficeHoursAttended] )
```

Date and Time Functions

CALENDAR

Definition

Returns a table with a single-date column that is a continuous list of all dates between the start date and the end date. This can accept DAX statements that would result with a date.

Syntax

```
CALENDAR ( <start_date> , <end_date>)
```

Example

```
DateRange = CALENDAR ( "01/01/2022" , "12/31/2022" )
```

DATEDIFF

Definition

Returns the count of a given set of intervals between two dates, where an interval can be SECOND, MINUTE, HOUR, DAY, WEEK, MONTH, QUARTER, or YEAR.

Syntax

```
DATEDIFF ( <start_date>, <end_date>, <interval>)
```

Example

```
DaysBetweenTerms = DATEDIFF ( MIN('UniversitySuppliedData'[Term Start Date]),
    MAX('UniversitySuppliedData'[Term Start Date]), DAY)
```

DAY

Definition

Returns the day of the month of a given date between 1 and 31.

Syntax

```
DAY ( <date> )
```

Example

```
DayOfTermStart = DAY ('UniversitySuppliedData'[Term Start Date])
```

MONTH

Definition

Returns the month of a given date between 1 and 12.

Syntax

```
MONTH ( <date> )
```

Example

```
MonthOfTermStart = MONTH ('UniversitySuppliedData'[Term Start Date])
```

TODAY

Definition

Returns the current date.

Syntax

```
TODAY()
```

Example

```
DaysSinceMostRecentTermStart = DATEDIFF ( Today(),
  MAX('UniversitySuppliedData'[Term Start Date]), DAY)
```

YEAR

Definition

Returns the year of a given date.

Syntax

```
YEAR ( <date> )
```

Example

```
YearOfTermStart = YEAR ('UniversitySuppliedData'[Term Start Date])
```

Time Intelligence Functions

DATEADD

Definition

Returns a table that contains a column of dates, either in the future or in the past by the specified number of intervals from the initial date.

Syntax

```
DATEADD ( <dates>, <number_of_intervals>, <interval> )
```

Example

```
ThirtyDaysFromTermStart = DATEADD ( 'UniversitySuppliedData'[Term Start Date],
    30, DAY )
```

DATESMTD

Definition

Returns a table that contains a column of dates in the current month to date.

Syntax

```
DATESMTD ( <dates> )
```

Example

```
MTDDatesOfTermStart = DATESMTD ( 'UniversitySuppliedData'[Term Start Date] )
```

DATESQTD

Definition

Returns a table that contains a column of dates in the current quarter to date.

Syntax

```
DATESQTD ( <dates> )
```

Example

```
QTDDatesOfTermStart = DATESQTD ( 'UniversitySuppliedData'[Term Start Date] )
```

DATESYTD

Definition

Returns a table that contains a column of dates in the current year to date.

Syntax

```
DATESYTD ( <dates> )
```

Example

```
YTDDatesOfTermStart = DATESYTD ( 'UniversitySuppliedData'[Term Start Date] )
```

Filter Functions

ALL

Definition

Returns all the rows in a table or column, ignoring all filter context for the selected table and column. Note that you can choose to not specify a column and use only the TableName portion of the function, effectively clearing filters on all columns for the chosen table. The following example demonstrates this. If you wanted to add specific columns to the ALL statement, refer to the full syntax, here.

Syntax

```
ALL ( ['TableName', [ColumnName1], [ColumnName2],...,[ColumnNameX] )
```

Example

```
%OfTotal = SUM('GradeScores'[Score]) / CALCULATE(SUM('GradeScores'[Score]),
    ALL('UniversitySuppliedData'))
```

ALLEXCEPT

Definition

Removes all filter context except for those columns specifically selected in the ALL EXCEPT statement.

Syntax

```
ALLEXCEPT ('TableName'[ColumnName1],[ColumnName2],...,[ColumnNameX])
```

Example

```
ScoreTotalOrByLastName = CALCULATE(SUM('GradeScores'[Score]),
    ALLEXCEPT(UniversitySuppliedData,UniversitySuppliedData[LastName]))
```

CALCULATE

Definition

Evaluates an expression with modified filter context. Remember, you will use this one a ton.

Syntax

```
CALCULATE(<expression>, {FilterCondition1}, {FilterCondition2}
    ,..., {FilterConditionX})
```

Example

```
AverageScoreAssignment1 = CALCULATE(AVERAGE('GradeScores'[Score]),
    'AssignmentDIM'[AssignmentID]=1)
```

Logical Functions

AND

Definition

Performs a test to determine whether both of the passed arguments are true. This function returns TRUE if both arguments pass, and otherwise returns FALSE.

Syntax

```
AND ( <logicalcondition1>, <logicalcondition2> )
```

Example

```
SpecificKingScoreForComparison = CALCULATE(sum('GradeScores'[Score]),AND
    ('UniversitySuppliedData'[LastName] = "King",
    'UniversitySuppliedData'[FirstName] = "Leonard"))
```

COALESCE

Definition

Returns the first expression that doesn't come back BLANK. If everything returns blank, BLANK is returned.

Syntax

```
COALESCE ( <expression1>, <expression2>,..., <expressionX)
```

Example

```
TotalScoreTreatingBlanksAsZeroes = COALESCE ( SUM ( 'GradeScores'[Score]), 0)
```

IF

Definition

Checks a given condition, returning one result if TRUE and going to a second result if FALSE.

Syntax

```
IF (<logical test>, <value_true>, <value_false>)
```

Example

```
CurveEligible = IF ('UniversitySuppliedData'[YearsAttended] <=2, "Yes", "No")
```

OR

Definition

Performs a test to determine whether either of the passed arguments is true. This function returns TRUE if either argument passes and otherwise returns FALSE.

Syntax

```
OR ( <logicalcondition1>, <logicalcondition2> )
```

Example

```
CountOfIndianaOrHawaiiStudents = CALCULATE(COUNT
  (UniversitySuppliedData[StudentID]),
  OR(UniversitySuppliedData[ResidencyState]="IN",
  UniversitySuppliedData[ResidencyState]="HI"))
```

DAX Operators

DAX has many operators that perform functions similar to what you would expect, but some have unique functionality. Table A-1 lists operator names, operator signs, and their function.

Table A-1. DAX operators

Operator name	Operator sign	Function
Plus sign	+	Addition
Minus sign	−	Subtraction
Asterisk	*	Multiplication
Forward slash	/	Division
Caret	∧	Exponential
Equal sign	=	Equal to
Double equal sign	==	Strictly equal to
Left caret	>	Greater than
Right caret	<	Less than
Right caret and equal sign	>=	Greater than or equal to
Left caret and equal sign	<=	Less than or equal to
Left caret right caret	<>	Not equal to
Single ampersand	&	Text concatenation
Double ampersand	&&	Logical AND operator
Double pipe	||	Logical OR operator
IN	IN	Logical OR condition for a given list of values

Some Favorite Custom Visuals

An incredible amount of development effort has been put into the creation of custom visuals in Power BI. In fact, in my last cursory count of custom visuals in Power BI's AppSource listing, I found 404! Many of the custom visuals in this list are 100% free to download and use. Some have free elements and then elements you can license to expand their functionality; for example, the xViz, ZoomCharts, and Zebra BI visuals work this way. Everything in the app store, to my knowledge, has at least some free components.

Something to think about when you use custom visuals is whether a visual is certified. Certified visuals have extra functionality in line with the prepackaged visuals from Power BI, including the ability to export their results to PowerPoint or embed the visual in emails from subscriptions. Just because a visual is not certified does not mean it's unsafe or a security risk. For more information on custom visual certification, see Microsoft's documentation on the matter at "Get Your Power BI Visual Certified" (*https://oreil.ly/igcx9*).

In this appendix, I'll provide a quick review on how to add custom visuals. I'll also review some of my personal favorite custom visuals. Finally, I'll introduce Charticulator, a free-to-use, no-code-required custom visual builder offered from Microsoft. For clarity, I will not include any visual that has a licensing component because, in full disclosure, I personally haven't used a lot of them and can't really speak to their prospective advantages over existing free options.

Adding Custom Visuals to Power BI Desktop

Adding a custom visual is a painless process if you know where to look. In the Visualizations pane alongside all the default Power BI visuals, look for an ellipsis after the last visual. Clicking this brings up a small menu that provides options to get more visuals, import a visual from a file, remove a visual, or restore default visuals. Before AppSource was as prevalent in the Microsoft ecosystem as it is today, many custom visuals were created as PBVIZ files. If you have a PBVIZ either from a custom visual you've created using TypeScript or an older version of a custom visual that you want to import from a file, you can select that option to access an Explorer window to navigate to the file and select it for importing.

If you select the "Get more visuals" option, an overlay will appear that will bring you to a list of custom visuals that are available in AppSource and custom visuals that have been added to your organization. Items from your organization will always appear before nonorganizational items in the list of all visuals. We can see what this overlay looks like in Figure B-1.

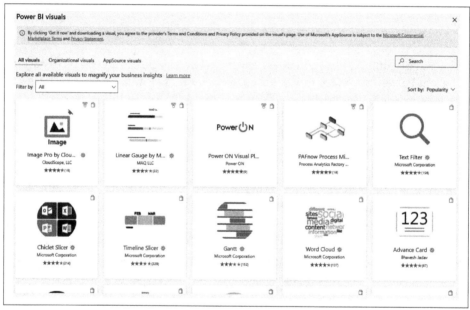

Figure B-1. The AppSource custom visual navigation window

You can see there are selection options for all visuals, organizational visuals, and AppSource-only visuals. There's search functionality. There is also the ability to filter the visuals categorically. These categories are Analytics, Advanced Analytics, Change Over Time, Filters, Infographics, KPI, and Maps. The filter categories aren't always helpful in defining what you're looking for, and this is particularly true in the Analytics category, which I find overly broad. However, you can use both filter and search together, which you might find more helpful.

Something else that is helpful in using each of these custom visuals from AppSource is that they all have a sample PBIX that you can use to see how they work and what they do. This provides a very low barrier to entry, as you can see the visual at its best, the defined use case from the creator of the visual, and decide if it is something that might work for you.

Ten of My Favorite Custom Visuals

I said there were 404 custom visuals in AppSource based on my last count. With that many, I certainly haven't had a chance to use them all, and frankly I don't know anyone who has. However, I keep coming back to certain visuals for different purposes time and time again, so I've composed a list of 10 that are either broadly applicable or that really do a good job of solving the problem they are designed to address. I'll provide you with a brief overview of each of them. I could've made this list two or three times as long, but I chose the ones I think are most helpful. Please note that in many cases, I'll demonstrate the use of these visuals by using the provided sample dataset.

- Advance Card
- Chiclet Slicer
- Drilldown Choropleth
- Forecasting with ARIMA
- Gantt chart

- Radar Chart
- Route map
- Scroller
- Sunburst chart
- Word Cloud

Advance Card

The *Advance Card visual* is not a radical overhaul of the basic card visual, but a straightforward enhancement. Advance Card supports additional features such as conditional formatting, conditional formatting based on another measure, easy text alignment, tooltip support, and background image support. We can see some of what that looks like from the example PBIX for the visual in Figure B-2.

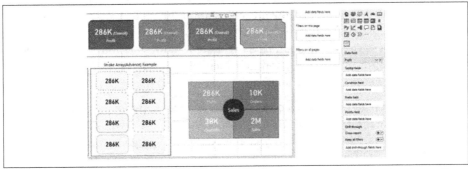

Figure B-2. The Advance Card is honestly just better than the regular card in basically every way

Chiclet Slicer

I love the *Chiclet Slicer*, which is a slicer that has controls for the number of rows and columns of values you want to condense your selections into. I personally just love the "button" feel of the Chiclet Slicer.

Another cool function of the Chiclet Slicer is that you can associate images with different "chiclets." A common example of this is a report about multiple countries, and each chiclet might display a national flag. Even without the additional chiclet formatting, I really like how the Chiclet Slicer looks and behaves.

Microsoft's initial announcement of the Chiclet Slicer back in 2015 used car company logos as an example. I like to store images for Chiclet Slicers in a OneDrive folder or SharePoint site and then have a column in my data model that calls those links as Image URLs. Figure B-3 shows Microsoft's car example of the Chiclet Slicer, alongside the visualization parameters.

Figure B-3. Chiclets aren't just a type of gum, they're also my favorite slicer

Drilldown Choropleth

I feel like I need to provide a warning first on this visual. It is not user-friendly to set up. You need to have TopoJSON files to identify how your maps should be shaped. Unlike the shape map visual, you will provide a link to the TopoJSON files you will use for your geographic drilldown in the visual's formatting pane. If you can't find a TopoJSON of the geographic boundaries you are looking for, you might be able to find it as a shapefile or GeoJSON, both of which have free online tools that will allow you to convert one type of file to another.

A *choropleth* is a map that uses color to show differences between geographic regions. The reason I like the *Drilldown Choropleth visual* is that even with its difficult setup, once you have everything working, you can allow users to go easily from one geographic level to another and keep all the context in a single visual. As you can see in Figure B-4, I go from the state/territory level of Australia down to the postal code level after going through the state-level filter to get to Western Australia, and my results remain contextual.

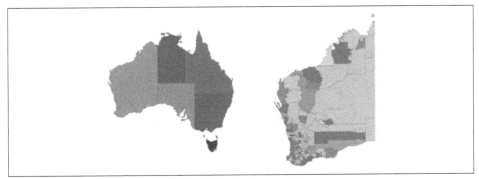

Figure B-4. TopoJSONs are powerful mapping tools, even if they're a pain to set up

Forecasting with ARIMA

Two of my favorite "simple" forecasting methods are exponential smoothing and Autoregressive Integrated Moving Average (ARIMA). It's important to note that this is an R-powered visual, which means to use it you will need to have R installed. The visual will prompt you to install the correct libraries when you first add ARIMA. The downside is that to refresh a data model that uses this visual, you will have to use a personal data gateway.

However, I like this visual because it is simple and provides easy-to-understand confidence intervals for the results. It also has several controls for more seasoned analysts to fine-tune the forecast to account for specific scenarios or parameters. For a more detailed explanation on ARIMA and its use in Power BI, I suggest downloading the sample dataset for this visual, as its report pages do a good job of explaining the ARIMA methodology. As a bonus, I think the visual actually looks pretty nice in its presentation. We can see what that looks like alongside its formatting options in Figure B-5.

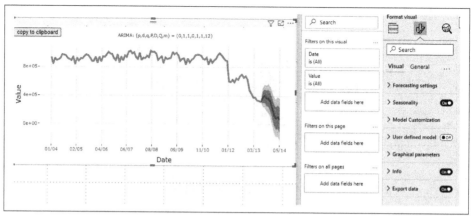

Figure B-5. ARIMA is not a universal bullet, but it provides a great starting point in your prospective forecasting

Gantt Chart

The *Gantt chart* has been around forever, and it's a staple of project management. It's a type of bar chart with a time series that helps you identify events in terms of estimated time to completion and the number of steps involved.

AppSource has a couple of Gantt chart options, but in this example, I'm specifically talking about the version from Microsoft. What I really like about this version is that it can be as broad or as detailed as you want to make it. This Gantt chart has 10 field selections you can add values to. The only field that is required is the task field.

The visual sample PBIX has an easy-to-read hints page that I often reference when I need to remember which field does what, since I'm not in project management that often. Honestly, I wish some of the formatting options in this chart were available in some base visuals, but you can also use the Gantt chart in "off-label" use cases to borrow some of that functionality for more classic bar chart use cases. We can see an example of the Gantt chart visual in Figure B-6.

Figure B-6. The Gantt chart is a powerful and surprisingly flexible take on the classic bar chart

Radar Chart

The *Radar Chart* is a visual that allows you to display multiple variables' worth of data to see a broader holistic picture across those variables. Generally speaking, the axes should not be considered comparative, as different variables will have different scales on their respective axis. For instance, the example in Figure B-7 shows the count of new employees by division versus the forecast number of new employees by division. We don't necessarily know what the absolute values are, but we can quickly compare how each group did with actuals to forecast in a broad interpretive sense.

One of my favorite examples of the use of the radar chart, not in Power BI, is in Street Fighter 5, where each character has a radar chart that shows their "stats" out of a rank of 5, quickly allowing you to see which characters have which general strengths. Want a character with a lot of life that hits hard or a quick character with many special moves? The radar chart works perfectly in that context as well, showing it's a chart type with broad applications. It's also easy to use in Power BI since it asks only for a category list and y-axis values.

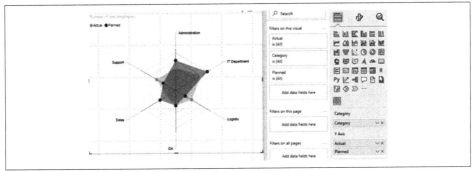

Figure B-7. The Radar Chart visual is for me an underrated gem

Route Map

The *"Route map" visual* helps visualize data that shows geolocation at different points across an axis, usually time. So, for example, if you were a trucking company and wanted to see the route your trucks were taking, you could get data from their GPS, model that data, and use this visual to note those routes and possibly run some optimization analysis.

My wife uses this visual with her geolocation data to map her runs. The visual does pass that geolocation data to a third-party service, which means it will not ever be certified, so that is something to keep in mind. You can see, though, that the map it produces in Figure B-8, from OpenStreetMap, is very readable.

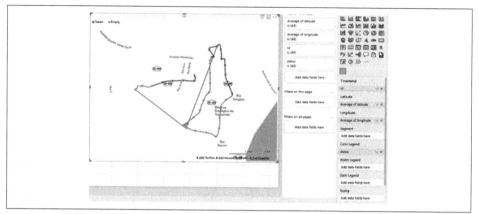

Figure B-8. The Route map is a visual that can really spice up geolocation data

Scroller

The *Scroller visual* is your classic ticker. It showcases data in categorical context with the option of adding a change measure. I like to use the Scroller visual to compare actuals with forecast values or against a previous day's individual value (say, product sales or shipments). I also like to use the Scroller visual when I have a report page that will be displayed and visible (say, a manufacturing floor). The Scroller visual can be used to provide repeating messages or other additional notices.

I had one customer who used it on a television display to remind employees of upcoming events, holiday notices, birthdays, anniversaries, etc. Everyone has probably seen a scrolling ticker at some point in their life, but the real power of having control over the data you put with this visual gives it so much flexibility. This implementation has controls over scroll speed, font size, and the ability to add color to status indicators and status text.

Sunburst Chart

A *Sunburst chart* is a circular chart (like a pie or a donut) with multiple "rings" that allow for different categorical combinations to identify an aggregation at any or all levels of the categorical split. Even though I generally don't like pie or donut charts, I like that for any given combination I select from the Sunburst, I get to see a specific value in the middle of the Sunburst that gives me numerical context to the combinations I'm looking at without having to guess. With multiple categorical options in the Sunburst chart, you can also use this to get to specific combinations of categories to filter other visuals on the page.

In Figure B-9, I have the Category 2 / SC2 / Asia grouping selected, and those values are passed to all the other visuals on the page from a cross-filtering perspective at once, as opposed to having to do three separate sets of cross-filtering. I also can choose any combination of those levels. All of Category 2? I can do that. Category 1 and SC1? I can do that. Category 2 / SC1 / North America? Yep. So it does have some pie and donut baggage, but it does enough differently that I think it's worth including in this list.

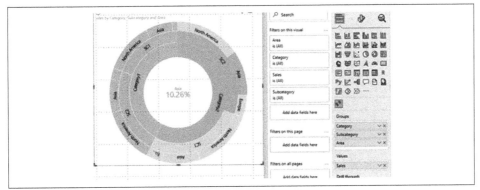

Figure B-9. The Sunburst chart, my hypocritical indulgence

Word Cloud

The *Word Cloud* is a visualization that we are seeing used more and more in a variety of contexts. A word cloud takes words and identifies how often they show up. I tend to use this visual most often in marketing analytics where I am trying to get some insight into consumer sentiment or understand what topics are dominating a conversation. Let's say we have a focus group and we're breaking down what the group members said about a product; I'd want to know the most common words used to describe my product.

This also comes up quite a bit in survey data. The count of how often a word was selected could also easily be visualized in a word cloud. This visual in its formatting also allows for you to choose words to exclude and has a default list that you can choose to disable to help keep the word cloud less cluttered. You also can control which words are excluded by providing your own words to remove in the Formatting area of the Visualization pane with this visual. I could add multiple words to the list as well, by using a comma. In this way, I can remove clutter.

In a sentiment analysis, certain words might have "weights." You can add these weights by using the values portion of the Visualization pane. From the download sample, you can see an example word cloud with default exclusions in Figure B-10.

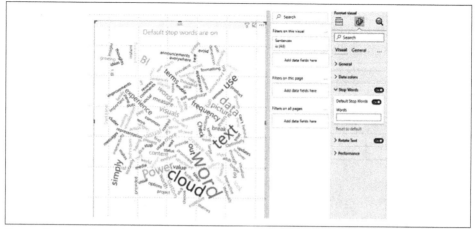

Figure B-10. Make judicious use of the Stop Words feature

Charticulator

Finally, we have *Charticulator*, one of the most exciting things to happen to custom visuals. Charticulator allows you to make custom visuals of your own without code. You can then import that visual you make at the Charticulator website (*https://charti culator.com*) into your Power BI report, and Charticulator is also completely certified for Power BI service.

Microsoft makes several video tutorials available, creating example visuals at Charticulator Video Tutorials (*https://oreil.ly/DDxS6*), and that is worth reviewing if you want to try creating your own visuals.

Generally, if I can choose between creating a custom visual from scratch in Charticulator versus doing a little extra work to get a visual to do what I want in Power BI Desktop, I'll choose the latter. However, if I have a unique client request, I will sometimes find myself in Charticulator to build that perfect piece of the puzzle.

Be aware that Charticulator does have a learning curve. However, it also has the advantage of not being a code-based solution, which would prevent, say, an R- or Python-based visual from needing a personal data gateway.

Charticulator is Microsoft's secret weapon in the Power BI ecosystem that not enough people seem to know about or use. As with any product, I suggest just getting your hands on it and trying it out. It does not require any licensing, and you can add your own data to work from. Charticulator might be that final tool in your tool belt, but it is an incredibly powerful tool.

Index

DirectQuery mode for SQL Server database, 18
donut charts, 90
    treemaps versus, 91
Drill through subsection (Visualizations pane), 35
Drilldown Choropleth, 274
Duplicate page option, 25
Dynamics, 20

E

earliest, 114
Elements subsection (Report view Insert tab), 26-28
    Buttons element, 26
    Text box, 26
elements, creating in Data Hub section of Navigate menu, 189
Enter Data option (Home tab of Power Query), 48
ETL (extract, transform, and load), 8
Excel
    analysis of datasets in, 187
    Excel workbook button in Data subsection of Report view Home tab, 18
    importing Excel files into Power BI, 128
    importing Excel files into Power Query, 43-47
    self-service BI with, 7
explicit measures, 114
Export Data (Bravo), 257
external tools, 232
    (see also tools, third-party)
External Tools tab (Report view of Power BI Desktop), 33

F

Field synonyms section, 169
Fields pane (Report view), 35, 73
filter context, 102, 123, 125
    CALCULATE function and, 118
    ignoring using ALL operator, 120
filter functions (DAX), 266-267
filters
    cross-filtering across filters, 75
    Filter option under Format tab, 76
    Filters pane in Report view, 36-37
    Show Panes subsection of View tab in Report view, 32
    on tables, 123

first, 113
flat visuals, 93-99
    card/multi-row card, 94
    gauge, 93
    KPI (key performance indicator), 95
    matrix, 97
    slicer, 98
    table, 96
Format pane, 35, 73
    Edit interactions button, 76
functions
    DAX aggregations, 117
    types in DAX, 103
    X functions in DAX, 123
funnel charts, 88

G

Gantt charts, 276
Gartner's Magic Quadrant for Analytics and Business Intelligence Platforms, 10
gauges, 93
GENERATESERIES statement, 173, 176
goals, creating and tracking in Power BI service, 5
grouping data, 41
    Group By option in Transforms section of Power Query Home tab, 51

H

Help section in Report view, 32
hiding tables, 145
Highlight option in Visualizations Format pane, 76
Home section (Navigation menu in Power BI service), 184

I

ideas for improvement of Power BI, 32
IDs, unique column IDs, 135
IF statements, 124
    nested, performance and, 154
Image button, 28
implicit measures, 114
Import mode for SQL Server database, 18
importing data
    first data import for a report, 127-132
        choosing and transforming data when importing, 128

About the Author

Jeremey Arnold is the senior analytics architect at Onebridge, a large data analytics consulting firm in Indianapolis, Indiana. Jeremey has worked in data analytics for over a decade and has been a Microsoft Power BI user since its release in 2013. His experience covers multiple industries including healthcare, finance, manufacturing, and the public sector, all with a focus on transforming data into insights and enabling truly data-driven environments.

Colophon

The animal on the cover of *Learning Microsoft Power BI* is an East African hippopotamus (*Hippopotamus amphibius kiboko*), an extinct subspecies of the common hippopotamus (*Hippopotamus amphibius*). Common hippos, also known as large hippos, currently inhabit the waters of sub-Saharan Africa's rivers, swamps, and lakes.

The name "hippopotamus" is derived from the ancient Greek for "river horse." Hippopotamuses have a bulky, gray-brown barrel-shaped body carried on squat legs and a head of considerable size (the mouth is typically over a foot wide and can hinge open 150°). Hippos are the third-largest living land mammal—after elephants and white rhinoceroses—with males weighing 3.5 tons on average.

Many of the hippo's physical features relate to its amphibious nature, allowing it to traverse land and water surprisingly swiftly and with ease. Their feet have webbed toes that distribute weight evenly and provide powerful propulsion through the water. A hippopotamus's weight allows it to walk underwater, and its ears and nostrils can seal shut, allowing it to remain completely submerged for about five minutes.

Originally thought to be closely related to pigs and similar even-hooved mammals, DNA and fossil records have since provided evidence that hippo's closest relatives are sea mammals: dolphins, porpoises, and whales.

While the hippopotamus subsists on nighttime grazing on riverbanks and surrounding grassland, it is considered to be territorially aggressive and has frequently been reported charging and attacking humans (among other animals), sometimes resulting in fatalities.

The cover illustration is by Karen Montgomery, based on an antique line engraving from Cassell's *Popular Natural History*.. The cover fonts are Gilroy Semibold and Guardian Sans. The text font is Adobe Minion Pro; the heading font is Adobe Myriad Condensed; and the code font is Dalton Maag's Ubuntu Mono.

O'REILLY®

Learn from experts.
Become one yourself.

Books | Live online courses
Instant Answers | Virtual events
Videos | Interactive learning

Get started at oreilly.com.

Printed in the USA
CPSIA information can be obtained
at www.ICGtesting.com
JSHW060950260324
59876JS00010B/260